Joanna Penglase is the co-founder of CLAN, a support and advocacy organisation for older care leavers, which helped to get up the 2004 Senate Inquiry into Children in Institutional Care. In 1999 she completed a PhD thesis which was an attempt to understand her own experience growing up in a Children's Home in Sydney in the postwar years. Joanna is the co-author of *When the War Came to Australia*, and has had a long career in documentary television as a researcher, writer and interviewer.

*This book is for all of us who grew up without the care
and love of our parents, in Children's Homes,
orphanages and other 'child welfare' institutions —
those of us who survived, and those who did not.*

Orphans of the Living

Growing up in 'care' in twentieth-century Australia

JOANNA PENGLASE

First published in 2005 by
Curtin University Books
a Fremantle Arts Centre Press imprint

Second edition first published 2007 by
FREMANTLE PRESS. Reprinted 2025.

Fremantle Press Inc. trading as Fremantle Press
PO Box 158, North Fremantle, Western Australia, 6159
fremantlepress.com.au

Copyright © Joanna Penglase, 2005

The moral rights of the author have been asserted.

This book is copyright. Apart from any fair dealing for the purpose of
private study, research, criticism or review, as permitted under the
Copyright Act, no part may be reproduced by any process without
written permission. Every reasonable effort has been made to seek
permission for quotations contained herein. Please address any
enquiries to the publisher.

Cover design Adrienne Zuvela
Cover image: Children in Dalmar Children's Home, Seaforth, Sydney from
the Wellings Local Studies Collection, courtesy of Manly Library, NSW.

A catalogue record for this
book is available from the
National Library of Australia

ISBN 9781920731663 (paperback)
ISBN 9781921696787 (ebook)

Fremantle Press is supported by the State Government through the
Department of Local Government, Sport and Cultural Industries.

Fremantle Press respectfully acknowledges the Whadjuk people
of the Noongar nation as the Traditional Owners and
Custodians of the land where we work in Walyalup.

Previous page: *Toddlers with a member of staff at the Methodist Dalmar Home, posing
for a photograph used in the 1958 annual report of the Sydney Home. Note the full
nurse's uniform, which was standard clothing for staff of Children's Homes of this era.*

Acknowledgements

My first and most heartfelt acknowledgement is to my analyst, Judy Spielman. Without her there would be no book. Without her I would not know myself or my own story. Thank you for caring about me, and for persevering through all the times when others would have given up.

This book has been a long time in the making, and along the way, so many people have helped me. I want to begin by thanking the 90 care leavers who shared their stories with me for my thesis and the many archivists and librarians who were of assistance, with special thanks to UnitingCareBurnside who allowed me access to their archives, and to their archivist Barbara Horton who helped me to use them. Anna Yeatman, who supervised my thesis in its final year, was invaluable for her insights, and for her personal support and advice. Other workers in the area of 'child welfare' shared with me useful and interesting information, in particular Donella Jaggs, Morri Young, the late Marie Wilkinson, and the NSW Department field officers I interviewed. I would also like to thank Pat Griffiths for her extra research for the book, and Kylie Norton, of Norton Design, for help with photos. Margaret Whiskin at Curtin Books and my editor Sarah Shrubb have both been lovely to work with — patient and insightful, and generous with their time and feedback.

A very special thank you to Leonie Sheedy. We founded CLAN together, and Leonie has never ceased to inspire and encourage me.

Others I particularly want to thank are:

Senator Andrew Murray for setting up the Inquiry into Children in Institutional Care, and all the other Senators on that committee who entered so compassionately into our experiences, along with the secretariat who worked so hard to do justice to them in the Forgotten Australians report.

All the people whose submissions to the Inquiry I have quoted from. I am sorry I did not have space to quote them all, as I would have liked to. Also the many care leavers I have met through CLAN who have shared their stories and their feelings with me.

Tony Taussig, my friends Pamela, Marie, Efe and Annie who have always been there for me, and other newer friends who also enrich my life now.

I want to thank my own dear family, for their love and care — my daughter Isabel, my sister Philippa and my nieces Meischak and Vivienne.

And finally I remember here my father and my mother, who did love me, and who would have kept me if they could have.

Note to the reader

A note on terminology
For clarity I have used the following terms throughout the text:

'**The Inquiry**' or '**the Senate Inquiry**' refers to the Inquiry into Children in Institutionalised Care, conducted over 2003–04 by the Australian Senate Community Affairs References Committee.

'**The Senate Report**' refers to the report of this Inquiry, the full title of which is *Forgotten Australians: A report on Australians who experienced institutional or out-of-home care as children.*

The '**Department**' refers to the government department that dealt with child welfare in whatever state I am discussing. (Departments had different names, as they do now, and they sometimes changed their name over the period of this book.)

'**Care leaver**' refers to anyone who spent time in or grew up in 'care' away from their family of origin — includes state wards, Home inmates who were not state wards, and people who were fostered.

Senate Inquiry Submissions
All personal submissions to the Senate Inquiry referred to in the text are listed, by name, at the end of the book (see page 357). These submissions are on the public record and can be accessed through the Australian Parliament website. Where a name occurs in the text but not in the list, this means that I am quoting somebody I interviewed for my PhD thesis and these names are pseudonyms.

Contents

Foreword	My story	9
Preface		29
Chapter 1	Speaking out at last	35
Chapter 2	Why Homes?	66
Chapter 3	'Complete and austere institutions'	102
Chapter 4	A window on the Homes	155
Chapter 5	'The Welfare': what happened when the state got involved?	215
Chapter 6	'A terrible way to grow up …'	256
Chapter 7	The aftermath	309
Appendix	Numbers of children in 'care' in 20th-century Australia	352
Picture credits		356
Senate Inquiry submissions cited		357
Notes		358
Bibliography		368
Index		375

My mother with her three children, c.1948: my sister Philepppa, my brother John and me, aged about 4. My mother's name was Eva Laurel Penglase, but she always called herself 'Eve'. We had been in the Home for at least three years when this photograph was taken by a street photographer — probably at Manly, New South Wales.

Foreword

My story

The persistent psychic problems of ... survivors arise out of the impossibility of telling others in a meaningful way what they have witnessed ... The unspoken experiences return in disguise, as symptoms, as uncomprehended behaviour, or physical disorders. And all the time there is a story that cannot be told.[1]

Dutch sociologist,
Abram de Swaan, on survivors of trauma

For as long as I can remember, I have woken up every morning with a feeling of dread. For me, the story that could not be told was the story of my early loss — the story behind my dread. I could not tell anybody what had happened to me because I did not know; I could not afford to know. Only my analyst could tell, on my behalf, the story that made sense of my life, of my symptoms, but until I met her there was nobody who was able to do that. That dread has only recently left me. It was exorcised by ten years of therapy which gave me a 'meaningful way' of telling my story for myself.

* * * * *

When I was eight months old, my parents put me and my sister in a Home, and although my mother visited, my father disappeared and neither of them came back to claim me. I had no idea that this mattered, and through years of therapy I resisted the fact that it did — I had no insight into my own life until I met Sydney psychoanalyst Dr Judy Spielman. I would not be here today writing this if she had not agreed to work with me. We have persevered through very difficult times, and I resisted all the way as she patiently insisted that facing the pain of that loss was the only way to get better.

I thought *all* my problems came from living in the Home, and undoubtedly some of them did. But they were layered onto that first early profound loss — the loss that squeezed the life out of me, stunted my emotional growth and took me close to death by the time I was fifty.

My family

I have managed to piece together a sort of family history by talking to remaining family members, but nobody can tell me about the sequence of events that led to our going into the Home. My parents married in 1941. There are a couple of photos of them from this time and they looked happy. The children came quickly: my brother in 1942, my sister in 1943, and then me, in 1944. By 1945 my sister and I were in the Home, 'just for three weeks while I get on my feet,' said my mother. This was one of the few statements about our fate she ever made.

I know next to nothing about my parents and I never talked to my mother about her childhood, her life as a young woman, her marriage, or her feelings about her husband. I never asked her what it was like for her to go, in the space of four years, from a bride to a single mother of three.

I don't know where my father was then or what he was doing. Did they both put us in the Home, or did my mother go alone, because he had left her? I have one photograph of the whole family, with me, then aged about two, sitting in my mother's lap on a beach, my sister in my father's lap, my brother between them. They must have visited the Home and taken us out for the day, but I don't know if they were living together then, had reconciled perhaps. I know that when my sister was three, they took her out of the Home and went to southern New South Wales to run a café; it didn't work out, and my sister came back. There is no later photograph with my father, but there is one taken by a street photographer, which shows just my mother with the three of us — in this one, I look to be about four.

I do know that my father eventually left New South Wales altogether and was not heard of — at least by me — for close to twenty years. I gather he moved around Queensland, working as a storeman or a salesman, apparently forming no ties. What had happened in his life that he could not bear the responsibility of a wife and three children and had to run away? He came from a family in Melbourne. His father had been a textile buyer for Myer, and had died relatively young of a heart attack. My father had four brothers, and had sung in the choir at St Paul's Cathedral School in Melbourne. He had come to Sydney as a young man — I don't know why. On my parents' marriage certificate he is described as a clerk in the Department of Air. Why hadn't he been in the war? I don't know his medical history, but perhaps the reason is there. I thought that he may have had a criminal record, and checked that recently, but he didn't. He seemed to have had trouble holding down a job and I do remember being told — by whom? my mother? — that he had had minor run-ins with the police for petty theft.

I met my father once, that I remember. I was nineteen. He turned up in Sydney in 1963 and we all met in a café: his three children, our mother and him. I was intensely disappointed by him — he didn't seem interested in us, and he blamed my mother for his life. So I made no effort to see him again; I didn't want to know him. He was in Sydney for quite some time before he returned to Queensland, but I never sought him out. He died, apparently of a heart attack, in 1968, aged fifty-three. He was found floating in the sea off Townsville. Judging by his death certificate, he had been an alcoholic in very poor health, but my sister is convinced he suicided. He had no identification on him, but was known to the police in Townsville.

Very recently I have started talking to my mother's half-brother about those early days, trying to piece together what happened. He told me that once my father had sent each of us a fountain pen. I don't remember receiving it, but when my uncle told me that, I did suddenly remember a fountain pen: I could see it — a dark mottled colour, and a rounded shape. I didn't keep the only present my father ever gave me, but I do remember it in another way: I have always used a fountain pen, for decades, even though it's really not practical when you are left-handed. When I finally, with my analyst, made that connection, my feelings about my father changed. I could see him as a person, not just the hated man who had abandoned me. I could think about what a lonely life he had had, drinking himself to death, alone in another state.

The particularly sad and awful thing about my father's leaving us is that my mother's father had also left her, although not intentionally. He died in 1919 (in the 'Asian flu' epidemic) when she was three, and her mother had remarried, so my mother and her younger sister had grown up with a stepfather and four stepbrothers. Some of her stepbrothers were still young when my mother's marriage failed, so her own family was not able to give her much support.

She was left to cope alone, and she did what thousands of parents in this situation were forced to do. She put the girls into a

Home, and my brother, aged three, in 'care' somewhere else, so that she could go to work. My brother — at age three, able to speak up for himself — apparently refused to stay where she placed him, and eventually my mother and my brother ended up back living with her family, in the family home.

What else could my mother do? In the immediate postwar era there was an acute housing shortage and very little government or community assistance. Women's wages were low and not equal to a male — a breadwinner's — wage. But how could my mother go to work, if she had found a job? Who would look after her children, one of them a baby? Even finding accommodation was difficult. She lived in a much stricter, more judgmental, moral environment than we do now, and women on their own — especially with children — were suspect.

I'm sure my mother never intended us to stay in the Home, but her options were almost non-existent. Like many women of her generation, she was not highly educated; she had been a clerk in a public utility before she married. But she was very resourceful, and she was an attractive, gregarious and friendly blonde who people warmed to easily. At some stage she got a job selling advertising space in magazines. Later on, when my brother was older, she also worked as a waitress in an inner-city steakhouse for several nights a week, to pay for him to attend a private high school. She wanted him to turn out better than his father, and she thought she would achieve this by giving him a private school education.

The Home

The Home where my sister and I spent our childhood was not typical in that it was a business, operated under licence from the NSW Department of Child Welfare. It was run by two women, the Taylors[2] — a widow and her unmarried daughter, Betty.

Neither of them had any training in child care but the mother had had two children. They were female and they were respectable, and the Department required no other qualifications.

The lives of all these women — the women who ran the Home and my mother — show how important it was then to have a male breadwinner, and how limited both life and work choices were for a woman without one. When Mrs Taylor's husband died in 1931 the older girl, Betty, had left school, at the age of fourteen, to help support the family (there was another, younger daughter who later married) and the mother and daughter eventually set up a sandwich shop in the city, which they ran for some years. It was very hard work, so they decided to set up a 'Children's Holiday Home', as they called it, instead.

Until I was four, the Home was quite close to the city, but then they moved to the house they had built on the waterfront about thirty kilometres north of Sydney. Although this is now a wealthy and exclusive area, when they set up the Home it was isolated and sparsely populated, two hours by road from the city. Setting up the Children's Home was an opportunity for the Taylors to both own their own home and make a living: women alone often survived this way then. But the move must have been a blow to my mother — now it was much further to travel to visit us.

The Home was licensed by the NSW Child Welfare Department to take twelve children at any one time: girls to any age, boys to just under five. There were three types of children in the Home. There were four other long-term inmates like my sister and me — the 'permanents'. One was the daughter of divorced parents who both worked, one had been left by her mother in her father's care, and he had placed her in the Home, and there were two sisters who must have been war orphans, 'displaced persons' from Europe who had been put in the Home by two women who were either relatives or friends of their parents and had taken on their care in Australia. Then there were children who came for longish periods, but not permanently, during a family crisis — when their mothers went into hospital for operations or new babies, or when they were not coping, and sometimes when parents were separating or divorcing. Finally, there was a changing population of children who passed through for holidays when their parents went away without them, which seems to have been common practice at this time. Children were left behind, as pets are now, while their parents had holidays alone together.

So unlike children in most other Children's Homes, I constantly saw children being picked up by their parents and taken home. It never occurred to me to hope that my mother might do that for me, and I had not even an image, let alone a concept, of 'father'. When I was put in the Home it was as if I ceased to belong to my parents, and they did not claim me. I never even thought about this until the day when my analyst asked me how I felt about it.

What happened when we went into the Home

My mother was weak and vulnerable. Weak in the sense that she had no money, no emotional support, no way of looking after her children; she herself had been abandoned. She needed help and Betty Taylor offered that help. My mother could never have imagined what would happen. Betty, who was almost exactly my mother's age, took me, the baby, as her own. In effect, she stole me from my mother. I could not acknowledge, until very recently, that I did get some good things from my 'care'; but I did, and without them I would not have survived as well as I did. I got one-to-one 'care', and babies can die or become autistic if they don't get that — as we have seen with the children in Romanian orphanages in recent years. I got attention and cuddles, which few children in Homes did. I got an education, which opened doors, got me good jobs, and gave me, eventually, the key to getting help.

Until I was six, Betty doted on me. I was *her* girl. She dressed me in starched frocks and polished shoes and tied hair ribbons in my hair, which she curled. I was the baby she could not have because she had chosen to stay with her mother and not marry. I have felt shame all my life that I let myself be owned by her, that I let her make me her creature. But I had no choice: my mother left me before I was able to survive on my own, and I latched on to the next person who came along so that I could go on living. This was a woman who was unable to leave her own mother, yet she told me that *I* did not need *my* mother and quite deliberately set about replacing her.

Betty made sure I depended on her approval for my very existence. She took advantage of my need, and my mother's need, to ensure that I would never be able to survive without her. This was perhaps the strongest message I got from her: I was hers, and without her I was nothing. I was not to dare to want my own mother, or to attempt to relate to her in any way. I accepted this.

But Betty was not at all interested in me as a person. I was a possession, a toy, a demonstration of the 'goodness of her heart', to use her phrase. 'After all I've done for you' was favourite phrase of hers. She used it to silence any hint of opposition, any different thought, or idea, or opinion, any expression of a desire to be a person in my own right. I dreaded hearing her utter this, because it meant that I had done 'the wrong thing' and could be at any moment thrown back 'into the gutter, where you belong' (and where I had been taken from). Every day I heard how lucky I was that they had taken me in when my mother did not want me (Betty's words).

The only way I could survive with her was to completely and utterly efface my own self and become a carbon copy of her, and that is what I did. I gave myself up entirely. I modelled myself on her, watched her, waited until she spoke to say what I thought (what she thought). Gave up my sister, my mother, my brother, any sense of a self that was separate from her.

She said that she loved me and I felt I loved her too. At the same time, I was frightened of her. I knew that her 'love' for me was totally conditional on my behaviour, would continue only if I was what she wanted me to be, and loyal to her over my mother. And she took pleasure in showing my mother that I preferred her.

In my earliest years, I was the focus of her relentless and possessive devotion, and I have some intense and apparently happy memories of that closeness. But these were and still are terribly confusing and shaming memories. People who are sexually molested in Homes sometimes say that, to their enormous and enduring shame, they did enjoy it because it was the only attention they got and it made them feel special. It's the same sort of thing for me, I think. I did enjoy the attention, being made to feel special, but all the same I was being used; it was primarily for *her* gratification, and it came with a huge price tag.

So although my Home experience is not like the usual one — in that I got one-to-one attention — in a more fundamental sense it is absolutely typical: I had lost my mother and father, so I could be used in whatever way my 'carer' wanted. Many children in Homes were used by adults for sexual gratification, or as punching bags, or as scapegoats for ill-temper and frustration. Staff in Homes picked on the most vulnerable, the ones they could have their way with most easily — the youngest, most fragile, most unprotected, most unclaimed. We were prey. Betty was using me for her own gratification, and all the things she gave me were things I didn't need. What I needed was my mum and dad, my sister and my brother.

My sister

My sister, aged two when we went into the Home, was given the opposite role to me. She was the bad girl, and Betty persecuted her mercilessly every day of her life until she left, at age seventeen.

'Persecution' sounds like an exaggeration, but it is the only word to describe how Betty behaved to my sister. She kept her under constant surveillance, and was always on the watch for an opportunity to find fault and punish her. She hit her with a wooden spoon, her bare hands, or any weapon to hand, she slapped her on the face, boxed her ears, shook and threw her about and once kicked her down a flight of stairs.

She singled out my sister for humiliation and public shaming and put-downs, told her 'no wonder your mother doesn't want you', since 'nobody could love you'. She appeared to hate my sister, and she never missed an opportunity to vent this hatred. This has been one of the worst and most enduring memories in my life, because along with it goes shame that I did nothing to defend my sister, shield her, that I did not ally myself with her. Yet how could I, when I was so young, and so in thrall to Betty? And how did I, as a child, deal with the two absolutely contradictory faces Betty showed me: her 'loving' behaviour to me, and her cruel behaviour to my sister? It's the sort of situation that drives you mad, and it did drive me mad. 'Your sister was a reminder of your family, that you weren't really Betty's,' said my analyst once, and that, finally, made sense of it for me.

I did not dare identify myself with my sister in any way. To show any feeling for her, or for my mother, was the most monstrous, criminal betrayal of Betty's 'goodness'. I had to collaborate in her assessment of both of them as 'bad', or risk further abandonment. So my sister and I lived in the Home as strangers to each other. My entire purpose in life, my reason for being 'a good girl', was to avoid further abandonment and avoid the treatment inflicted on my sister (and, to a lesser degree, on certain other children in the Home). This involved the most minute surveillance of my every thought and action. I gave up any sense of self in order to survive. I lost my sister, and I did not really find her again until we were both close to sixty, though this was not through any fault on her side.

We saw quite a lot of each other over the years, but I kept an emotional distance from her through my total inability to face my feelings about what had happened to us as children.

My mother

It is only through my therapy with Judy Spielman that I have connected with the feelings of abandonment and loss, the bottomless despair and grief of that little girl. I was frightened when my mother came to see us because I knew I must behave as Betty expected me to and show loyalty to her, not to my mother. I found it hard to think of my mother as mine; I felt that she belonged to my brother — I suppose because he was the one she had kept. I remember feeling frozen when she came to see us, going out with her and behaving like the robot I was, feeling dazzled by her apparent gaiety and smiles. My sister told me that every time we returned from one of these outings with my mother I vomited, but I have no memory of it.

I don't remember how frequently my mother visited us in the Home, but I think it was quite often. It was always on a Sunday, her only day off. She didn't have a car, and she used to catch the bus to the Home, a journey of at least two hours each way. I remember very little about her then, except the picture in my mind that I have of her — a blonde, glamorous lady with a cigarette, always chattering, always smiling, with bright pink or red lipstick and very long fingernails painted in the same colour. She would take us to a café for afternoon tea, or to the beach, then return us to the Home. How did she feel as she sat in the bus on the way back, travelling further and further away from us? She never told us. She never said she missed us, and I never saw her cry. She did not seem real to me.

Only now can I think about her life. I wonder how she managed to keep going. She had very little leisure time, and the money she earned was never enough, no matter how hard she worked. She had a whole list of throwaway lines — '*toujours gai*' was the catchphrase, then 'every cloud has a silver lining', 'there's something good just around the corner' and 'some day I'll meet a wealthy fella'. She was not '*toujours gai*' underneath. She had at least two emotional breakdowns for which she was hospitalised. The first time she was given shock treatment for depression — this was in 1954, when I was ten. I think she probably kept telling herself that soon she would get the girls out of the Home, soon she would be in a better financial position (or soon she would 'meet a wealthy fella'), one day she'd have a home and we would all be together. She was always an optimist, but she was not very realistic, especially about money. She had a great sense of humour and she was very gregarious. She loved the theatre, and music. She loved smoking and called cigarettes her little friends; they reminded her of good times, she said. In 1969, she followed my brother to England. Once again, we girls were left behind, but we both eventually followed her there, at least for a time. I didn't stay, but my sister did. I returned to England in 1977 when my mother was in a London hospital with lung cancer. I would not believe she was dying, and I felt so angry with her that although I'd come all the way from Australia to see her, I went off to a Greek island for a holiday. When I returned she was dead.

The price

This is the price I paid to survive in the Home: I became a robot. I had to be part of Betty's family, not my own. I had no relationship with my mother, I had nothing to do with my sister, and I had no friends in the Home, since I was always being puffed up as superior to the other children. Judith Herman, in her book, *Trauma and Recovery*, could be describing me when she says that the child in an abusive environment often, in order to survive, becomes 'a superb performer', 'attempts to do whatever is required of her', and may become an academic achiever and 'a model of social conformity'.[3] I became all of those things, and one of the good consequences was that I got an education. However, that too came at a price, as Herman says: 'None of her achievements in the world redound to her credit, for she usually perceives her performing self as inauthentic and false.' Children in such environments, she says, 'attempt to appease their abusers by demonstrations of automatic obedience' and 'many develop the belief that their abusers have absolute or even supernatural powers, can read their thoughts, and can control their lives entirely'. I did believe this until I was well into my teens.

I had no understanding, as a child, of what I was doing; it was a survival mechanism that was completely automatic. I came across a description of Betty in RD Laing's book, *The Divided Self*, the parent whose child has to consent to being engulfed, colonised — cannibalised, as I've sometimes thought of it — as the price of being looked after. I stole Laing's work from a shop in Brussels in 1972, during my kleptomania phase, and when I read it, I felt relief and amazement, because for the first time I found somebody who understood what had happened to me. Laing describes how people growing up in an emotional scenario like mine — though he is describing a parent/child relationship — develop what he calls the 'false self' which operates above all through compliance with what we think others expect of us, 'an excess of being 'good', never doing anything other than what one is told, never being 'a trouble', never asserting or even betraying any counter-will of one's own'. This is purely for survival, prompted by the dread of what might happen to you if you were actually yourself.[4]

How many of us survived in Homes by reacting like this? And how many of us, in our adult lives, have suffered from the consequence of doing so, which Laing goes on to describe: 'the haunting sense of futility' which goes along with not being yourself.[5] When you feel abandoned by your parents you do whatever you have to to survive, and the younger you are, the more entrenched your survival behaviours become. I was lucky to get somebody who would look after me when my mother could not, but I was unlucky in the sort of person she was, and in what she did to me. Part of her 'training' of me was, I know, to try to ensure that she would keep me forever, as 'hers', since one of the mantras I heard from her constantly was, 'after all I've done for you, you'll only go to your mother'. This was always a signal to me to redouble my efforts to prove how 'good' and 'obedient' I was. That response became even more intense when she got another baby to look after: this happened when I was six. I was abandoned once again, for although she still called me her 'pet', this baby replaced me as the first object of her interest and devotion.

Living in the Home

In *Banished Knowledge*, psychoanalyst Alice Miller speaks of childhoods that, she says, 'resemble a totalitarian regime in which the only authority [is] the state police'.[6] This describes the atmosphere of my childhood in the Home. The older woman, Mrs Taylor, was a relatively mild presence: she encouraged my reading and study, and bought me books — and how lucky I was, for books were my great escape. But Betty used her power to intimidate the children in her 'care', in particular my sister, as I have described. This atmosphere, characterised by physical violence, or the threat of it, is what in other contexts is described as 'domestic violence', and psychologists compare it with the experience of living in a war zone. I never felt safe.

Children were physically punished, hit and shaken and thrown around, though not with the degree of violence meted out to my sister. I sometimes heard the two women discussing how they would explain to a parent the bruises on a child, and asking,

'What if the Welfare find out?' Children were also forced to sit for hours on a stool, and younger ones were thrown into cots and left alone to cry behind a closed door. Verbal abuse and personal humiliations were commonplace, as they seem to have been in all Homes. At the same time, there was a sort of hierarchy of treatment. The holidaying and the shorter-term children were often from families that were well off, where the parents were professionals. These children were unlikely to be hit, and Betty would often, in fact, speak to them quite differently. Children of 'common' or 'lower-class' parents, parents who spoke 'badly', were poor, sent cheap clothing with their children, and had few worldly achievements or possessions, got the worst deal.

Physically, however, we were very well cared for. Betty was obsessive about cleanliness and spent most of her time cleaning and washing, which she insisted on doing entirely herself. She would not have a washing machine and she refused to have paid help because nobody would achieve her standards. We had regular baths, clean sheets and clean clothes, and always went out the door looking immaculate, in spotless starched and ironed dresses or uniforms and shining neat hair. We were well fed because Mrs Taylor was a good cook.

Boredom, but maybe it was really depression, or just sadness, is a very strong memory of my childhood. I was treated differently from the others, and given books and dolls and some space of my own (a luxury in a Children's Home), but like all the other children there, my horizons were extremely restricted. We did very little physical activity, but I also remember that even as a child I never had much energy. Time was to be got through with as little noise and fuss as possible. There was absolutely no spontaneity allowed, no free exploring of our environment, no initiative in anything. It wasn't just that it was forbidden, though it was. It was worse than that. For me at least, it did not have to be forbidden because I had internalised the belief that I must not exist outside the formula I had been given: you must never ever do anything unless you had been told to, or without asking permission. I heard another care leaver relate once how there was a sign in her Home that said, 'Don't think, ask'. That could describe my Home too.

Books became my escape, not only from boredom, but from the unbearable tensions of the atmosphere around me, which often culminated in Betty's flying into an explosive rage with no warning. Reading was an escape, but I did not think this at the time, I just knew that I needed books; I felt bereft and frightened without them. Reading also gained me approval (good girls are readers) and approval was something I craved like a drug. It meant I was safe. I became a know-all, determined that nobody could tell me anything. I had to be one step ahead of everybody so that I could protect myself from surprise attacks. It's no wonder I had no friends in the Home. I was always held up as an example of perfection, and that separated me from the other children — who no doubt despised me. I was like the prisoners who suck up to the prison guards. But I was also, as my analyst pointed out one day, like the prisoners in the camps who went through the motions of living but were dead inside.

It was an insular life. It was the 1950s. I lived in a house of females, and most of the teachers in my single-sex high school were women. I had one male teacher in my primary school years and the only other men I encountered were tradesmen who came to the Home, and occasionally, briefly, the fathers of girls in my class or fathers who came to the Home to pick up their children. The Department inspectors who came to the Home were always women. I had no hobbies and no outside activities except Sunday school and church. Unlike most care leavers, I have no memory of feeling stigmatised at school because I came from a Home. Perhaps this was because I interacted little with other children, since. I just didn't know how to; but also, by setting myself up as an academic achiever, I gave myself an alternative identity. In class my only concern was to anticipate and carry out to the letter the teacher's wishes, and this type of compliance was well rewarded in Australian schooling in the 1950s — which also reinforced my belief that being 'good' was the only way to survive in the world.

I was the only child in that Home who was never taken back, eventually, by somebody, whether parent or relative. The holidaying children and the longer stayers all went home, the 'permanents' too (including the 'displaced' children) were all claimed by somebody. Even Betty's second 'baby' was, after some years, fought for and reclaimed by her own mother. My sister left the Home at seventeen and went and lived with our mother. I didn't leave until I was almost twenty-two, and I was only able to because the friend I had made at Sydney University got a flat for the two of us. It didn't occur to me to go and live with my mother; I wouldn't have dared to anyway, because I was so trained by then to believe I belonged to Betty. It was too late for me to connect with my mother without a lot of help.

The consequences

The depression started when I was eighteen. By this time, my mother was renting a large house where my brother and sister lived with her, and she took in boarders to help with the rent. I won two scholarships to Sydney University, and I took the one that gave me a living allowance (along with a bond to teach, which I later paid back), so that from then on I paid my own way — but I still could not leave the Home. I had no idea how I would do that, or even that I could. It was when I was at university that I did begin to spend time with my mother, and with my brother and sister, but I could not relate to them as people who mattered to me. I barely knew my brother, and I felt guilt about my sister. I could not/would not let my mother get near me emotionally.

Although I kept on going to my mother's house, I still felt I ought to belong to the Home, and particularly to Betty.

The year my depression started, I also began to develop anorexia nervosa. I was well on the way to skeletal perfection by the end of the year I turned nineteen. That was when I met my father. Then the anorexia turned into compulsive eating and starving, which went on for the next fourteen years. It ended quite abruptly when my mother died. That was in 1977, when I was thirty-three and she was sixty, the age I am now.

I got through my twenties with anti-depressants, tranquillisers, sleeping pills and alcohol. At twenty-two I sought out a psychiatrist. Besides the pills he gave me, we did have sessions of talking, and I remember how it took a long time for him to get through to me that my childhood in the Home had been a bad experience. I was amazed. I did not connect any of my symptoms to my past. I still told myself that I had been so lucky to have 'her' and my 'care'. But the psychiatrist did not understand that the major reason for my debilitating symptoms was the still completely unacknowledged loss of my parents. He did not try to help me to reconnect with my mother. And when he gave me all those pills, they stopped the symptoms and made me feel I could be 'normal'. So I never looked into the void; I just worked harder at papering it over.

These were the years when I travelled overseas, taking terrible risks, not looking after myself and living with bouts of depression, panic and fear. In the decades after my twenties I didn't take any pills — it was just alcohol. I used alcohol the way a lot of people do, as an anaesthetic: to dull pain, fear, insecurity, emptiness.

Getting to the end … but also the beginning

It is an understatement to say that being a wife and mother was difficult. I loved being a mother but I didn't know how to be one, although I thought I did. You learn to be a mother by having one, so I made all the mistakes that 'Homies' often do — too close or too distant, no boundaries or too many, no idea at all just what is good for children and what isn't. And having a child triggered off in me something which had been lurking for years. I had always been chronically anxious about the safety of boyfriends, ringing up hospitals and police stations if they were running late, always fearing the worst. It was a hundred, a thousand, times worse with a child, especially as she got older. I feared she would disappear as my own mother had disappeared — inexplicably, catastrophically (though I did not make that connection then). But it was also as if I feared that I would fail my daughter as my mother had failed me, that I would not be there when she needed me. When she was five I had a dream in which she had been kidnapped and was in a room alone somewhere. She telephoned me, but she was too young to be able to tell me where she was, and so in the dream I never found her. This was my waking fear, not merely a nightmare.

* * * * *

It was this crippling anxiety that finally made me seek serious therapeutic help. I did not feel I would survive my daughter's adolescence. I knew I had to let her go, let her grow up and become independent, but I didn't know how I would be able to do it. I felt I would literally die from anxiety. What I must really have been feeling was that I could not endure much longer the pain I had buried inside me from my own childhood; it was *that* pain that would kill me. I was in the middle of writing my PhD thesis, and in doing the interviews with other Homies I was confronted daily with feelings I'd tried to keep at bay all my life. Although nobody would have known it from my outward appearance (working, studying, shopping, smiling), I was close to total breakdown when I finally sought help. I was fifty when I did that, and when I knocked on her door on an afternoon in May 1995 I was barely alive inside. My life felt unbearable but I had no idea why. I was wearing a fake fur coat in bright parrot colours, my façade that said 'I'm fine'. This was my first visit to the psychoanalyst, but she saw straight through the parrot coat. How incredibly lucky I was that I met Judy Spielman. If at this stage in my life I had met a therapist who had not understood, I would not now be here to write this.

Preface

It was a terrible way to grow up. You think, how could that have happened?

Jilly Marsh,
on growing up in a Children's Home in the 1950s

… it is highly likely that every Australian either was, is related to, works with or knows someone who experienced childhood in an institution or out of home care environment.

Forgotten Australians, report of the Senate Inquiry into Children in Institutional Care, 2004

This is a book about a forgotten chapter in the history of Australian childhood: growing up in institutional care. It was an experience that close to half a million Australian children had in the 20th century, and it is one that affects us all.

However, it is a history that has not been spoken; it has remained hidden. The first public recognition came with the report of an Inquiry conducted by the Australian Senate during 2003 and 2004. The Inquiry took evidence from all over the country and received more than 600 submissions — 'the largest volume of highly personal, emotive and significant evidence of any Senate Inquiry'.[1] The people who wrote the submissions had been in both state and non-state institutions across Australia between the 1920s and the 1990s.

Forgotten Australians, the Report of this Inquiry, contains a powerful and graphic overview of the experience of institutional care. The stories of care leavers, said the committee:

> outlined a litany of emotional, physical and sexual abuse, and often criminal physical and sexual assault. Their stories also told of neglect, humiliation and deprivation of food, education and health care. Such abuse and assault was widespread across institutions, across States and across the government, religious and other care providers.
>
> But the overwhelming response as to treatment in care, even among those that made positive comments, was the lack of love, affection and nurturing ... [provided for] young children at critical times during their emotional development.

The Report states unequivocally that, with regard to the institutional care system:

> The Committee considers that there has been wide scale unsafe, improper and unlawful care of children, a failure of duty of care, and serious and repeated breaches of statutory obligations.[2]

It would be impossible to exaggerate what *Forgotten Australians* means to care leavers. We have been waiting all our lives for this recognition, for something that would take the place of the denial and disbelief we are all so used to hearing. There are many angry and sad voices in that Report, expressing the feelings of people living still, as adults, within the prison of their childhood pain. Until very recently we have all had to explain our anger and our pain in subjective terms, as if it indicated 'something wrong' with us. The Senate Inquiry marks a turning point — we can finally see and understand our individual histories within their social and political contexts. *Forgotten Australians* confirms what we have always felt and tried for so long to tell others: that our childhood in 'care' scarred us for life.

In 1990, long before the Senate Report was released (which happened in August 2004), I had begun researching this history in an attempt to understand my own childhood experience of growing up in a Children's Home in Sydney. My research, much of it based on interviews with other care leavers, became a PhD thesis. Soon after I submitted it in 1999, I met up again with Leonie Sheedy, one of the women I had interviewed, and together we started a national support and advocacy group for older care leavers like us — 'Homies' and 'wardies' (state wards). We called the group Care Leavers of Australia Network (CLAN). From small beginnings CLAN has grown into an influential national organisation, even though it is still has no ongoing funding by government and thus depends entirely on donations. There is no other national forum for care leavers; in fact, as the Senate Report notes, there is very little support, and there are few services of any kind, in any state, for these Australians.

Leonie and I gave evidence, on behalf of CLAN, at the Senate Inquiry into Child Migration that reported in 2001. There we met Australian Democrats Senator Andrew Murray, the man who was responsible for the establishment of that inquiry. Like the other senators sitting on the inquiry committee, and like most other Australians, Senator Murray was unaware until CLAN's evidence at the hearings that institutional care had been so common for Australian children. Having heard what we had to say, Senator Murray decided that it was time for what he called the third inquiry of the trilogy — after the HREOC (Human Rights and Equal Opportunity Commission) inquiry into the experiences of the stolen generations and the child migration inquiry. It took over a year of intensive lobbying by him and by CLAN to get the proposal for the inquiry through Parliament: to convince enough politicians of the pressing need to put care leaver issues on the national agenda. All care leavers owe Senator Murray a great debt, for without this one man who thought our experiences mattered, there would have been no inquiry into institutional care.

* * * * *

But what lies behind the events documented in *Forgotten Australians*? How could this happen? What was this system of 'care' that treated children so badly, for so long and on such a huge scale? Although I can offer no definitive answers to these questions, this book is my attempt to put the experience of institutional care into context. Uncovering this history has been like looking at a photograph in developing solution. The picture has always been there, but for a long time it has been submerged. Now, gradually, its details are beginning to be revealed, and very slowly it is being put onto the public record and into public consciousness. This was also true for the stolen generations, and for the child migrants. The people who lived these histories always knew them, but the histories were not, until recently, a part of what is recognised as 'history'. *Forgotten Australians* has begun to change that, and this book, I hope, adds to this process.

I should say at the outset what this book is *not*. It is not a history of Australian orphanages, Children's Homes and other children's institutions. Nor is it a history of the policies and laws that governed them. It is not a history of child welfare in Australia or even a history of institutional care for children. My purpose is to present, through the voices of the people who lived it, the experience of growing up in a Children's Home, and to give this experience a social, political and economic context. So I do discuss the social environment which allowed children to end up in institutional care, and the attitudes to these children and their families which rubber-stamped institutional care for so long as an acceptable solution — and which also made the system so impervious to both visibility and accountability. I hope that other publications will follow this one and bring together the many other dimensions of this history: this book is only a beginning.

The sociologist Zygmunt Bauman, in his 1989 study *Modernity and the Holocaust*, suggests that we can treat such apparently inexplicable events as the Holocaust as either a picture or as a window. A picture is static and finite, he says, whereas a window offers many possibilities — depending on where you choose to look. Similarly, we can choose to see the institutional care of children in the 20th century as a picture on a wall, in which case we need only the histories written by the agencies that ran the Homes. Or we can think of it as a window through which, as Bauman says, 'one can catch a rare glimpse of many things otherwise invisible'.[3] This book is that window for those prepared to look, for although this 'care' history is made up of tens of thousands of childhood histories, it is also a social and political history, which illuminates the time during which these events occurred.

In telling this history, it is inevitable that I talk about the sexual and physical abuse of children, but my purpose is not simply to catalogue once again the horrors visited on 'helpless' children by 'sadistic' adults. That perspective immediately puts this history into a specialised category – 'child abuse' – and robs it of any other context. Histories of children's experiences can only be fully understood by inserting them into mainstream history. So we must start by seeing the subjects of these histories as *people* — not just 'children' — caught up in a human tragedy that parallels others in the same era. These events are not bad because they happened to children; they are bad because of their inherent inhumanity. Only when we can fully appreciate this can we go on to say that what makes it worse is that they concern children, and children even more vulnerable than most, since they were without their own families to care for them.

So although children feature on almost every page of this book, it is not only, or even primarily, a book about children. It is a book about our own society, and about ourselves in that society. It reveals aspects of our past that are a part of who we are today. There will be people who will not want to hear what this book relates, just as there are people who do not want to hear about our past policies and actions towards Aboriginal people. But denying the truth of all these histories will not make them go away; nor can it erase the fact that they have occurred. Those who lived them are still with us, and the effects of these events are still with them. Which is perhaps why the senators conclude their executive summary in *Forgotten Australians* with this statement:

> This report is not just concerned with the past, it is very much about the present and it informs the future of our nation.

* * * * *

The Senate Report begins with a quote from Nelson Mandela: 'Any nation that does not care for and protect all of its children does not deserve to be called a nation.' In other words, the way a society treats *all* of its children throws a searchlight on its values and priorities. Let us now turn that searchlight on.

Chapter 1

Speaking out at last

First of all I want to say that, after 40-odd years, at long last somebody is listening to us. At long last we can talk about these events that happened to us ... When I first came out of the Home, it was the sort of thing you could not talk about. At that time, who would listen to you? It has only been in the later years that people have been able to come forward and have their say because there are people listening at long last.

Brian Hart, who grew up in a Salvation Army Home,
WA, in the 1950s[1]

I have found it very difficult to write my own story, to relate those painful events and to expose so much of myself in such a personal way. But at some point I realised that however difficult it was, I had to describe what had *really* been going on for me over the years — mostly hidden, but more real than anything that was visible. I have spent my life hiding, but I don't want to do that any more.

In a more general sense, speaking out is very difficult for all of us, and the Senate Inquiry has done us an enormous service just by inviting us to do so. People who have grown up in 'care' are often afraid to speak up, and indeed unable to do so, because in the very roots of our being we feel, because our experience has taught us this, that we don't matter to anybody and so have no right to speak. So writing a thesis was a great struggle for me. I feared that a thesis written in my own voice and based on my own experience was not valid because *I* was not valid. I was sabotaged daily by the question, 'Who do you think you are?', a question I heard constantly throughout my childhood, addressed not only to me but to all the other children in the Home. The answer for us as children was: nobody, nothing.

So every day, while I was writing the thesis, I battled with the split in me between wanting to speak out and feeling absolutely prohibited from doing so, fearing I would be ridiculed and in some way punished. It felt dangerous to expose what I thought and felt, and the first time I gave a paper at a conference, in 1993, my voice shook so much I could barely get the words out. I had been trained quite ruthlessly in the Home to associate being 'myself' (rather than a self identical with my carer) with danger. In *Self and Others*, RD Laing says, 'The act I do is felt to be me, and I become "me" in and through such action ... [so] there is a sense in which a person keeps himself alive by his acts.' As a child, I had never learnt to keep myself alive by my acts. In fact I had been trained to do the opposite: it was only safe *not* to act on my own initiative.[2]

In these fundamental ways, then, despite the fact that my own childhood experience is in many ways not a typical one, I identify with the histories I read and hear from other care leavers, which tell of the more usual type of institutional experience; I feel the same as they do. What resonates, of course, is the loss of parents — and of their love and their care — and the consequent feeling of being unwanted. There is also a feeling of extreme vulnerability to the behaviour of others when you grow up in a situation where you are dependent for your care on non-kin. The feeling that you are never safe in the world, that nothing seems to add up; you are always watching your back, always feeling frightened, always expecting something terrible to happen. Your memories are of uncertainty, fear and, often, the possibility of violence.

How this book came about

In my switched-off state, I had no idea what I was getting into when I began my PhD in 1990. I saw it as an attempt to understand how I had come to have the sort of childhood that I had, but I was really looking for the answer to a personal question: why did my parents not want me? Why did they give me away? I could not face that question at the time, though, so I set out to answer a more manageable 'academic' question: how could the Department charged with the welfare of children in New South Wales have licensed the Home I lived in? What sort of society, what sort of attitudes to children, could allow that? As Jilly Marsh, one of my interviewees, said to me: 'It was a terrible way to grow up. You think, how could that have happened?' These were the feelings I was wrestling with.

So I wrote the thesis, initially, as I had lived my childhood — with my feelings split off from my actions. It took a long time for me to put myself into my work. I could not do it until I had help with my feelings about my parents, about losing them, and about what had happened to me because of that. I was lucky that one of my supervisors encouraged me to defer further work on the thesis until I had found the help I needed to support me through it. That was when I found my analyst. Once I resumed the thesis, this supervisor also encouraged me to put myself into it as a personal narrator — even though this is not conventional academic practice.[3]

This book is based on my thesis, but I have expanded the study to make it an account of the institutional experience right across Australia. I have therefore eliminated much of the detail of the original research, but kept the insights into policy and practice which my study of NSW child welfare gave me. I interviewed ninety 'Homies' and 'wardies' for the thesis; other voices in this book are from the hundreds of written submissions which have been made by care leavers to the Senate Inquiry, or from those who gave oral evidence at the hearings in Perth, Adelaide, Melbourne, Sydney and Brisbane in late 2003 and early 2004.[4] The terms of this Senate Inquiry into Children in Institutional Care were designed to target the people whose histories had not been covered by the previous inquiries (into the Aboriginal stolen generations and the child migrants): the 'forgotten Australians' who had grown up in institutional care. 'Care leavers' is the term which is now commonly used to describe us — it includes people who grew up in Children's Homes and other institutions or in foster care, and covers both wards of the state and children who were never wards of the state, like me.

In their submissions to the Senate Inquiry, people from Homes all across Australia speak of their experiences, and their accounts both support and amplify what I had learnt through my own research, and also through running CLAN. In this book I have used the Inquiry submissions to expand the history beyond New South Wales, plus other material, including legislation and one representative annual report from the relevant Department of each state. I chose the year 1956 to provide a snapshot taken mid-century. I use pseudonyms for all my interviewees, but I use real names when quoting from written submissions, as people did when they made them, and because those submissions are now on the public record. I use a capital 'H' when speaking of 'Homes' because I think it is important to differentiate the word irrevocably from 'home'. Although the word 'orphanage' was generally replaced in the postwar period by the term 'Children's Home', little else changed. A Home, like an 'orphanage', was an institution characterised by the absence of all that life within a family home implies.

My focus in this book is on Homes for dependent children simply in need of care — children whose parents were unable to care for them and so put them in Homes, or who had been removed from their parents by the state. Child welfare was (and still is) a state responsibility, so legislation, policy and practice were specific to each state, and in all states there was a clear divide between the government and the non-government sectors. State governments took children into 'care' (usually making them state wards), sometimes ran Homes, and also fostered children, and the ultimate responsibility for 'child welfare' rested with them. However, it was the non-government sector — predominantly churches and charities — that did most of the actual 'care' in Australia in the 20th century, and most of that was institutional. Even in New South Wales, where the state avoided using the non-government sector to 'care' for state wards, and had a high rate of foster care, there were, as well, thousands of children in institutional care run by the charitable sector. I will expand on this in later chapters. The period I am talking about in this book is the decades of the 20th century up to the late 1970s, when to be 'put in a Home' was the commonest form of out-of-home care experienced by Australian children — as well as being one of the major 'solutions' to family breakdown. That is why there are so many of us: close to half a million in the 20th century alone, according to the estimates of the Senate Inquiry.

By the 1970s, looking after children in large institutions was well on the way to being phased out in favour of small family group Homes, cottage Homes, or foster care. There are no longer any orphanages or Children's Homes of the generic type that I describe in later chapters, at least in the West.

Many people who grew up in out-of-home care in this era had a mixture of related experiences, so in this book, as well as people like me, who grew up in a Home, there are others who spent time in Homes combined with time in foster placements, and people who 'graduated' from Homes (and/or fostering) to 'training schools'. 'Training schools' were correctional institutions run by state governments and some non-government organisations (see Chapter 5), where children who were considered potentially 'delinquent' or who had actually committed criminal offences — even if often very minor ones — were placed, usually (but not always) as a result of court determinations. The earlier name for such institutions was 'reform school' or 'reformatory'. I cannot do justice to this experience or its complex history, which needs its own account,[5] but it is inevitably woven into this book — as it is into the report of the Senate Inquiry — because it was not uncommon for children to go from being 'in care' to being detained in 'training schools'.

One striking aspect of this history of institutional care is that the experience seems to be a very widespread one. Canadian, British and Irish narratives written by 20th-century care leavers, for example, tell the same story as Australian accounts. The similarities in these stories are quite explicit, regardless of where and when they occurred in the Western world. In other countries too, in very recent years people have begun to speak up and demand recognition and social justice, and governments and past providers have had to begin to face these issues.

Uncovering this history

In an article written in 1981, the American scholar Peter Lyman asks, 'How do we learn from the history that we live?' He answers his own question like this. We learn, he says, 'not from the formal chronicle of events, but from the subjective feelings and thoughts with which we experience the events of our everyday lives'.[6] There is no other way to write the history that I relate in this book. The 'subjective feelings and thoughts' of people who grew up as inmates of Children's Homes are the only evidence we have to place beside the official histories of institutions — which are written in a way that renders the inmates of the Homes invisible: as narratives of 'rescue' by benevolent adults of 'unfortunate' children. The great achievement of *Forgotten Australians* is that it presents this history from the perspective of the people who lived it (although admittedly filtered through their adult selves). In this book, I too am writing from the perspective of the 'children', which means I am painting a very different picture from the 'official' one.

There is little systematic documentation of the central role that institutional care has played in the history of child welfare throughout much of the 20th century in Australia. This became apparent when I first set out to look for material on Children's Homes for my thesis. When I began this research, I assumed that in the NSW Department's archives there would be a file on every Children's Home but I could not have been more wrong. This was a highly bureaucratised department[7] and there must once have been a file on all Homes licensed by it, but they have obviously been destroyed, since what remained was six small boxes. Where files had been kept, it seemed to be when a Home had come to the Department's attention because of a problem — for example, non-compliance by the Home with licence regulations about hygiene, diet and facilities. In these few remaining files there was almost no comment on children or staff.

To say I was disappointed not to find a file on my own Home is an understatement; I remembered inspections by officers of 'the Welfare' and had been looking forward to reading their reports. I just could not believe there was no file, and I kept hoping I would find one. I had been relying on finding it and seeing something written there which would give me some clues as to why they had thought the Home suitable — clues to how 'the Welfare' 'thought'. My experience in the NSW archives was symptomatic, as we have subsequently discovered through CLAN, of an Australia-wide indifference to this history.

It is, indeed, only in the last seven years that any of the states of Australia have made an attempt to catalogue their delivery of institutional care in the past, whether statutory or charitable. To put it another way, it is only very recently that it has occurred to the Departments responsible for out-of-home care in the past that this kind of record-keeping might be an *essential service* that they should be providing as a matter of social justice to the thousands of Australians who grew up as their responsibility. The purpose behind such directories is that in their pages, former inmates of Homes can find the institutions they lived in, and use the contact information supplied to request their personal records (which may, however, no longer exist). To understand the significance of these records to care leavers, we must remember that they are sometimes the only information they will ever have about their childhood: there is often — perhaps even usually — nobody in their lives they can ask to fill them in about what happened to them as children.

The NSW Department of Community Services published the first directory, but only in 1998. Called *Connecting Kin*, it is described as 'a guide to help people separated from their families search for their records'. It lists all the NSW state institutions and all known Children's Homes run by charitable organisations or churches, with an indication, where known, of the location of their records. Not all Homes are there, as we have discovered through CLAN. Homes such as mine, a private business, are not recorded. *Connecting Kin* is almost the only proactive publication: all the ones that have followed have come about as the result of the recommendation of an inquiry, and without this prompt, they may not have been compiled at all. For example, as a result of the 1999 Forde Inquiry, Queensland in 2001 published *Missing Pieces*, a similar register to the NSW one, also listing both state and non-state institutions. Guides to records were produced by both the Catholic and the Anglican churches as a result of the 1997 inquiry into the stolen generations.

In 1999 the Catholic Church issued *A Piece of the Story: A national directory of records of Catholic organisations caring for children separated from families*, which lists 130 institutions across Australia operating over 160 years. In 2003 the Anglican Church published *For the Record*, noting that although its brief was to provide indigenous people with information about their records, ultimately it had to cover all Anglican agencies providing residential 'care' to children from 1830 to 1980. This was because, while doing the research, 'it quickly became evident that it would not be possible to reliably distinguish between those agencies which provided 'care' to indigenous children and those who did not'. So without haphazard record-keeping on the part of this 'care' provider, Australian care leavers who are not Aboriginal would still have no guide to their records of 'care' in Anglican Homes. As it happens, the Anglican Church has now anticipated one of the recommendations of *Forgotten Australians* (number 14), 'that any agency or state government that has not compiled a directory of records do so now'. Many care leavers might, however, feel excluded when they pick up this guide, since the cover features an Aboriginal painting and the guide is described as 'Background information on the work of the Anglican Church with Aboriginal Children' with, as the second part of this sentence, 'and Directory of Anglican Agencies providing residential care to children from 1830 to 1980'.

The latest publication of this type is the WA Department's *Signposts*, a very comprehensive guide to records from 1920; as yet there are no publications from other states. *Signposts* came about, as the co-ordinator of the project related at its launch in 2004, after she heard Leonie Sheedy, who founded CLAN with me, speak at the Australasian Conference on Child Abuse and Neglect in Perth in 1999. It was listening to Leonie's account of growing up as a Victorian state ward, she said, that helped trigger 'our thinking about how we could make improvements to our systems for children in care', and one area they identified was the need to improve access to information for care leavers.

In a more general sense, even the historical fact that as a matter of deliberate social policy half a million children grew up in institutional care in Australia in the 20th century is merely a footnote in mainstream history. Apart from a very few personal accounts, there are no books on the shelves of Australian bookshops on the experience, or the history, or the character, of institutional care for children in Australia — but we are not alone in this. In a recent (2000) British account of this history in the United Kingdom, *Forgotten Children: The Sexual Abuse Scandal in Children's Homes*, Christian Wolmar, a UK journalist, notes that his is the first attempt to 'document and explain' a series of scandals that has occurred in British Children's Homes over the past 30 years, the first account, apart from government reports, to take this history seriously. Yet, as he says in his opening pages, what has happened in Children's Homes, and what he sets out to document in his book, is, on the face of it, inexplicable:

> A modern western nation with a tradition of caring for the weak, indeed the very birthplace of the welfare state, houses thousands of children in residential homes where they end up battered and sexually abused.[8]

It is certainly the case that many institutions and agencies have written their own official histories; and in recent years more and more care leavers have written their own accounts — but most of the latter are self-published and therefore not available in bookshops.[9] There are some valuable Australian works on child welfare generally,[10] and many academic articles, theses and monographs which illuminate various aspects of this history – though rarely what it was like to experience it. But this type of childhood does not appear, except peripherally, in works about children in Australia. It does not feature, for example, in a recent general work by Jan Kociumbas, *Australian Childhood: A History* (1997). Kociumbas is sensitive to the lived experience of children, but there is no mention of the hundreds of thousands of Australian children living out vastly different childhoods from the one documented in her book. Similarly, in another recent Australian work, *The Country of Lost Children* (1999), the author, Peter Pierce, proposes that 'Australia is the place where the innocent young are most especially in jeopardy',[11] but again, though the work ends with a couple of pages each on the child migrants and the stolen generations, there is nothing about all the other children institutionalised via the mode of 'caring' that has been most common for most of Australia's history. If ever there were 'lost children', they are surely these. Perhaps, however, we have to excuse the ignorance of these authors: how, after all, would they know about this other, unacknowledged, history? The Senate Inquiry is the first time a significant number of people have given voice to their experience of this *other* childhood, and that the extent of these experiences has been revealed.

The effects of institutional care on children

What did authorities of this era think about children in need of care? What made them believe that long-term institutionalisation was appropriate? Institutions, after all, have throughout history been used to house people who are regarded as potentially dangerous, either to themselves or to others, or who, at the very least, need to be contained in some way. And we have actually known for a very long time about the detrimental effects of institutionalisation on children; that knowledge simply appears to have had little lasting impact. As long ago as 1855, the Governor-General of New South Wales wrote of the 'utter inefficiency' of orphan schools — the contemporary term for orphanages — to 'produce any good effect upon the children maintained in them'. The 1873–74 NSW Public Charities Royal Commission made this point:

> The farther the life of these young people differs from that of the work-a-day world, the more difficult will they find it to accommodate themselves to its demands when they go forth and earn their living.[12]

In the 19th century, some of the concern was about the moral effects of institutionalisation, but it was not only that: even then, authorities recognised that institutions were 'mechanical, anonymous, de-individualising'.[13] Large, barracks-style institutions were not conducive to the production of self-reliant, hardworking, virtuous citizens, who would go out and reproduce self-reliant and hardworking families of their own. The 19th century response was a movement to 'board-out' (foster) children, which developed in Britain and Europe and had arrived in Australia by 1872.[14] There was much enthusiasm for boarding out, and there was considerable success with it in all states, in terms of the numbers of children boarded out instead of institutionalised, but it did not totally replace orphanages, and it did not last. It was only in New South Wales that it became longstanding official policy, and this was the only state that maintained a high rate of foster — as opposed to institutional — care for state wards. In other states there was a gradual drift back to institutional care, and in the years of the Depression and World War II, when specific social pressures undoubtedly increased the number of children in need of out-of-home care, the proportion of children placed in institutions increased steadily across the country.[15] By the postwar period, the NSW Department's fostering policy was in marked contrast to the policies and practices of other states, in which only a very small proportion of state wards were fostered — the majority were institutionalised in non-government Children's Homes.

It is poignant, in view of what we now know of how 'child welfare' has operated on children, to read the words of Catherine Helen Spence, the South Australian social reformer and chief advocate of the boarding-out movement, who in 1907 wrote:

> Here under the Southern Cross, it is the law of the land that children shall be brought up in homes not institutions; that the child whose parent is the state shall have as good a schooling as the child who has parents or guardians; that every child shall have not the discipline of routine and red tape, but the free and cheerful environment of early life, preferably in the country, going to school with other young fellow citizens, going to church with the family, having the ordinary duties, the ordinary difficulties, the ordinary pleasures of common life, but guarded from injustice, neglect and cruelty by effective and kindly supervision.[16]

The clear message that the institutionalisation of children was to be avoided at all costs was delivered again in 1946 in the Curtis Report, which set out the findings of the Care of Children Committee set up by the British Government after World War II to investigate conditions of children in care at that time. In postwar Britain, it was this report that provided the impetus for reshaping child welfare policy around a commitment to de-institutionalisation.[17] But although mid-20th-century Australia was still heavily under the influence of 'the mother country', Australian states did not pick up on this report and use it as a model for different practice. The Curtis Report spoke out strongly of the 'dangers of institutional life' to children, *'even in the most well managed of institutions'* (emphasis added), dangers which arose out of 'the tendency to a lack of interest in the child as an individual and to remote and impersonal relations'. The committee was convinced, both from its own observations and from those of other witnesses, that:

> on the human and emotional side, [children] continually feel the lack of affection and personal interest. The longing for caresses from strangers, so common among children in Homes, is in striking and painful contrast to the behaviour of the normal child of the same age in his parents' home.[18]

In a British parliamentary debate following the publication of the Curtis Report, Godfrey Nicholson, MP, said it was not the horrors detailed within the report that moved him most — he believed that 'you have only to focus public attention on those Dickensian scenes to get them remedied'. He continued:

> I am much more moved by the paragraphs that deal in more moderate tones with the lack of background and of private life, the fact that children in institutions have nowhere to put what my children call their 'treasures'; the fact that there is lack of stability. All that is a far greater condemnation of our attitude of mind than are certain isolated horrors ... It is a melancholy, ugly picture.[19]

Nicholson was clearly particularly struck by the emotional sterility of such a life and, even worse, by the acceptance of it as tolerable. Even today, 60 years later, there is still a tendency to focus on the 'Dickensian scenes' in our understanding of the institutional experience — on the abusive actions perpetrated by adults rather than on the 'melancholy, ugly picture' of parentless children living in the dehumanising institutional environment.

What Nicholson's comments suggest is that he thought of his own children, and knew that what he saw in institutional life was not what he would want for them. He therefore did not think it was good enough for other children either, whoever they were — but in this he appears to have been unusual for his time.

There have also been not a few past inquiries in Australia into what happened to children in 'care', particularly in New South Wales. The McCulloch Report, which followed one such inquiry in 1934, expressed surprise that so many of the problems uncovered by that inquiry were old ones, identified time and again and yet not acted upon. These were problems such as 'inadequate training and staff levels, cruel and excessive punishment and poor organisation'[20] — the same problems that are described in *Forgotten Australians*, 70 years later. As *Forgotten Australians* points out, for over a century inquiries into both management practices and abuse have condemned children's institutions in Australia.[21]

In 1956, the Ross Report, following a major British investigation, criticised many facets of Australian children's institutions, including their lack of homely style, isolation from the community, lack of trained staff and poor educational and employment opportunities. The Australian government would not allow publication of the Ross Report until Australian authorities had conducted their own inquiry. The Australian inquiry disagreed with Ross's unfavourable conclusions, prompting the response in the United Kingdom that 'as we feared, the Australian authorities focus only on material things like bathrooms and carpets, and ignore what has been said about atmosphere and management'.[22]

Closer to our own time, there have been three inquiries that have given ample evidence about the experience and the effects of institutional care. One was the HREOC Inquiry into the Separation of Aboriginal and Torres Strait Islander Children from Their Families (1997). Another was the Senate Inquiry into

Child Migration (2001). And there was also an inquiry — the 1999 Forde Inquiry into the Abuse of Children in Queensland Institutions — which was quite specifically concerned with assessing the institutional care of children in that state from 1911. The Forde Report documents an almost total failure of duty of care, involving thousands of children and covering decades, by both the state and the religious organisations that provided that 'care'. The report stated that in Queensland institutions for children, excessive corporal punishment was common, emotional abuse went far beyond neglect — all the way to mental cruelty — sexual abuse occurred in almost all institutions and children were consistently harmed in a range of ways by the very system that was meant to care for them. Breaches of the statutory regulations in relation to food, clothing, education and corporal punishment were 'commonplace'.[23]

In all these reports, sexual, physical and emotional abuse in Homes is a dominant feature.[24] What they also clearly describe is an institutional culture, a standard regime and set of practices, that was apparently characteristic of Children's Homes for decades and which created a depersonalising and punitive living environment in which nobody *of any age* could thrive. Institutions for the care of children appear to have displayed all the features of what is now termed 'systems abuse', defined as 'harm done to children in the context of policies or programs that are designed to provide care or protection'.[25] The dehumanising environment of the institution itself is the primary 'abuse', and from this stem all the other more easily classifiable abuses, such as sexual and physical abuse. There has been little interest, however, in this dimension of institutional care, which has meant that the day-to-day experience of living in an institution has remained almost invisible. The Forde Report in fact represented the institutional care experience in all states of Australia, but when it was released no one asked whether or not its findings might be relevant to other states — and it did not prompt those other states to set up their own inquiries. All that had to wait until the 2003–04 Senate Inquiry and *Forgotten Australians*.

Forgotten Australians estimates that at least half a million children grew up in institutional care in Australia last century. And we have to bear in mind that each child represented in these statistics had parents, siblings and other relatives who were affected by that child's removal into care and its ongoing consequences. There were a maximum of 7500 child migrants to Australia,[26] and it is estimated, perhaps conservatively, that 20,000 to 25,000 Aboriginal children were separated from their families between 1910 and 1970. Those figures in themselves are shocking. As Robert Manne says of the Aboriginal children:

> Given the stunning cruelty and injustice so often involved, and the ripple effect of removals on parents, siblings and extended families, 20,000 or 25,000 separations seems to me a far from trifling sum.[27]

Nothing I say here is meant to detract from the horror and injustice of both those histories, or to claim that the history I am writing about here is more significant. I cite those figures only in order to raise this question: why have we paid so little attention to the experiences of these other, even more numerous children? Why have we been so reluctant to acknowledge the 'cruelty and injustice' which characterise the experiences of all children unfortunate enough to be caught up in the 'welfare' systems of this era?

I can only suggest reasons, not definitive answers. One reason might be that it shows us a childhood so contrary to what childhood is 'meant' to be — carefree, happy, uncomplicated, nurtured — that we do not want to know about it. As the writer and poet Diana Gittins says, 'it could be argued that … the stories adults tell of childhood and the images they create of it may bear almost no relation to the actual experiences of many children'.[28] That is, childhood is often idealised, with a corresponding resistance to accepting as true accounts which challenge that idealised picture. Documenting the Home experience makes visible a type of childhood that does not fit into any narrative of childhood generally regarded as 'typical' in Australia. On the contrary, it offers evidence of a childhood that many do not want to believe was possible in our country.

When I was interviewing people for my thesis, in 1992–93, many of those I spoke to found it incomprehensible that their experience was so little known and so difficult to make known. Sylvia Baker said: 'I feel the injustice when I read accounts like of the Aborigines — I want to say, "But it happened here too."' Sylvia was not denying the devastation wrought by government policies on Aboriginal people, or the uniqueness of their history. What Sylvia meant was that as a child she had suffered experiences as traumatising as had the Aboriginal children, with similar lifelong consequences, and yet there was no forum in which her experiences could be heard, no context in which they could be understood. Similarly, Ray Flett, a NSW state ward, in his submission to the Inquiry, said:

> I have suffered the past few years during the inquiry into the stolen generations with whom I share a commonality of experience. The memories and pain that resurfaced listening to their stories were particularly distressing.

Sylvia was simply 'in a Home': not forcibly removed from her parents, not even sexually abused or physically assaulted, merely emotionally devastated both at the time and for all her adult life by the experience and the effects of growing up in the type of 'care' characteristic of that era. Other care leavers, such as Ray Flett, *were* removed from their parents by the state system — and like so many Aboriginal people, never saw their parents or, in many cases, their brothers and sisters, again. The standard 'welfare' policies and practices of the day devastated the lives of the children and families of thousands of non-Aboriginal families just as the racist policies did Aboriginal people. Ray was removed from his parents by the NSW government in 1957, at the age of three:

> [By the age of six,] I had been denied all knowledge of my natural family and indeed had forgotten about the existence of my siblings, aunts, uncles, grandparents, mother and father. I had no knowledge of the history of my predecessors, who I was or where I belonged.

Where children are removed from their parents in the service of racist policies, we can see very clearly, from a contemporary standpoint, the injustice and the cruelty of such policies. Non-Aboriginal children were usually removed on the grounds of 'neglect', and this has been taken to be so self-evidently necessary and 'right' that it is never questioned. What we do not remember, or perhaps never knew, is that 'neglect' was very broadly defined in Child Welfare Acts, and these Acts gave all states comprehensive jurisdiction over the behaviour of both parents and children. So while some children were undoubtedly removed from unsatisfactory family circumstances, many other children were removed either for reasons we would now regard as insubstantial, or from circumstances where, with even temporary support for the family, removal would not have been necessary. Removal of children from their parents by the state was often an inappropriate response to a crisis situation, but it was the only response available. This, I am sure, is why relatives (or the remaining parent) would often move quickly, in a family crisis, to 'voluntarily' place children in non-state Homes: to avoid the state intervention which could result in the loss of their children altogether. This possibility was particularly likely in New South Wales, as I discuss in Chapter 5.

There is a further powerful convergence of the black and white histories in the fate of children once they were in care. There are the same stories of indifference and cruelty, the same denial of children's feelings and of their parents' feelings, the same callousness towards vulnerable and dependent human beings. When the stolen generation histories started to emerge, I was struck that there was so little discussion of how Aboriginal children were actually treated once they had been so cruelly removed from their families. Few people asked, 'But why institutional care?' and, even more pertinently, 'Why was institutional care so unremittingly appalling?'

Most children in institutional care were not orphans — they often had at least one parent, along with siblings and other relatives — but they were effectively disconnected from them on entry to a Home. Hence my title, *Orphans of the Living*.[29] All children who are removed from parents — by whatever means and for whatever reasons — suffer the same feelings of grief and loss: they suffer as all children do who lose their parents. When the HREOC Report on the stolen generations was released in 1997, Senator Rosemary Crowley remarked that this was a report that, along with recording the histories of the children, also 'lists the broken hearts of thousands of women, of thousands of families'.[30] Alongside those grief-stricken Aboriginal families we must put the thousands of white families whose children were, similarly, lost to them, often forever, through state intervention. We will never hear of the broken hearts of these other women and men who had their children removed by 'child welfare' authorities, never to be returned, or who, through a total lack of other options, had to place their children in institutions. We have only just begun to hear of the broken hearts of their children.

Another similarity between the care leaver history and the stolen generation history is in the readiness of people to deny its significance. Care leavers who speak of their experiences are often met with disbelief and denial. They are also confronted with a great reluctance on the part of the past providers of institutional care — governments and charitable organisations alike — to acknowledge the extent of the damage. But like our treatment of Australia's original inhabitants, this is part of our nation's history. To deny it is to refuse to acknowledge that this is part of being Australian, however unpalatable that might be.

'Child rescue'

When you read the hundreds of histories of care leavers' experiences which are now available, the single most striking feature, the one which stands out above all, is how cruel adults were to children. So perhaps another reason we do not want to know about this history is because it indicates that adults cannot be relied on to be benevolent to children. That is a challenge to some very fundamental beliefs about our social values. We would like to think that only some adults — *other* adults, perverted, sick, disturbed adults — harm children, and it is difficult to face the fact that harming children may be within the range of 'normal' behaviours that all adults might be capable of, under certain circumstances and conditions.

Harry Hendrick, the historian of English child welfare, once observed that 'much of the history of childhood is really the history of what adults have thought about and done to children'.[31] Social policies applied to children, he argues, are motivated by what he describes as 'ageism', which seeks to both repress and oppress young people. Older people are prejudiced against children, a prejudice shared by all classes; and while children are undoubtedly 'dependent, ignorant, vulnerable, untutored and very often threatening' at different stages of their lives, the important issue, he says, is *what adults do to children on the basis of these conditions* (emphasis added). Hendrick claims, and I would agree with him, that all these attributes of children and of childhood have been used to justify the repression and oppression of children 'for their own good'. This, I think, has been particularly the case where children were not contained within their own family, which is why it is most visible in child welfare measures.

What links all the childhood histories which have been the subject of recent inquiries is that they are part of a long tradition of 'saving' children from situations constructed as 'undesirable'. The Aboriginal stolen generation experience, along with all its other highly specific aspects, is part of that tradition. The racial and genocidal dimensions of the policies towards Aboriginal people were grafted onto a tradition already well established by the white rulers of Aborigines, in relation to a specific group of children in their own society. From the 19th century onwards, there was a growing impetus to remove children from their poverty-stricken, usually urban, working-class parents 'for their own good'. It was also to prevent them from becoming 'a threat to society': as Anthony Platt observes in his history of 'child rescue', 'The child savers should in no sense be considered libertarians or humanists.'[32] Under this rhetoric of rescue, as well as being removed from genuine squalor and ill-treatment, children could also be removed from parents regarded (often because of their extreme poverty) as inadequate; and adolescents who did not conform to adult expectations of dependence could be reconceptualised as delinquent and subjected to training and correctional programs characterised by loss of liberty, enforced labour and militaristic discipline — in the interests of, as Platt describes it, 'the inculcation of middle-class values and lower-class skills'. Or, as Kociumbas puts it:

> child rescue has never been without an economic or political agenda, rendering the objects of so much concern in danger of being considered less than human, like animals to be trained or put out of the way.[33]

These interpretations of the 'child saving' movement are not uncontested, and there has been considerable debate about the motivations of its activists.[34] This is a debate that misses the point entirely in terms of the perspective of the children involved, since it is interested only in the adults in the story. It cannot be denied that children were often 'saved' with good reason, and 'saved', often, by people who felt for children and genuinely wished to improve their lives, but that is only half the story. No-one ever asks, as part of this narrative, 'But what happened next? Were these children better off — or just badly off in a different way? How did *they* feel about their "rescue"?' To use the terminology of today, we never ask about 'outcomes'; we just assume that since the adults concerned 'meant well', the children must have been better off. The children involved are invisible, they are simply objects — the focus is always on the rescuing enterprise run by 'benevolent' adults, not on the child's own experience. The American sociologist of childhood, Frances Chaput Waksler, has observed that 'adults routinely set themselves up as the understanders, interpreters and translators of children's behaviour'. This is so common that the absence of children's explanations is rarely even noticed, because, as she says, their 'very existence is not recognised'.[35] It is to be expected, then, that older accounts of 'child rescue' would be blind to the children involved. But Waksler, writing in 1991, claims that we still find it very difficult to acknowledge that in any account involving adults and children there are two sides to the story. What this means in the 'child rescue' history is that even *today* we do not notice, until it is pointed out, that the narrative does not include anything about how children themselves experienced their 'rescue' or how they felt about it. So while Dorothy Scott and Shurlee Swain, in their recent work, *Confronting Cruelty: Historical Perspectives on Child Protection in Australia* (2002), do recognise that, 'Paradoxically, the voices of the children remain almost inaudible, detectable only through other's descriptions of their suffering',[36] even they do not confront the cruelty perpetrated on children in institutional care by the adults who had 'rescued' them.

If we take seriously the evidence we now have, we would have to say that one of the greatest risks to children in Western society is abuse by the adults entrusted with their care — *whoever they are*. This risk is rendered all the greater when the adults so entrusted wear the halo of respectability and 'good works', because their behaviour is less likely to be scrutinised. Public servants, philanthropists and religious personnel operating in their official capacities are much harder to render visible as abusers of children than poor working-class parents, exploitative employers or paedophiles. Acknowledging that the former are just as likely to perpetrate cruelty against children as any other adults meets with strenuous opposition *even now* (see Chapter 7). Legal theorist David Archard has observed that 'relying on love alone to secure the well-being of children shows a misguided and perilous optimism':[37] relying on 'benevolence' and 'altruism' would seem to be even more fraught. I would argue that one of the greatest cruelties visited on children in both the 19th and the 20th centuries has been the welfare measures — whether state or charitable — designed to 'protect' them, and the interventions that have implemented that 'protection'.

When we cannot avoid acknowledging the unacceptable behaviour of adults responsible for the care of children — in the wake of inquiries, for example — we seek to contain it within a paradigm of 'abuse'. We turn what we find into histories of victimisation by 'vicious' adults of 'innocent children', where the focus is yet again on the adult behaviours. This is another way of letting adults *in general* off the hook, of retaining the delusion that adults do always know, and do, best for children, and it's just a few 'bad apples' who spoil it for everyone. Perpetrators of abuse are pathologised and individualised as 'sick' or 'perverted'. This has several effects. First, it puts this behaviour outside the range of 'normal' behaviour, so that it is not about 'us' — even though the high incidence of child abuse suggests otherwise. Second, individualising these events obscures their social and political context: there is an unequal power relationship between adults and children which some adults exploit and which means that children have little redress when adults choose to treat them badly. Finally, by focusing on abuse alone, we lose sight of the appalling bleakness of the life in which that abuse occurred. We do not put ourselves in the shoes of these children and ask, 'What would it be like to be treated as if I were not a human being with the same feelings as other human beings? What would it be like to live in that sterile and loveless institutional environment?'

So sexual abuse of children by priests and other clergy is guaranteed coverage, but it is only one dimension of this story, and there is little or no interest among journalists, even since the release of the Senate Report, in pursuing the broader context. Obviously, I am not denying that what adults 'did' to children is an important part of the story; but we need to understand that it is precisely because children in this situation were invisible as people that adults were able to abuse them with impunity. If, in attempting to understand how it happened, we continue to focus on adult behaviours rather than on children's experience, we extend that invisibility into the present. What is missing here is an understanding that how we treated children in the past and how we treat them now are reflections not just of individual behaviours but of social values. Waksler, whom I quoted above, points out that children's lives and experiences, along with adult relationships with children, are rarely analysed as a means of providing 'insights into the social world as a whole'.[38] Which implies, she says, that we have nothing to learn from children as subjects in their own society.

Since there has been so little reflection on the subjective experience of institutionalisation, it is not established as a category of traumatic childhood experience which needs explanation. It is not part of 'everyday knowledge' that to grow up in institutional care is *in itself* a traumatic and damaging experience *for any child*, regardless of whether or not that child has been 'abused'. There is a clear demonstration of this ignorance in the ruling on the first NSW stolen generation case, that of Joy Williams, which ran in 1999.[39] The judge quite patently did not believe Joy Williams' own account of her life in the two Homes in which she had spent her first 18 years; he chose instead to accept the accounts of those who ran the institutions. Even more significantly, the comments he made in support of his ruling demonstrate that he had no knowledge or understanding that life in an institution, after having been separated from parents and everything familiar, cripples the psychological and social growth of a child. This is a fact quite apart from whether or not a child is abused (as in fact Joy Williams was); abuse merely magnifies the desolation of a life which is already desolate. I am not claiming that this would have influenced the outcome of the case in terms of legal points, but that the judge's statements indicated his ignorance of what should by now be common knowledge — that children are traumatised by growing up in institutions. The judge was concerned only with the measurable physical standard of care, which he found no fault with.

The reaction, in some quarters, to the stolen generation history is a similar example of this same adult-centred perspective. Throughout the debate which followed the 1997 release of the HREOC report, *Bringing them Home*, the fact that Aboriginal children were often taken from conditions of material and physical neglect or poverty was stated frequently, as if it 'proved' that it was a reasonable policy, and outweighed all other considerations.[40] There are, then, still many people *today* who think, as the writer David Horton observed, that 'if you put children into a (H)ome, with clean clothes and food to eat, that [is] all that [is] needed'.[41] Here again we see the inability, or perhaps refusal, to acknowledge the feelings of children. In this conceptualisation of what children 'need', food and shelter not only eliminate all other considerations, but receiving them disqualifies the children concerned from being entitled to anything else. It apparently does not matter, in this interpretation, that the children of the stolen generations lost their parents, their kin network, their country and their identity, and that their alternative care was usually institutionalisation. Not only were they not supposed to grieve for their losses, but they were also obliged to be grateful for what they had been so 'generously' and undeservedly given. These same attitudes were applied to other children removed by 'the Welfare' in this era, and were shared by the managements of Children's Homes.

I am not denying that significant numbers of children went into institutional care because their families failed or even deserted them. Similarly, the state often stepped in quite appropriately to remove children from dangerous family situations. Hector Davis, born in 1926 in Victoria, sums up his family situation like this: he was one of 10 children, with a father unemployed for most of his working life, and the family lived, says Hector, 'in what may best be described as a slum dwelling', in conditions of 'great poverty'. Hector, at the age of 10, with his parents' consent, 'because of neglect, truancy and behavioural problems', was placed at the Burwood Boys' Home in Victoria, where he remained until about age 16. Hector believes that in comparison with his experiences in his family setting, he was better off in institutional care. Many people who grew up in care say that they know they would not necessarily have been well brought up by their parents. Such statements are sometimes used to justify institutional care of children, but they do not justify it; nor do they justify the neglect and cruelty perpetrated on children in that 'care'. They also do not justify the blindness of adults to the feelings of children. And even if individuals acknowledge that they were better off in care, that does not cancel out the sadness and sense of loss that all children suffered when they were not able to be brought up by their parents — whatever those parents were like.

What a story like Hector's shows most graphically is the poverty of our response, historically, to situations such as his. If the children removed by the state were taken from parents who were deficient, surely this was an argument for ensuring that once removed, they were provided with a high standard of care to make up for what they had suffered already. One would expect this particularly where Christian charities were in charge of the care. In fact the opposite appears to have been the case: children in this situation were treated as if they were fortunate to receive even a minimal standard of care. With few exceptions, what they came from, although assessed as inadequate, was used as the yardstick to determine the standard of care they should then be content with. So while some care leavers would concur with Hector, there are many others who say that however 'bad' their parents were, they could not have been worse off with their parents than in the care environments they were subjected to once the state became their parent.

In her submission to the Senate Inquiry, Kate Gaffney, who has researched the Victorian child welfare system,[42] said that she often encountered members of the public who, when told of the abuse of children in institutions, said that 'the children were lucky to be there and should not complain'. This was a response, she argued, which 'seek[s] to justify treating vulnerable children as second class citizens'. All children were entitled to the same standard of care, said Gaffney:

> to say that a child should be treated differently on the basis of his or her parents or socio-economic circumstances at birth should be abhorrent. No child should be expected to be grateful for the opportunity to be abused.

Nor, I would add, for the opportunity to be deliberately and systematically depersonalised. Another common response is that 'times were different then', that people 'thought differently' about what was acceptable behaviour towards children, and we are judging the past by the standards of the present. But times were never so different that it was acceptable to flog, rape and torture children.

Yet another form of denial is to argue that because the care system did not intend to produce the consequences that it did, those consequences are somehow cancelled out, washed away. 'They meant well' is offered as a way to gloss over the effect of institutional care on survivors and to deny our right to protest. This response silences us once again, just as we were silenced as children. People can mean well and still have a horrendous effect on others. In *Neglected and Criminal* (1986), Donella Jaggs prefaces her account of the foundations of child welfare legislation in Victoria with a quote from American social analyst Steve Marcus which expresses exactly this point:

> We can degrade people by caring for them; and we can degrade them by not caring for them; and in matters such as these, there are neither simple answers nor simple solutions ...
>
> Dependants, precisely because they are dependent and often unable to help themselves, deserve more than others to be protected from the unintended consequences of our benevolence and the incalculable consequences of our social good will.[43]

Good intentions do not cancel out bad outcomes; nor can they be used to excuse cruelty to children. A child who would have starved if left with his poverty-stricken parents is nevertheless not well-off in an institution in which he is emotionally neglected, beaten and sexually molested. Or even in an institution where he is well cared for physically, and not raped by his carers, but where he is deprived and neglected emotionally. A child who suffers so much at the hands of his parents that he has to be removed from them is all the more in need of a caring childhood to compensate him for that devastating loss.

Whatever people 'meant' or intended at the time, the care

system for much of the 20th century damaged the children who experienced it. Many of the people working in this system did do their best for children within the scope of their ability and their own understanding, and within the 'common knowledge' of their era. They meant well and they tried to *do* well by children. Many other people working in this system did not mean well by children and used the almost limitless opportunities it offered to inflict at best a callous indifference, and at worst, cruelty and every kind of violation of body and spirit. The children who survived this treatment became adults condemned to a life sentence of reliving their pain over and over.

Georgina Fraser, a NSW state ward, remembered in her submission an occasion as an adult when she enrolled to do a training course through her work. On going to the address where the course was to be held she discovered it was the Children's Court where as a child she had been charged with neglect. 'I was so traumatised I could not get out of the car,' she related, and when she finally managed to walk through the doors, she 'almost fainted'. Worse was to come when she discovered that the lecture was to be held in the very courtroom where she had been charged. 'I left there that day and sat in my car and sobbed,' said Georgina. 'How does anyone come to terms with such a traumatic childhood that still confronts you today in your workplace?'

For me, the term 'Children's Home' has the same emotional atmosphere conveyed by Solzhenitsyn's term for the Soviet camps, the 'gulag archipelago'. It stands for the loveless, desolate lives that children led in such places, motherless and fatherless, isolated from the community, a prey to assault and rape or simply casual and arbitrary cruelty, knowing there was nobody to turn to — and knowing that the sentence had years to go. It is not a prison system we are describing; indeed it apparently had quite contrary intentions of charitable goodwill. Yet most Children's Homes were run like prisons, and they were experienced in this way by their inmates. Managements of Homes (as distinct, often, from the staff employed in them) often had a sincere desire to do 'the best' for children. But, as a US lawyer once observed, 'while paying lip-service to the platitude, best interests of the child, horrible tortures have been perpetrated on children'.[44] For most of the 20th century the definition of 'the best' completely disregarded the need for children in the welfare system to be treated like human beings. It condemned them to a loveless existence, isolated from their families and communities: layer onto this a superstructure of physical and sexual abuse, and the emotional desolation of the children living in this environment is complete.

Perhaps another reason this history has not been told is that governments and charities do not want to recognise that the standard system for looking after children in need of care was for so long both abusive in itself and also a haven for abusers: that as a society, we got it so wrong. In order to understand how this could happen, we need to recast this history away from a psychologised paradigm of 'child abuse' into a social and political perspective. In the following chapter, I discuss the reasons children went into institutional care, and the social context in which it seemed appropriate care for children without viable family. Chapter 3 describes the characteristic features of the institution of this era, and in Chapters 4 and 5 I describe the context within which 'child welfare' was administered by, respectively, the charitable sector and the state. Chapter 6 relates what it felt like to grow up in such an environment. My final chapter, Chapter 7, is an attempt to describe first the consequences of this childhood for survivors, and second the reaction to date of the organisations and governments responsible for those consequences.

Chapter 2

Why Homes?

There is no such thing as a single parent's pension — you either robbed banks or you had a job.

Bruce Randle, Mt Gibraltar Home, Bowral, NSW, 1958–1966

The social context of the Home history

In the institutional era, the wellbeing of children within families, children who were to all intents and purposes 'owned' by their parents, was a private matter, and if, in a family crisis, a parent or relative put children into a Home run by the private charitable sector, the state had little to say about it. All it concerned itself with was licensing the Home and monitoring physical standards. However, parents who did not — or could not (perhaps through poverty) — maintain 'community standards' could expect the intervention of the state child welfare Department, and if their children were taken into state care, they lost their parental rights. While the state took its duty of care towards children privately placed in charitable institutions lightly, once children came under state control it took its duty seriously. As care leaver accounts show, the state was a strict and often punitive guardian, particularly in New South Wales.

How were children placed in Homes?

There were three ways children could go into care, which usually meant going into a Home. First, a parent or relative could put a child in a Home following a family crisis, as my mother did. This was called 'voluntary admission' in government reports, although there was little about it that was voluntary when there were so few other options available. The second way was removal into care by the state. The child removed this way was usually made a state ward and disposed of according to state child welfare policy, which in most states was institutionalisation. In New South Wales children were first 'processed' through the state receiving 'depot', then generally placed into foster care. If this broke down, they went into one of the government institutions — only rarely did they go to non-government Homes. However, this state differed quite markedly from all others (see Chapter 5). The third way was when parents approached the Department in their state and relinquished their children into state care. This too could be termed 'voluntary' relinquishment, but my guess is that it was usually the action of a desperate parent or parents, of people who knew they were no longer in a position to look after their children. It is difficult to tell just how many parents took this path, but there is evidence of it in submissions to the Inquiry and in my interviews.

Some children also entered Homes as Commonwealth wards. Bernard Brady's Inquiry submission related one such story. He and his younger sister were referred to as Repatriation wards: their parents had both served in World War II, but by 1952 both were dead, so the children became Commonwealth (not state) wards under the *Repatriation Act 1920*; since they were a Commonwealth responsibility, the state government was not accountable for them.

James Luthy's submission showed just how vulnerable children were when their families fell outside accepted social norms. James was born in 1951 to an unmarried woman who had four much older children, and who died when he was four, leaving him in the care of his sister. Eventually a neighbour, a single woman unrelated to him, said that she would care for him — but, he says, 'her rules were that unless my family wanted me to be put in a children's Home they would stop seeing me'. This was a completely informal arrangement, with no government involvement at all. James was 'physically, mentally, verbally and emotionally abused' by this woman. 'It was akin to a custodial sentence,' he said, '[for] there was no-one to go to, and there was nowhere to go to':

> I had no choice but to remain in this situation because no-one would believe how I was treated, and due to my background, no-one really cared. My carer was a schoolteacher and involved with a church, and so she was

seen as a pillar of society who was doing her best to give a chance to a 'poor orphan' who came from an unfortunate background.

Soon after James started high school the woman sent him to the Salvation Army's Gill Memorial Home at Goulburn. The Home took him, apparently with no questions asked, even though he was unrelated to the person who had committed him. James has since obtained his admission form, and it makes no mention of his remaining family members — who, he says, were not notified of his changed circumstances. When in 2003 he attempted to get some answers from the Salvation Army, they told him that they 'could not determine whether checks were undertaken' before his placement in their care, and they did at that time take 'voluntary placements from responsible next-door neighbours'. James's conclusion is that 'if they were paid, it would seem that the Salvation Army would lock any child away in one of their institutions without any thought, care or check'.

Very few parents from this era are on record to tell us how they went about placing their children in Homes. We might assume that they chose Homes that matched their religious affiliation, and that sometimes the local priest or minister was involved in helping them find them. One parent I interviewed said that she had chosen Burnside because 'it was such a big Home I thought the Welfare would be checking, not like in a small Home where they might be whipped' — her confidence was entirely misplaced, as she discovered later. I gather that my mother heard about my Home by chance, from somebody who was a neighbour of the women when they were just starting it — my sister and I were its first intake. It is likely that many parents, operating in crisis mode, simply placed their children wherever there were vacancies.

The care history of Joy Hill,[1] one of my interviewees, shows what might have happened if my mother had not found the Home where she placed us. Joy said that when her mother deserted her father in 1944, leaving him with three daughters aged from 18 months (Joy herself) to four years, her father had tried, unsuccessfully, to keep his family together with the aid of his mother and sisters and an unreliable housekeeper. He then tried to have the children admitted to various church Homes, of several denominations, but all were unable to help him. Mr Hill then applied for assistance to the NSW Department, which took the children into care as state wards, and fostered them out. Joy lost one sister immediately, but was fostered with her other sister. She was separated from this sister too after some years, and only found her again 30 years later. Joy's 'care' experience ran the full gamut of welfare interventions, from abusive foster placements to several periods in government institutions, culminating in a stint in the state 'training' school for girls at Parramatta. Note here that her father tried other avenues before contacting the Department. His apprehension about finally having to do this was justified, for he never managed to get his children back, despite more than one application, and he eventually dropped out of their lives.

Joy's story began in wartime, but it seems that in the years of the baby boom following World War II it was still difficult to find a vacancy in a Children's Home. The 1956 annual report of the WA Department says, for example, that 'All institutions are filled to near capacity most of the time'. And a newspaper article in June 1957 in Sydney's *Sun-Herald* claimed that 'more than 100 distraught parents ring or call the Church institutions in Sydney each week with the plea: "Please take my child"'. There was a demand for many more Homes, said the article, and this is borne out by statistical evidence: in New South Wales, for example, there were 296 non-government Homes in 1956, and 383 only two years later. This shortfall in available places is one of the reasons for care leaver histories often showing siblings being accommodated in Homes far apart — on the opposite sides of the city, or in rural locations far from any family connections — which contributed very significantly to the fragmentation of families.

'Normal' families

Charles Waterstreet was eleven in 1961, when his parents kept a hotel in the large country town of Albury, in New South Wales. Charles later described life with his mother, who was addicted to both alcohol and non-prescription drugs:

> Mum's drinking was a family secret confined to a circle the size of Antarctica but we never spoke of it. It was a given. The thing not said ... But we — me, Katherine Ann, John and Peter — were kind of drug couriers between the pharmacy and Mum. She had seasonal changes of medication. In summer it was handfuls of Relax-a-Tabs; autumn, Bex; winter, Veganin and in spring, Vincent's powders ... Dad threatened the chemist physically by lifting him off the ground by his white lapels with one of his huge trout-spotted fists. But there were other chemists and children ready to walk miles for their Mum ... We never blamed her ... She was not a drunk like the others at the pub. They were drunks. She was sick. She was Mum. We were mum.[2]

A great deal is revealed in Charles's description. There is the loyalty of children to their mother, whatever her behaviour: 'she was Mum. We were mum'. There is the unexpressed desperation felt by many women cast in the role of homemaker — it wasn't until two years later, in 1963, that Betty Friedan published *The Feminine Mystique*, which attempted to pin down 'the problem that has no name' — and the availability, and use, of analgesics to assuage that despair.[3] And finally, there is the silence about 'unspeakable' matters in this era, so different from our confessional age, where so many people seem prepared to air their most intimate personal problems on daytime television.

Charles's story also shows that being embedded in a loving network of kin is what was required if children in his situation were to avoid going into care. He came from a large family, which included three maternal aunts, Faith, Hope and Charity — Aunt Faith was his 'home away from hotel'. He also had a father who was prepared to support his family and to make up for his mother's absence in her children's lives when it occurred, and it often did. Without this family support, there were two possible outcomes for the Waterstreet children. One was that a relative or perhaps the local priest would have suggested that the children be placed in a Catholic Home, and that is where they would have gone. The other is that Mrs Waterstreet would eventually have come to the notice of the NSW Department because her children were visibly neglected. 'Neglected' could simply mean that they were occasionally absent from school, or trying to look after themselves without adult supervision.[4] This would very likely have happened had she been without family support, or had a husband unprepared to fill in for her, and it would have meant the removal of her children into state care.

Author Helen Townsend gives a succinct description of the social norms of this period in the following passage from her book, *Baby Boomers*:

> In general, mothers and fathers came appropriately paired. They didn't have much choice. Social security didn't look after single-parent families. Married women were barred from many jobs and were paid less than anyone else if they were allowed to have them. Adultery and cruelty were the grounds for divorce. Divorces were reported in lurid detail in the evening newspapers. Most couples chose to stay together.[5]

Postwar Australia was a deeply conservative, insular and isolationist country — in the words of one British visitor, 'in many ways, still essentially a Victorian society with a mid-20th century economy and culture'.[6] The 1950s and 1960s also, observes historian Janet McCalman, saw the 'world gone mad with marriage'.[7] What is often described as 'the traditional family' became firmly entrenched as the only 'real' family: a male breadwinner and a female homemaker who looked after the children and did not go out to paid work. All other family forms were regarded as deficient. However, in a highly conservative social, political and moral climate, this model became an oppressive norm. As Townsend reminds us, divorce was stigmatised and avoided, no matter how appalling and difficult the marriage was, and where it occurred it created a 'broken home'. This model family type was, furthermore, regarded as the 'natural' and indispensable socialising agent for children,[8] and families who 'failed' to meet these standards were pathologised as contaminating, because they did not provide the 'right' influences for children. This could ultimately invite drastic remedies, such as state intervention.

Part of the stigma felt by children living in institutional care during this period is that they were excluded from membership in this ideal, the only 'normal' social status of the time. Shame, embarrassment and secrecy are the reactions that care leavers commonly speak of. Many have never told the families they now live in, would never tell friends or workmates, and regard it as something to be hidden and forgotten, a shameful past that marks them as worth less than other people. Children outside 'normal' families had no place in society, and people went to great lengths to dispose of 'unwanted' children in socially acceptable ways. One woman I interviewed, Marion Tucker, was an 'illegitimate' war baby, born in 1940, and was fostered out informally to a family after her grandfather advertised on the radio for a home for her. Marion's story, like James Luthy's, above, shows how casually such children were disposed of — there was no consideration of their feelings or their sense of identity. They were simply a problem for which a solution had to be found. That in 1947 there could be a book entitled *The Psychology of the Unwanted Child*[9] shows that for this generation, this was a self-evident category of children.

The babies of unmarried mothers, for example, were all described as 'unwanted', and children who had to go into Homes ended up with a similar evaluation of their worth. What the terminology glosses over is that these babies and children were unwanted not by their parents and families, but by their society.

This was also an era in which the worth of an individual was assessed with little or no regard for the social and economic factors that affected that person's situation. Poverty, unemployment, mental illness and other circumstantial misfortunes tended to be attributed to personal failings such as 'weakness of character', and people were judged accordingly. Women, as a matter of custom, were less educated and vocationally trained than men; they also suffered restricted entry to many jobs and professions, and were usually paid two-thirds of a male wage — on the incorrect assumption that they did not have to support families. The social security and community support available were based on the assumption that the family model of breadwinner/homemaker was a fact — as a result, there was seen to be little need to provide for situations other than the norm. This left a huge gap in service provision which was filled by charities: thus assistance was experienced by the 'less fortunate' not as an entitlement, but as a gift bestowed out of somebody else's 'goodness'.

The last resort before the Home: state assistance

Given this social environment, there was a high risk that families would cease to function if two parents were not available. 'There was no such thing as a single parent's pension — you either robbed banks or had a job,' said Bruce Randle. When his mother was deserted by her husband, Bruce, who was one of seven children, ended up in a Home without his siblings — they went to other Homes; the family scattered. Until the sea change that came with the Whitlam Labor Government (1972–75), there was meagre assistance for women — or men — left to cope as sole parents. The Commonwealth-funded Deserted Wives and Widows' Pension, as historian Jill Roe points out, had defined women by their relationships to men (as did women themselves, not surprisingly) — it was extended, in 1947, to deserted *de facto* and legal wives as well as widows, but not to unmarried mothers. Evaluating the worth of women on the basis of their marital or quasi-marital status meant that 'women unable to fit that category became once again undeserving, emphatically so in the period after World War II', says Roe.[10] I think this stigma flowed on to include women with children who had no men around, even if they had once been married — like my mother, who never admitted to being divorced, and always said that her husband was a tobacco farmer in Mareeba, Queensland.

All the states did, however, provide some financial assistance — often called 'relief' — to (mainly) women struggling to raise their children alone. Since there is little or nothing said in Departments' annual reports about sole male parents, it appears that women were the main recipients of government 'relief'. The assistance, like the widows' pension, was meagre: it embodied the strongly entrenched belief — fundamental to the British Poor Law and developed throughout the 19th century — that state assistance ran the risk of absolving recipients, including parents, of their responsibility to support themselves.[11] The Departments also helped out with medical, pharmaceutical and dental needs, and school requisites.

In 1956, the families of just over 3000 Victorian children were being paid 'relief' of this kind, ranging from 5 shillings to 35 shillings a week. Of the 1189 parents involved, the reason for payment in over half the cases was 'desertion'. The children who make up those statistics are not the subject of this book; they are the ones whose mothers, or other relatives, managed to keep them.[12]

The state took a serious view of the responsibility of men to maintain their children. In New South Wales, for example, an allowance was available to a woman only once she had taken out a maintenance order against her husband (or the putative father of the children, if she was not married) and it had not resulted in payments from him. The Victorian Department's report noted the significant increase from the preceding year in the number of deserting fathers (an increase of 25 per cent), and that there were almost double the number of fathers in gaol compared with the previous year. The Queensland Department's annual report for the same year said that although 'the problem of the deserting husband' was causing concern, 'efforts are always made to locate him'. Court action was taken against these men once they were found, but 434 children that year became the financial responsibility of the state because their fathers had deserted.

The South Australian Department had a whole branch — the Prosecution and Maintenance Branch — whose functions were to investigate maintenance on behalf of wives and children and process affiliation orders where children were 'illegitimate'. The branch was kept extremely busy enforcing orders and mounting prosecutions against non-payers. 'Every possible endeavour' was being made, according to this Department's 1956 annual report, 'including extensive inquiries and also proceedings interstate and overseas to obtain maintenance for women and children', and officers were in court every day on matters arising from the work of the branch.

Fathers who did not keep up-to-date with maintenance payments were gaoled in some states, including New South Wales. I only learned a few years ago that my mother at some stage had taken out a maintenance order against my father, and I wonder whether this was why he eventually left New South Wales for Queensland: NSW law was not enforceable in other states, at least at the time he left my mother.

Applying for assistance appears to have brought families under considerable surveillance: the SA Department's 1956 annual report said that inspectors visited the families involved and 'looked into their welfare', and 'many inquiries and special reports were provided by police officers, town and district clerks'. Women applying for maintenance from their husbands did not appear to feel they were calling on an entitlement, as this 1951 NSW account by a mother of three children (aged four months, three years and four years) shows:

> The first time in court was terrible for me. It made me feel humiliated and guilty as the magistrate was not sympathetic. He asked me why I had left my husband and made me feel that I should have stayed. It was as if I had committed a crime. I didn't get any money for myself, and the amount the magistrate ordered my husband to pay towards the expenses for my baby didn't even cover the cost of Lactogen [an infant formula].[13]

It is clear that despite the fact that there was some state assistance available, for a sole parent in this period there was a clearly defined choice between work and child care; it was rare for both to be possible. A parent with a job could not look after children, because there was no before-school or after-school care, kindergartens and other child-care centres were not common, and there were few community support structures for struggling families. From the statistics in the state Departments' annual reports, it appears that many women did manage, somehow, solely on their state allowance: this is another history that has not been told. But my mother's decision, to put her children into a Home and go to work, is the same decision that thousands of other mothers — and fathers — all over the country made.

Reasons children went into care

The majority of care leavers who were placed 'voluntarily' in Homes relate histories that repeat the reasons in my own history.

Bill Cremen's submission to the Senate Inquiry showed how rapidly things broke down once there were no longer two available parents:

> My young brother and I were placed in St John's Home for Boys at Goulburn, NSW [a Catholic Home]. I am not sure of the year, it would have been about mid 1940s to 1949–50. My mother had just been divorced and could not afford to look after us. We had a good home life before the divorce, growing up in Annandale and Balmain, never went without anything, my mother never had to work, but when we moved to Balmain into a house owned by distant relatives, we had an upstairs flat. These relatives were strict Catholics and we were Protestants, at the time I think my brother would have been about 3–4 years old, myself about 7–8 years. Now at the time there were no childcare centres, so that's how we ended up at Goulburn, we were forced to become Catholics so we could go to St John's so my mother could go to work. I was told only for a short time, till she could afford to bring us home.

And Douglas Mann's account, in his submission, of going into care in Western Australia demonstrated the same reasons again — and that in this state the government appeared to be less successful in compelling men to support their families:

> When my parents separated in 1947, my father refused to pay any maintenance. He was involved with another woman who he later married. With no social security payments back then, my mother was forced to put me and my brother and sister into the Parkerville Children's Home ... My mother got a job as a sales assistant so that she could pay for our keep at the Home. She did not get any help at all from the Mann family and had to live in a one-room boarding house ...

What were the specific factors, or combination of factors, that sent children into Homes? The typical reasons are indicated in the 1956 annual report of the Queensland State Children's Department, which sets out in full the causes for admission to institutions of the 2106 children taken into care in that year.

There are some interesting points about these figures. First, there are only 18 orphans out of more than 2000 children. Second, the absence of viable fathers is the major factor precipitating children into care. Or to put it another way, it is the major predictor of a child's entering care in this era. The category 'father dead/father deserted, mother unable to support' accounts for 1011 children, just over half. If we add the situations where the fathers are insane, in gaol, in hospital or invalids, we get a further 469. Where births are ex-nuptial, and fathers appear to be out of the picture, again children go into care. However, where absence of the mother is the main factor, the figure is only 132 in total. Third, there is an interesting variation in the terminology: mothers are described as 'unable to support' when the father is not around, whereas in the reverse situation, fathers are described as 'unable to look after'. Yet, as I have noted, when one partner disappeared (for whatever reason), the remaining parent, whether male or female, was in the same predicament: he or she could work or look after the children — it was not possible to do both. Presumably this terminology simply reflects an assumption of the day — men can't, or don't, look after children.

The reasons given in the Queensland table occur in care leaver histories from all states, and in my original study. Only detailed comparative research — which has not so far been done — could determine whether or not there were any significant differences between the states in terms of the prevalence of some reasons over others. In my NSW study, for example, one-third (31 of the 90 interviewees) were in care because of the death or desertion of their mothers — this is a considerably higher proportion than in the Queensland statistics.

My original research, both in interviews and in other material I found, puts a human face on the categories in the table above. When I read the minutes kept by the Ladies Visiting Committee which assessed children for admission to the large Presbyterian Homes complex in Sydney called Burnside, there were, over and over, family histories of death, desertion, separation or divorce, illness and accident, in conjunction with little or no support from other members of the family. Sometimes aunts or grandparents had attempted substitute care but it had not worked out. The most extreme situations were revealed in the Burnside Arrears of Maintenance files, where the parents listed had disappeared, attempted suicide, died, entered 'mental' hospitals or, occasionally, gone to gaol.

Another point which came out in my interviews — and which recurs in Inquiry submissions — is that people often didn't know why they went into care; seven of my interviewees had never found anybody to explain it to them. Sally Fenton, for example, knew only that she and her sister had been put into the Waitara Foundling Home in Sydney in 1940. 'My parents were not around,' Sally said. 'I don't know how this came about — and I even wonder, was [she really] my sister?' Similarly, Dorothy Ashby related in her submission that although there is a record of her placement in the Goodwood Orphanage, Adelaide, in 1946, at the age of two and a half, there is no reason given. For a further nine of my interviewees, almost 10 per cent of the total, the circumstances in which they had entered care were somewhat hazy: they had not understood at the time what was happening, but ultimately both parents had abandoned the children either by death or actual desertion. This not knowing why they went into care is a common experience for care leavers from this era, a time when little or nothing was explained to children.

When I began my research I assumed, generalising from my own experience, that it would be, as the Queensland statistics indicate, the death, desertion or at any rate absence of fathers that

Reasons for admission to care in Queensland, 1955–56

Causes for admission	Total
Both parents dead	18
Both parents deserted	31
Parents divorced	22
Parents unable to accommodate	32
Parents unable to control	17
Mother dead, father unable to look after	22
Mother insane, father unable to look after	10
Mother in hospital, father unable to look after	42
Mother deserted, father unable to look after	53
Mother invalid, father unable to look after	5
Father dead, mother unable to support	590
Father deserted, mother dead	13
Father deserted, mother unable to support	421
Father in gaol, mother unable to support	124
Father insane, mother unable to support	57
Father an invalid, mother unable to support	221
Father in hospital, mother unable to support	67
Father dead, mother deserted	8
Ex-nuptial, mother unable to support	131
Ex-nuptial, child an encumbrance	18
Ex-nuptial, mother deserted	9
Ex-nuptial, mother dead	2
Committed by court	117
Released on probation by court	74
Notice of default	2
	2106

Source: *Annual Report 1955–56, State Children Department, Queensland.*

sealed the fate of children and sent them into care. Often it was, but there were several fathers in my NSW sample who were very different from my father, and who tried hard to keep their families together after the death or desertion of their wives — but had to accept finally that it was simply impossible. Margery Chandler, who was in the Dr Dill Mackey Home in Sydney, remembers that 'it was always Dad who cared for us' during her mother's sporadic desertions, and that when he ultimately had to put Margery and her sister into a Home, he checked out several Homes first and refused to take them to one where, when he walked through the dining room, he saw children eating off chipped plates and drinking from tin mugs. 'He couldn't bear to think of his children doing that, so we didn't go there,' said Margery. One of my interviewees came from a family who had been immigrants from Germany, which meant that when her mother left them, there was no family network to draw upon. This was Else Ferguson, who was in the Baptist Roslyn Hall Children's Home, in Rockdale, New South Wales. Her mother had left them in 1963, when Else was nine, her sister younger. Her father could not afford a housekeeper, and 'men didn't look after daughters in those days', said Else, so 'Dad put us in a Home.' Else thinks that 'the Welfare might have threatened to remove us' and would have separated them if her father had not 'voluntarily' put them in a Home, where in fact they did remain together.

Then, as now, women often had to flee their homes because of violence: Pippa Corbett's submission showed particularly vividly how great was the effect of men's behaviour on women's and children's lives. This was in 1957, in Sydney:

> My father, a severe alcoholic, gambler and violent towards my mother and I, threw us out into the street. He opened the front door of the house we lived in, in Jannali, Sydney, and pushed out my mother, my sister (five years old), my brother (two months old) and myself (eight

years old at that time). Then he threw my brother's pram on top of us. My poor mother, after years of violent abuse, walked to Central [Station] with us, and we sat in the park, waited and worried what would become of us. We sat there for thirty-six hours until the police came, then the Salvation Army came and forcibly took us from our mother, breaking her heart.

All three children were subsequently placed in a Home at Bondi — Scarba House, run by the NSW Benevolent Society. In a scenario that is still common, Pippa's father continued throughout her childhood to determine — by his absence, or his violence when present — what sort of life his wife and children led.

Many children went into care simply because of family poverty, the sheer lack of enough money to keep the family. Hector Davis describes vividly how in the 1930s very poor families survived:

As there were little or no Government social benefits program, the family was very much dependent on the help given by the Churches, the 'people who lived down our street' who cared, and the small amounts of money the children earned selling newspapers, sweets at the football ...

But as some accounts indicate, even if poverty was not the reason for entry to care, it was often a shortage of *enough* money that determined the fate of the children. The professional fathers in my interviews would probably have sent their children to boarding schools rather than to Homes, had there been a bit more money. This would not necessarily have been a happy solution for a child — boarding schools of this era were also commonly run on punitive and repressive lines. However, children in boarding schools knew their families, and had homes to return to. Also, they — and their parents — were not stigmatised as those in the care situation were. In fact it was quite the reverse, as boarding school was often viewed as a privilege which conferred social cachet.

The NSW Department noted in its 1956 annual report that 'the children coming to the Department are not necessarily under-privileged economically, but come from many walks of life' and this seems to be borne out both by my interviews and by some of the submissions to the Inquiry. Anne Martin-Smith, who was in the Church of England Girls' Home at Carlingford from 1932 to 1946 (from age three) came from a family who ran a sheep station in the 1930s. In a series of misfortunes, the property was destroyed by two bushfires in succession, and with no insurance, the family lost everything. Her father became a park ranger, but Anne and her sister were put into a Home anyway:

> [because] my mother became ill after the birth of her third child, another daughter, and collapsed. It was what today would be called a nervous breakdown but you never talked about those things in those days. The family doctor said we must be put somewhere.

Note the role of the family doctor here — he may well have known of a Home and made inquiries on their behalf. In Catholic families, it might be the local priest who performed this service.

What is evident in so many care leaver histories is that with some community or government support, many children would not have had to go into Homes. As late as 1974, the director of the Catholic Family Welfare Bureau, John Davoren, observed that 'our welfare system is mainly concerned with crises and casualties' and that 'community development that seeks to reduce the crises and casualties by addressing itself to their causes is still in its infancy'.[14] Institutional care involved no investment in children or their families so it saved money at the time — but the costs to the children, to their families, and to society were enormous.

Average age of entry and length of stay in a Home

Perhaps not surprisingly, most children went into institutional care when they were very young. Two-thirds of my 90 interviewees, 62 in all, were aged between birth and seven years when they went into care. Of these, 11, or more than 12 per cent of the sample, were babies aged one year or less; with only two exceptions, all the rest were aged 11 years or under. The average length of stay in a Home was seven and a half years, but some spent much longer — 29 had been in a Home for 10 years or more; some of them, like me, had been there for their entire childhood. Only seven interviewees were in Homes for less than three years. So most people spent a very substantial number of their childhood years living in an institution. From subsequent CLAN histories and submissions to the Inquiry it is clear that these findings are typical of the era. One of the saddest statistics is the number of babies' Homes. Victoria had, between 1962 and 1964, 12 babies' Homes, housing a total of 470 children, none of them aged over three; the largest, the Catholic St Joseph's Broadmeadows, had 91 of these infant inmates.

'Better off in a Home'

My discussion so far refers to the Home as the only resort in a crisis. My interviews showed, however, that there were other situations where 'putting the children in a Home' was apparently seen as an *appropriate* course of action. The parents of Rebecca Feinstein, who was in the Isabella Lazarus Home for Jewish Children in Sydney, had separated, and both worked, which was an identical situation to that of Rachel, the child in my Home who had divorced parents. Since both parents had to work and neither could make 'a proper home', they apparently decided that Rebecca, aged five, would be 'better off in a Home'.

In other situations, children were sacrificed — the only appropriate term, it seems — to 'propriety' or to service a family feud. Sylvia Baker, one of four children under 10 in her family, recalled that after her mother died, the family had often moved house, in order, Sylvia thought, to avoid the interventions of her maternal grandmother, who 'had never thought our father was good enough for her daughter'. Her grandmother eventually asked the NSW Department to investigate how the children were being cared for, which resulted in the children's being placed in a Home — not by 'the Welfare', but in order to prevent 'the Welfare' becoming further involved. Sylvia's grandmother clearly believed that the children were better off in a Home than with only their father and a housekeeper. As Else Ferguson observed (above), looking after children was not considered appropriate work for men in this period; indeed a woman of Sylvia's grandmother's generation — late Victorian — might well have seen it as 'unsuitable' that a father should look after daughters.

Divorce took a heavy toll on children, and on their mothers. Bob Medway's parents divorced in 1944 and his father won custody of the children: girls aged three and six and Bob, aged four. This presumably means that Bob's mother was 'the guilty party' and so considered an 'unfit mother' (the term used at the time), who would morally contaminate her children. In an Australian case in 1966, a woman who left her husband for another man lost custody of her very young child, the judge saying, in support of his decision, that not only had her conduct broken the marriage, but she had also 'been intimate' with her husband before their marriage.[15] In Bob's case, the children were put into Salvation Army Homes, the girls at Bexley in Sydney, and Bob, by then aged eight, in its boys' Home in the country. Bob did not see his mother again until he was 21, and saw his sisters only when he went home at Christmas time — as a consequence he developed no significant relationship with them. He was deprived of his entire family for the rest of his childhood, and Bob's perception of his fate was that he had received a prison sentence: 'I hadn't done anything,' he said, 'yet [I was] treated as if [I] had.' The Home that he was sent to — the Gill Memorial Home in Goulburn — would only have reinforced that feeling (see Chapter 4).

For parents of large families, the Home was sometimes, apparently, the only way to cope. Gabrielle Fanshawe, a Catholic interviewee, in St Martha's Girls' Home, Leichhardt in the late 1940s, said that in St Martha's, some children were there specifically 'to relieve the pressure on large families'. In the Home, so the thinking went, the nuns would do well by the children and ensure that they got an education: it was the Church's obligation to care for its own. Also, said Gabrielle, some Catholic families earmarked one of their children for the religious life, and this was seen as a preparation.

There is another reason which is much harder to understand from a contemporary perspective: there also seems to have been an apparent acceptance of the institution as, at times, a necessary remedial environment for children. I first realised this when I interviewed Ray Lennox, who, soon after World War II, was sent to Australia from Britain — when he was 11 years old — under the Fairbridge scheme because he'd got into 'bad company' after his mother died. Even though his father was alive and securely employed as a London fireman, and he had sisters old enough to have homes of their own, *his own family* felt that the main thing was to get him into a situation where he would come under 'better' influences, the influences needed to make children 'turn out' right. Fresh air, wide open spaces, hard work and exercise — these would 'make a man' of him. Ray was sent to Australia 'for his own good'; his attachment to his family was apparently not considered important.

This same set of beliefs can also be found in comments which occur regularly in the Burnside Ladies' Committee Admissions file, referring to single-parent families, such as, 'Mother has to work and has no one to care for him and he is getting out of hand.' Such comments seem to express not merely the apprehension but also the conviction of parents that once the family was 'broken', the children could 'run wild' or even become 'delinquent'. In this scenario, children, so the thinking went, were 'better off' contained within the structured discipline of the Home environment. This perspective on institutional care has to be understood within a constellation of beliefs about children that were paramount until probably well into the 1970s.

As I discuss in Chapter 5, the words used to describe children's behaviour in the Child Welfare Acts and annual reports of the era — such as 'uncontrollable', 'wayward', 'delinquent', 'falling into bad associations', 'exposed to moral danger' — are never explained; they may have been regarded as self-evident. Given this, it is perhaps understandable that the order and discipline of a routinised existence with regular meals and bedtime, church on Sundays and 'a lot of other children to play with' were seen as the best thing for a child whose family was under pressure. It could even be regarded as an acceptable, almost 'normal', solution for a family in crisis — children were 'better off in a Home' especially where the mother was absent, or where 'mother has to work', since it was the mother's job to bring up children.

In a 1953 file in the NSW Department archives there is a very clear expression of these contemporary beliefs. A woman wrote to the director of the Department to complain about some local children whose parents had 'no control' over them: they were throwing stones at her grandson and were 'a menace' to the street. 'Both those kids want putting away in an institution,' she said, 'as they are neglected.' The assertion that children are neglected if they are 'uncontrolled' by parents is characteristic of child welfare literature of the period, but it was also, as these comments show, a generally held belief. The Department took this complaint seriously, and sent out a district officer who checked the details and concluded that there were no real grounds for it. He made an unannounced visit to the family, and his report makes interesting reading for what it reveals about how he came to his conclusions. He noted the type of house the family lived in, the number of rooms (including bedrooms, which he checked against the number of people living in the household), the cleanliness and tidiness of the house, and the occupation and wage of the male breadwinner. He checked school attendance and interviewed the teachers for their opinion of the children — luckily for them, he recorded that they were 'well mannered and teachers speak highly of both'. He noted that:

> Mrs L ... admitted that occasionally she had a drink with her husband, but denied that she drank to excess or that the children's meals were ever later than 6 p.m. She said that the children do not use filthy language (this was confirmed by reports from the school).

The district officer assessed the family in terms of respectability, willingness to work, regular habits, and conformity to 'normal' roles — the attributes known to produce what he would have described as 'normal children'. The neighbour's role in this incident is interesting, and points to what appears to be a high level of surveillance of the behaviour of other people — or, perhaps, of other people's children. A statistical survey of children committed to state care in New South Wales in the early 1950s states that of 1748 cases of alleged 'anti-social behaviour' reported to the Child Welfare Department in 1950–51, 700 were reported by 'private persons not related to the family in question', with a further 117 the result of anonymous letter or telephone calls. This appears to indicate that almost half the children were brought to the notice of the Department by people who were strangers to or, at best, acquaintances of the children concerned.[16]

Routine, stability, discipline, hygiene and 'training' in manners, morals and religion were the highest priorities in the upbringing of children in this period. The annual reports of the NSW Department stress that children who come into its care lack these indispensable factors in their lives, and it is clear that the Department saw it as its responsibility to provide them. Underlying this attitude is a general consensus among adults about what children 'need'. Burnside's 1952 annual report expressed beliefs that would have found general acceptance at this time: 'It is every child's heritage,' it said, 'to have a happy and healthy childhood free from the discord of broken homes and squabbling parents'. This is hardly arguable even now; what is less explicable to us today is a statement such as that found in the Home's 1955 annual report, that some children might be better off in Homes than with their own families. Speaking of the superior environment provided to 'their' children, the report claims that 'many would not receive the good moral and spiritual training that is given at Burnside even if their homes were not broken'.

The ability to provide children with material things appeared to be regarded at times as more important than children's feelings. This perhaps helps to explain why parents who had to work did not feel that they could provide the 'right' conditions for their children. Norma, one of the parents in my research study, said that her children did not go home (from the Home) for holidays but instead were fostered out to strangers. Her husband was occasionally hospitalised for an intermittent mental disorder, and the family was not well off, but even when he was well, the children did not come to them for holidays. This, said Norma, was because:

> They [the Home management] told me that there were couples that were very willing to take a child for the holidays, to make a child happy — you know, to give it all the little extras that parents couldn't provide ... and so I was happy for them to go to them.

Norma related how sometimes the foster carers would agree to meetings with the children once or twice in the holidays, 'on neutral ground', and how 'the children always seemed very happy and well-dressed, and were always happy to tell us all these extras that they got, ice-creams and rides on ferries'. Norma was typical of parents of this time in that she saw the material advantages her children got from their foster carers as more important than spending time with their own parents. Her daughter Jennifer's recollections, however, were not of the treats and outings, but of how she had *felt* with these foster carers, and how much she had longed to be with her own parents.

'Good' children are seen, not heard

Children's voices at this time were unable to be heard; nor was it considered necessary that they should be. 'Nobody pondered the process of growing up,' says Townsend, speaking of the three decades after World War II, the baby boomer era, or 'thought about what went on in a child's mind or attempted to understand it'.[17] It was usual in this era for children to be told little, if anything, about events which affected their lives or the lives of other family members. They often did not go to weddings, almost certainly did not go to funerals, and did not always accompany their parents on holiday, hence the 'transients' in my Home. It was considered inappropriate for children to know too much, because a significant feature of the demarcation between adulthood and childhood was childhood 'innocence' (or perhaps ignorance of things adults preferred them not to know about). The labels which the national Censorship Board applied to films at this time applied equally to life, for children. There were some matters that were 'For General Exhibition' and others that were 'Not Suitable for Children'. It is not necessarily different now — we still speak of childhood 'innocence' — but the distinctive characteristic of the earlier era is that the line between these two categories was drawn in a way that eliminated all but the blandest of information from children's knowledge, regardless of how much this distorted reality. For children in institutions, one major consequence of this was that to speak up about being sexually molested was *literally* unthinkable, since it was 'wicked' to know anything about sexual matters. The child who was forced to know about sex through being violated, had to take on, as well, the guilt of knowing about sex.

It is useful to remember here that over the past 30 or more years, there has been a quite radical shift in the way we think about children. The 1989 United Nations (UN) Convention on the Rights of the Child asserts that children are entitled to their own 'wishes and feelings', and to self-determination and empowerment as persons in their own right. But a right such as this was quite unthinkable in the time of my childhood. An earlier UN Declaration, in 1924, had emphasised the importance for children of 'socialisation to serve others', while the 1959 UN Declaration 'expressed no recognition of the child's autonomy, or understanding of the importance of a child's wishes and feelings; the child is an object of concern, rather than a person with self-determination'.[18] This set of beliefs about children describes quite accurately the commonly accepted dehumanising attitudes towards children up to the 1970s. The standard phrases used about children in this era demonstrate how completely adults, including parents, construed children in terms of what they required children to be, on the assumption that children's needs were identical to their own — 'children soon forget', 'children get over things quickly', 'children need discipline', 'you spoil children if you give them too much', and so on. The psychoanalyst and writer Alice Miller offers a useful analysis of relations between adults and children up to and including this institutional era. The repressive child-rearing practices which are often described as 'traditional', she says, are better described by the term 'poisonous pedagogy', since such practices are actually no more than an ideological exercise whose purpose is to control children in the interests of sustaining and perpetuating adult dominance. 'Poisonous pedagogy' can be used to rationalise any behaviour by adults towards children, since under its rubric, adults are always right, and children, if they resist, are always wrong. Children are disciplined through moralising rules and regulations, which interpret any expression of self, any resistance to the desires of an adult, as wilful and wicked. Any feelings that do not conform to adult requirements — particularly anger — are forbidden and punished, often very severely, but this can always be rationalised as being 'for the good of the child' (and sometimes as being for the good of the child's soul). Under this sort of treatment, children learn to repress their feelings, and eventually to hide them even from themselves; this is a major handicap to developing an authentic sense of self. As Miller observes, '*overt abuse* is not the only way to stifle a child's vitality' (emphasis added).[19]

When attempting to understand the punitive character of institutional care, we must remember that the adults of this era had themselves grown up through the social upheaval and material privations of World War I and its aftermath, the Great Depression. Furthermore, both during their own childhood and until well afterwards, emotional deprivation was a crucial part of child-rearing practice. From the second decade of the 20th century, child-rearing was dominated by a particular expression of Miller's 'poisonous pedagogy': the puritanical regimes of Truby King — once described by the writer Leila Berg as 'a big stick to keep babies in order'. King, says Berg, became 'the figurehead of a puritanical authoritarian cult which gripped maternity hospitals, clinics and homes' for about 50 years.[20] His approach to the care of babies and children was characterised by rigid adherence to routine, the deliberate rationing of feeling, and an obsessive insistence on cleanliness and hygiene. This was a philosophy which reduced children to their physical selves, but it obviously appealed to this generation, for as Berg notes, King exerted a powerful influence on child-rearing practices over several decades: his ideas began to lose power only in the 1960s. As one writer has observed, King's philosophy both limited the ability of adults to be permissive, and led them to expect devotion — and enduring gratitude — when they did manage to be indulgent.[21] In other words, parents of this generation struggled to care unconditionally for their *own* children: how much more conditional, then, would their care have been when it was given to children who were not their own, and whose own parents were seen as having reneged on their duty?

Miller could be speaking of this generation when she notes (in another work) that:

> the more one-sided a society's observance of strict moral principles such as orderliness, cleanliness, and hostility towards instinctual drives and the more deep-seated its fear of the other side of human nature — vitality, spontaneity, sensuality, critical judgement and inner independence — the more strenuous will be its efforts to isolate this hidden territory, to surround it with silence or institutionalise it.[22]

This generation was firmly convinced that too much affection was 'bad' for children, that it spoiled them by making them overly demanding and intolerant of frustration. John Bowlby, a psychoanalyst and pioneer chronicler of childhood feeling,[23] points out that no evidence of substance has ever been presented to support this theory, and that in fact all the evidence points the other way; nevertheless, he observes, it was a very widely held conviction during the first half of the 20th century, and it died hard.[24]

These attitudes are revealed very vividly in a 1993 study conducted by sociologist Kerreen Reiger, who interviewed several Australian women from different generations about changes in child-rearing practices and attitudes. A woman who reared her children in the 1940s and 1950s spoke of the differences she had noted in her own daughter's relationship with her children:

> Perhaps they're communicating with the children better than we did. I think they know what's going on in the children's minds that we didn't know ...
>
> One thing, we weren't conscious about them being happy ... I was more conscious of them doing the right thing, speaking properly, respecting other people, respecting other people's property, and of course, religion.[25]

Underlying these beliefs — and perhaps not even thought about because it was taken for granted — was the assumption that if you inject the right values into children it will follow 'naturally' that children will turn out to be good, honest, well-functioning citizens. Happiness would follow on from that, but it was not one of the objectives of parenting. Quoting this interviewee, Reiger called her study 'I don't think we worried about whether they were happy...'. This does not mean that parents did not love their children, or hope that they would be happy in life; it just means that they thought about them differently from the way we do today. Children were seen in functional terms, and had no identity as social or emotional beings. Child welfare authorities, teachers and parents all collaborated in constructing the 'well-adjusted' child, and it was the responsibility of adults to ensure that they produced this, which accounts for the disapproving tone of the state Departments when speaking of the parents whose children had come to their attention. Children deprived of the 'correct' influences would axiomatically, in the view of welfare authorities, turn into 'juvenile delinquents'. It is easy to see how this constellation of emotionally harsh attitudes could lend itself to a particularly punitive interpretation in the institutional context, where the children involved had no claim to the affection or love of their carers to mediate the harshness.

Religion

The 1958 Burnside annual report advertised its work as 'a practical expression of Christian love', but Christian 'love' in Children's Homes appears most often in the guise of punishment. Religion and punishment are intimately connected in the Christian tradition, with its doctrines of original sin, hellfire and damnation, and eternal punishment — and the belief that the will of the child must be broken for the good of the soul. This belief, coupled with the particularly insular and repressive character of religious practice which appears to have been characteristic of these years, meant that religion was a useful — if not indispensable — tool for disciplining children. The guilt and sin of Catholic doctrine, the dour, anti-pleasure ideology of the evangelical Protestants — Methodists, Presbyterians, Salvationists — and the chilly austerity of the Anglican Church all found expression, in Children's Homes, in a practice that had little to do with love or comfort and much to do with the repression of all feeling.

Historian Phillip Greven analysed this deeply rooted tradition in his 1992 work, *Spare the Child: The Religious Roots of Punishment and the Psychological Impact of Physical Abuse*. As Greven observes, we tend to forget how profoundly the Judeo-Christian tradition has shaped our beliefs:

> [Even today,] most secular issues involving punishment cannot escape the enduring assumptions and perspective generated over the centuries by American and European religious rationales. So embedded are these assumptions in our minds and culture, and so familiar are they to most of us, that it is often almost impossible to discern their actual influence on us.[26]

In Children's Homes – including state-run Homes — this religious rationale was visibly present and unquestioned; even where carers were not personally religious, they operated within the cultural norms described by Greven. Queensland's Forde Report comments that where children were cared for by Christian organisations, there was the comfortable belief that they would be cared for with kindness and compassion, the Christian virtues.[27] However, as Greven observes, the interpretations of Christianity that have dominated in our culture promote not kindness and compassion, but the physical abuse of children. Christianity provides a religious rationale for this abuse — Miller, indeed, locates the roots of 'poisonous pedagogy' in religion. The religious foundation of Children's Homes is one factor which helps to explain the almost unremittingly punitive attitude towards children within the institutional context which I describe in the next chapter: Children's Homes were punitive towards children *because of* not *despite* their religious origins. The primary use of religion in Children's Homes was as a tool to inculcate in children a belief in their own inferiority, and to rationalise punishment. Children were 'wicked', or 'evil', and this had to be beaten out of them. Brian Cronin described his life in the 1960s at the boys' orphanage run by the Sisters of Nazareth in Ballarat, Victoria:

> I was dragged — 'brought' — up and told I/we was a piece of trash and of the devil's work, a common terminology used 100 times a day by any nun at any given time of the day.

Variations on this statement are very common from care leavers, and not just from inmates of Catholic Homes. As Greven points out, this type of religious rationale is drawn predominantly from the Old, not the New Testament. Jesus, says Greven, 'clearly felt a deep love and compassionate concern for children',[28] which means that the staff attitudes to children which can be seen in the institutional culture of this period are a distortion of the tenets of Christianity as taught by Jesus himself. It is pertinent to ask here why it is that in their dealings with children, adults have been predominantly drawn not to the New but to the Old Testament.

There were two related assumptions about religion, in this era, that made life in institutional care inherently dangerous for children. The first was that religious people and organisations were by definition benevolent and above reproach; the second was that religion was somehow linked to a love of children. The fallacy of these assumptions is demonstrated *ad nauseam* by the behaviour of professedly religious people towards children in Homes, in every state of Australia. However, given that they were almost universally and unequivocally accepted, it is not surprising that children in institutions run by churches and other religious bodies (such as the Salvation Army) could be abused with impunity. Anybody professing religious commitment would never be suspected of the behaviour of which many thousands of religious personnel were in fact guilty. This also goes some way to explaining why society tolerated the lack of transparency and accountability of church-based Homes, and also why children felt it inconceivable to accuse their abusers.

Children as commodities

There is another factor which is relevant when we are looking for reasons for the specific character of institutional care. This is the sense in which children in this era — a time before the recognition of 'children's rights' — appear to be a commodity; and like all commodities, their value can rise or fall. A newspaper article in 1957, for example, speaking of the availability of children for adoption, commented that 'orphans are snapped up for adoption like bargains at a winter sale'.[29] That was because *these* children were highly valuable: the means for a childless couple to 'complete their family'. Once children were adopted they were deemed, by a legal fiction, to belong to their adoptive parents as surely as if they had been born to them. But when children had no 'normal' family, or persisted in behaviour that put them beyond the pale of 'normal' ('innocent', obedient, conformist) childhood behaviour, their value dropped. A passage in the Victorian Department's 1956 annual report expressed this quite unequivocally. The report observed that 'there is and there always will be, need for the group care of very many children in institutions', among them 'the delinquents' and 'children with defects in habits and behaviour and, generally, children unattractive to foster-parents'. The report then noted how hard it was to interest people in becoming foster parents when they could not be guaranteed 'permanent and undisturbed custody (as is the case with adoption)'; for — leaving aside how likely this was to happen — parents were legally entitled to reclaim their children from the state once they could prove they were eligible to do so. By contrast, 'many arms are outstretched to enfold' the ward who is available for adoption — 'providing the child is normal, of tender age, and not unattractive'.

Hopewood

Perhaps the most extreme example of the degree to which 'unowned' and therefore 'unwanted' children could be commodified can be found in the Children's Home called Hopewood at Bowral in rural New South Wales, a Home which is unlike any other. Although it was conducted under a conventionally Christian ethos, Hopewood was established primarily as an experiment in both eugenics and social engineering, an attempt to breed a new 'super' race of Australians. It used 'illegitimate' wartime babies reared from their earliest months in an environment totally controlled by the founder of the Home, Sydney businessman LO Bailey,[30] who subsidised it through the string of Chic Salon underwear stores that he owned in New South Wales. Hopewood was licensed by the NSW Department, and established and managed by Bailey through his Youth Welfare Association of Australia. Bailey's stated motivation in setting up the Home for children was a desire to amalgamate what were, according to his biographer, 'two of the driving forces in [his] life ... his love for children and his interest in better health'.[31] His overall purpose, in fact, was to produce better human beings: the rationale for the experiment was that Australia needed not only more population, but a *superior* population, to combat the threat from 'inferior' races such as those to the north.[32]

Bailey obtained babies for his experiment through the fortunate (for him) circumstance of World War II: almost all the babies were the result of the mother's liaison with a serviceman, and this, historian Deborah Ambery notes, offered 'some guarantee that the fathers were physically fit and free from any sort of genetic deficiency'.[33] Bailey's long-serving assistant, Madge Cockburn, once revealed that 'we did get babies from the Child Welfare Department after we became established, but in the beginning we had to go out searching for them'. This was achieved through circularising the medical profession and asking doctors to refer women to the maternity home which Bailey ran in Sydney.[34] Eighty-six babies, all born between 1942 and 1947, became the 'Hopewood children'. Bailey did not adopt the children; he entered into an agreement with each mother to the effect that the Youth Welfare Association of Australia would care for the child until maturity. Mothers had the right to reclaim their children at any time, but could not then return them; the mothers of the babies who remained left their children and apparently did not return.

Part of Bailey's experiment involved raising the children free of contaminating influences, that is, the influences of the 'outside' world. Isolation was important for this goal, so in 1944 he bought Hopewood, a large rural property about 135 kilometres from Sydney. The children grew up there as a 'family', under a regime that expressed Bailey's belief in vegetarian food, cold showers, fresh air and outdoor activities as the basis of superior health. Bailey had hoped to school the children at the Home in order not to expose them to 'unfair temptations', but was prevented in this by the NSW Department, which insisted the children go to the local school. As well as the Home at Bowral, Bailey had small properties to accommodate groups of six to eight children at Manly, Narrabeen, Moree and other NSW locations. Children were periodically moved to one or other of these, without notice or consultation, for quite long periods. The 'Hopewood children' I interviewed spoke of this as a difficult feature of their lives — and some had very disrupted schooling as a result.

In recent years, allegations of sexual and emotional abuse have divided the 'Hopewood children'. The allegations involve staff members at the Home (and at the various smaller Homes, particularly the one at Moree) as well as Bailey himself, who some of the 'children' claim to have been an anally obsessed sexual deviant. Others have discovered that relatives tried to reclaim them but were told the children had been adopted; one woman was presented with a bill for several thousand pounds if she wished to take her child away.[35] Bailey himself conceived of his project as philanthropic, and this is how it was viewed at the time,[36] but this view was only possible in a social context that saw 'unwanted' children as appropriate subjects for scientific experimentation. And despite its unique rationale, accounts by Hopewood children suggest that this Home was not very different from the characteristic institutional norm, which I describe in the next chapter.

Chapter 3

'Complete and austere institutions'

I felt like I was serving time in prison. At least I still had a mother that would one day take me from this place. This is what I told myself and the hope of this event is what kept me going. I would often think about the other kids who were in there for good. If that happened to me, I thought I would die.

Bette Formosa, in Methodist Dalmar, Sydney, in the 1950s

WORK, FLOGGINGS ... FLOGGINGS, WORK was my whole life at the homes, which now seem to me nothing but concentration camps.

Ken Carter, Victorian state ward in the state Home Turana, and in the Salvation Army Boys' Home, Box Hill, Victoria, in the 1950s

When people were talking to me for my thesis, about their lives in Homes, I very soon began to see a clear pattern in what they were telling me. Even though there were nearly 80 Homes in all in my study, and they varied in size, location and in the organisation that ran them, the histories that I collected showed the same living environment — regardless of whether it was a state Home, a church Home or a charitable Home. This pattern is repeated over and over in the histories I have continued to hear, through CLAN and through the Senate Inquiry. What they all indicate is that there seems to have been a formula operating: children of 'this kind' — without family to care for them — fell into a specific category of beings, and had to be dealt with in this way.

I recognised the formula when I read *Asylums: Essays on the Social Situation of Mental Patients and Other Inmates,* published in 1961 by the American social theorist, Erving Goffman. Goffman's book was based on a study he had conducted of life within an institution for the mentally ill — from the patients' point of view. This was unusual for the time, because as he commented in his preface to the book, 'almost all professional literature on mental patients is written from the point of view of the psychiatrist'. He described the institutional setting that he observed as a 'total institution', which he defined thus:

> a place of residence and work where a large number of like-situated individuals, cut off from the wider society for an appreciable period of time, together lead an enclosed, formally administered round of life. Prisons serve as a clear example, providing we appreciate that what is prison-like about prisons is found in institutions whose members have broken no laws.[1]

Goffman's conclusion about 'total institutions' such as orphanages, mental asylums, prisons, army barracks, boarding schools and monasteries was that they were 'the forcing houses for changing persons; each is a natural experiment in what can be done to the self'. When I read Goffman's work I recognised the system he was describing — it tallied very well with what I was hearing from people about their Homes, and what I knew from the Home I grew up in. I am not talking here of the actual objectives of Children's Homes but of how they operated, and how their inmates experienced them.

The pattern was enforced more rigidly in some Homes than in others but the essential ingredients were the same in all of them — they were 'prison-like' institutions 'whose members have broken no laws'. The major characteristic of 'total institutions' is what is contained in the word 'total'. We are on the same ground here as 'totalitarian', a word which describes a closed system serving its own ends, ends which may not coincide at all with the ends of the people who live within it. There is no room here for individual selves, since all units in such a system are interchangeable.

Contamination

One of the purposes of the 'total institution' says Goffman, may be the 'protection of the wider community from pollution'.[2] The methods of dealing with Home children, and in fact with all children entering care, including state care, do indeed suggest fear of a contamination that has to be contained: every child entering a NSW non-government Home had to have a medical certificate stating they were 'free of infectious diseases'. On a practical level this is a sensible precaution; but on a deeper level it seems to brand children in this situation as likely to contaminate others. A preoccupation with hygiene, both outer and inner, and with contamination and contagion, was characteristic of this era generally, and rooted in the medicalisation of childhood, which itself had arisen from centuries of high infant mortality.

These concerns were intensified in the Home environment because of the low status of the inmates. In a later work, Goffman says that when we encounter somebody whose status is threatening, 'we construct a stigma-theory, an ideology to explain his inferiority and account for the danger he represents'.[3] These children were believed to be from contaminating families — poor, mentally ill, alcoholic, unable to manage, 'feckless', 'lazy', 'weak in character' — and they were also a threat to social order, because they were not contained in their rightful place, within families which 'owned' them. The carers and managers of Homes in the postwar years had grown up in a time when eugenics — the equation of 'poor stock' with social 'inadequacy' and intellectual weakness — had widespread credibility. These children, then, were 'polluted' by their parents' 'inferiority' and 'failure', which had led to their being placed in care, making them the responsibility of other than their rightful 'owners'. This whole construction was underpinned by a concept of children and of children's 'nature' that was based on the punitive Christian ethos discussed in the previous chapter.

There are highly specific methods used by total institutions to handle their inmates, and in this chapter I describe how they operated in the typical Children's Home of the institutional era.

Fear

> Us kids were brutally treated and betrayed and savagely beaten to within an inch of our lives by our carers and providers [like] something straight out of the 16th century, ie the Poor Sisters of Nazareth, whose method was to inbreed fear into us by 'supervision by aggression'.
>
> Brian Cronin, in St Joseph's, Ballarat, Victoria, in the 1960s

It is no exaggeration to say that most children living in Children's Homes felt fear on a daily basis. This was not necessarily the intention of the Home but it was an inevitable by-product of the way Homes were run. The very environment in which children were placed could not help but be frightening, indeed threatening, to children already frightened — to put it mildly — by losing their parents and everything familiar. Sometimes, however, it *was* the intention; there were Homes which appeared to set out to rule their inmates by fear. Ralph Doughty's description of life in the Salvation Army's Gill Memorial Home in Goulburn, New South Wales, provides the template:

> The generation of FEAR was the active ingredient used by the officers against the boys in the orphanage. Standing before the officer(s) and waiting for him to attack often caused a boy to wet or dirty his pants. Fear was with you 24 hours every day. You have a painful lump in your solar plexus and the pain gravitates into your neck.

Ruling by fear is very effective, but it is also very destructive to a developing person. Being frightened for much of your childhood colours forever how you see the world, and it becomes an integrated part of how you normally feel. Terry Langham, in his evidence to the Inquiry in Adelaide, described how he tried to cope with the fear:

> Surviving in those places, you develop a survival mechanism. You be quiet, you do not say anything. You make yourself a small target. You learn to be quiet and you carry that into adulthood. You become withdrawn … It took many years for me to get over that. I suppose sometimes it still comes out because I lived in constant fear.[4]

Clearly, the fear does not always leave when you leave the Home. Lorraine Rodgers concluded her submission with this: 'After all these years, I still got that terrible FEAR in me, I cannot explain it any other way.' Being frightened all the time is my primary memory of my childhood. This is the prison that confines us long after the walls of the Home have been left behind.

Control

> A daily routine was methodically carried out, rigid rules you were expected quickly to adapt to, know and obey. A place that implemented methods of control adopted from the criminal system.
>
> David Walshe, also in the Salvation Army Gill Memorial Home, but more than 20 years after Ralph Doughty

Harry Hendrick, the historian of British child welfare, has observed that social policy in regard to children could be described as 'the history of the imposition of adult will upon children's bodies'.[5] The four primary forms of control he identifies are food and feeding, medical inspection and treatment, the 'ordering of the body in movement and the tongue in speech', and the infliction of physical pain. Control in all of these areas was intensively practised in Children's Homes, and was used not only to control but also to eliminate individual differences between inmates. The destruction of a sense of self began as soon as children stepped over the threshold of the Home.

Goffman notes that admission procedures are an important aspect of the total institution because they must impress on new arrivals immediately that they are 'merely an inmate' and so must give up all claims to a sense of self. New arrivals must, he says, be 'shaped and coded into an object that can be fed into the administrative machinery of the establishment to be worked on smoothly by routine operations'. Mavis Devereaux-Dingwall described several characteristic aspects of procedure in all Homes when she talked of her admission to Bidura, the NSW

Department's main receiving Home in Sydney in 1943, following her court appearance:

> I was then separated from my brothers, as they were sent to Ralston [Royleston], a nearby Home for boys. Going through the medical checks were to a young girl of seven years both invasive and embarrassing. There I was sitting in a bath whilst two of the female staff members went all over me and talked as if I was not there ... After the humiliating bath I was given a uniform to put on which was about three sizes too big for me. I experienced the same with the shoes that were allocated to me. I was told they were out of my size and I would just have to wait until they had ones to fit me.

Mavis was then handed a broom and told to sweep the pathway and verandas, and was hit around the head and face by the matron when she used her initiative and put the broom away. In one brief sequence, her sense of an individual self was cancelled, as she inexplicably lost her siblings, her bodily privacy, clothing that fitted her body, and the right to use her own mind. 'Each time you entered, you were reduced to a manageable unit, private property was removed and never seen again, government day clothes were issued and you were given a number,' said Peter Brownbill, who was admitted several times to the NSW Department's receiving depot for boys, Royleston, Glebe, in the 1950s and 1960s. The same procedures applied in other states and across all denominations. 'Our clothes were unpacked and taken from us. Nothing belonged to you after you arrived in the Home; everything was communal,' said Christine Lang, about arriving in Rathgar, a United Protestant Association (UPA) Home, in 1952; 20 years later, when Lesley Simmonds entered the Church of England Girls' Home in Burwood, NSW, little had changed — 'They cut my hair off. "We have short hair here," they said.'

This type of depersonalisation, as children were processed through cleansing rituals both external and internal, is standard in all accounts. Children were routinely given carbolic baths, and had their hair washed in chemicals to kill nits. Margery Chandler remembered how her skin was burnt by the kerosene or phenyl they used, 'and we were always being given doses of horrible things for various reasons — like senna tea, and castor oil'. It seems to have been a longstanding feature of Homes — Iona Owen, who was working at Havilah, a NSW Anglican Home in 1936, said, 'The children were kept spotlessly clean. All of Saturday morning was spent cutting toenails, bathing, and cleaning hair for nits.' The woman who ran my Home, like those running Havilah, was obsessive about keeping the children, their clothes and their bedding 'spotlessly clean'. Children who were due to be returned to their parents would be dressed in their own clean clothes and then told to sit on a stool and wait, in case they got dirty.

These practices endured over decades, turning up again and again in care leaver accounts, with greater or lesser severity. The admission procedures for Queensland's Wilson Youth Hospital, a 'correctional facility' opened in 1961, for example, are an intensified version of this same routine. Girls had to strip naked, shower, often in the presence of male staff, and have all their orifices examined. They were then deloused with the highly toxic insecticide DDT, regardless of whether or not there was any evidence of insect infestation. All personal possessions were removed and institutional clothing was issued.[6] Like many of the girls in 'correctional facilities' all over Australia, the girls subjected to these sexualised procedures had often been incarcerated because they were on the run from incestuous or otherwise abusive families.

In many Homes, children had numbers. 'Nothing was personalised. Everybody had a number — mine was two, my sister was one, and I still remember my best friends' numbers,' said Cheryl Hannaford. 'Every boy was known and referred to by his number,' said Ralph Doughty, in the Gill Memorial Home from 1941, and 'for the next 10 years, I was known as boy number 59. That number was "me" until I left the orphanage.' Caroline Carroll recalled that Miss Davies,[7] the superintendent of the NSW government Home, Lynwood Hall, 'rarely addressed us by name; when she wasn't calling us sluts or whores she called us by a number'. Children often had their names actually changed: Cheryl, one of my interviewees, had to answer to Hazel (the colour of her eyes) because there was already a Cheryl in the Home. What was being made clear to children in this process was that their names were just labels for identification, not individual possessions that identified them as their own selves. (Children who were fostered could end up with a succession of names to match each set of foster parents. As NSW state wards, Marion Tucker had four different surnames and Joy Hill had several different complete names.) Mavis Devereaux-Dingwall described her arrival at a Catholic Home in Erskineville, NSW:

> the nuns tried to humiliate me by taking away my name. I remember only too well, on my first day being called to the front of the class by a Sister Michael. What is your name? She asked. 'Mavis Devereaux,' I replied. How do you spell it? was the next question. 'D.e.v.e.r.e.a.u.x,' I replied. Sister Michael snapped, 'There is no such name or spelling. You made it up, didn't you? Your name is Connolly the same as your mother, isn't it?' And so I started school as Mavis Connolly, being baptised under that name, making my communion under the name Connolly.

There was another agenda going on here: the nuns would not recognise Mavis's father's name because he was Presbyterian, and in their eyes the marriage of her parents was not recognised and she was therefore 'illegitimate'. 'Losing your name can be a great "curtailment of self"', says Goffman, and David Forbes expressed exactly what that means when he related how after a period in the care of the NSW state, never being called by his name, he almost forgot what it was: 'When you are never called by your name it sends you a clear message — you don't have the right to be yourself — you are nobody — you may as well not even exist.'

Communal clothing is also a reminder to inmates that they are 'nobody' — they are interchangeable with all the other children in the Home. Ellen Brown, when she was taken to Bidura in the early 1960s, wore her best dress, since her mother had told her they were going on 'an outing'. On arrival at Bidura, her dress was taken away from her and she never wore it again; when, as sometimes happened, the children were taken out of the Home, for example to church, 'I can remember waiting to be given the clothes to wear and I was too terrified to ask if I could wear my dress that I could see hanging up.'

In many Homes children wore donated clothing — this was often necessary, since many had parents with few resources, or no parents on the scene at all. Less necessary was the way this clothing was used by some staff as yet another way of reminding children of how interchangeable they were. 'Clothes for the next day were issued each evening. If someone nice was on duty, you could choose; if not, too bad,' said Rosemary Bartlett, of the UPA Home Rathgar, New South Wales. 'If you were lucky enough to get a pair of undies that fitted you thought all your Christmases had come at once,' said Christine Lang.

Kerry Geldard explains in her submission why 'private ownership of anything was impossible'. When her mother bought her comfortable shoes because she had none, another girl in the Home simply took them and wrote her name in them, and no staff member intervened. In my Home, the carer kept a large drawer of old clothes in which she dressed the transient, 'holidaying' children — so that they would not dirty or tear their own clothing. But even when children had not worn their own clothes, she would wash and iron them to her own high standard before returning them. Thinking about it now, I wonder if this was intended as a message about her care of the children themselves. If their clothes were so beautifully cared for, how could parents think the children themselves were not?

'The personal possessions of an individual are an important part of the materials out of which he builds a self,' says Goffman;[8] but if you want to run an efficient institution you cannot afford to allow inmates to have personal possessions. The more you dispossess inmates, the more easily they can be managed by staff — which means, as Goffman says, that for all total institutions there is a constant conflict between humane standards and institutional efficiency. In Children's Homes institutional efficiency appears almost always to have been the major consideration. The visible, material dispossessions were layered on top of the invisible dispossessions that children had already suffered — of membership of their own family and of brothers and sisters. Those dispossessions were only invisible because the institution denied that they were important, so that children were also dispossessed of their feelings about them, and had to hide or even deny them.

Humiliation

Humiliation and shaming were standard techniques of control, as well as being particularly effective in reminding children how easily the 'territories of the self', to use Goffman's term,[9] could be violated. It is difficult to retain a stable self-image in the face of constant denigration. Some humiliations had undeniably sexual overtones. In the Church of England Girls' Home, Burwood, New South Wales, 'they'd take your pants down in front of everyone else and smack you — this went on up to age 16,' said Lesley Simmonds, who lived there from 1972 to 1978. Some humiliations had overtones of a torture ritual. Pearl Webster, in a rural Catholic orphanage, recalled the punishment for talking one night at dinner:

I was brought out the front to stand on my toes, with my hands on my head and my tongue poking out, for the duration of the meal. Each time my toes gave way and my heels dropped to the floor and my tongue withdrew, the cane was made visible as a threat.

Ralph Doughty, in his Salvation Army Home, described a form of punishment that involved standing in line for hours on end without moving. Even if a boy fainted, he was left lying there until he recovered and got up to resume his place in the line:

> If you had to urinate or defecate and called out or raised your hand to request permission the officer invariably refused the request and added time on for the group because the boy had moved or had spoken without receiving permission. Naturally, the boy wet himself or wet and shit himself. This torture of standing in lines and rigidly at attention did not last for just ten minutes or even half an hour, but went on for hour after hour, and if a mealtime intervened then the torture started again after the meal-break and would stop only when the officer decided or there was work to be done.

Here, to the physically gruelling ordeal is added the humiliation of soiling yourself, which would be particularly shameful for older children, as these boys were. To be reduced to the status of a young child who cannot help but soil himself is a cruel humiliation for any human being. Similarly, at St John's, a Catholic orphanage also in Goulburn, an inmate relates how once a week the boys were all given a dose of Epsom salts in the morning. However, he said, 'There were 200 odd boys and about 12 toilets.' The result was that the boys 'shit in the urinals, drains, on the grass and in our pants. We would then be punished by being belted for doing this.'[10]

The focus by staff on children's elimination functions in these examples is common in many accounts. More than one inmate talks about 'undie patrol' — having to check other children's underpants for 'skid marks'. Leesa Stevans described being potty trained as a very young child in the Catholic Nazareth House in Victoria, in the 1960s:

> We all had to line up in a row next to a row of potties and sit down and do our business, then when finished we had to wipe ourselves. Then we had to stand next to our potties and bend over so as a nun could check our behinds to see if we had wiped ourselves properly. The next thing I remember is being hit hard with what they called a switch; my bottom then bled and bled. I had never seen so much blood before and thought I was going to die.

These behaviours — repeated in Home after Home — form part of what Judith Herman, in her book *Trauma and Recovery* (1992) describes as a characteristic pattern of totalitarian control: their objective is to rid inmates of any sense of self.[11]

Lack of choice and lack of privacy

> You ate and slept with 60 other kids; there was no privacy and no choice.
>
> Mary Owen, of her life at St Brigid's, Ryde, NSW, 1965

> The inmate is never fully alone; he is always within sight and often earshot of someone, if only his fellow inmates.
>
> Goffman 1978: 33

Not only not alone, but also often exposed, naked, and forced into spatial intimacy. Helena Dam, in Catholic Nazareth House in Brisbane in the 1930s, recalled bath time at the Homes as 'horrendous':

We used to bath only once a week. The water wasn't changed at all. If you went in first the water was very hot, hot enough to scald you. If you were one of the last ones in the bath the water was usually cold and muddy, as it was never changed.

Many inmates of both sexes talk of showering naked, no matter what their age — which, incidentally, exposed the blue welts on those who had been beaten. Others had to line up naked to wait for their turn in the bath. At Lesley Simmonds' NSW Church of England Girls' Home, throughout the 1970s, although bathing was more frequent than it had been in Helena Dam's Home, 40 years earlier, there was still no privacy at all. Everyone washed together, until age 15 or 16, in open showers, she said. This shows how entrenched and how resistant to change these procedures were.

Children commonly slept in dormitories, with no personal space to call their own. Lack of personal space and privacy was one of the most significant markers of the fact that a Home was not a home. It was this absence of the possibility of a 'private life' that so moved and horrified the British MP, Godfrey Nicholson, in 1946, on reading the Curtis Report, because it is above all a marker of the status of such children as merely 'inmates'. Physical confinement was accompanied by emotional claustrophobia — 'There was absolutely nowhere to be by yourself, or sleep by yourself,' said Cheryl Hannaford. 'You got so irritated with each other, being in a confined space with nowhere to get away to,' said Sylvia Baker. 'There was no privacy at all, even when you had your periods, everyone knew, even at 17.' At the NSW state 'training' institutions at Parramatta and Hay, and at Victoria's Winlaton, girls had to show their soiled sanitary pads to staff before they were allowed fresh ones. In many Homes toilet paper was rationed — in mine, each child was allowed two pieces per visit for 'number 2'.

Another way of impressing on children the fact they did not exist as individual persons was for adults to 'talk about you as if you weren't there'. This was standard practice in this era generally, but in the institution, the feeling of being already 'unwanted' made children particularly vulnerable to the pain of this experience. One woman remembered how the matron of her Home would tell prospective foster carers, in front of the children, that she and her sister were 'no-hopers'. Mim McKew recalls a similar situation, when the matron of her Home said:

> Yes, I'm afraid she does have a difficult time. Her parents don't want her, and she is such a sullen, fidgety child. We're so very sorry you had a problem with her, and we will make sure we provide a child more suitable for you next time …

Former state wards spoke of similar experiences, particularly when they were fostered — it sometimes felt like being 'handed around like baggage', one of my interviewees recalled. This kind of treatment tells children, yet again, that they do not exist except as objects, and objects which can be used however adults determine.

Food

Food was mass-produced, of course; with dozens of children to feed, how could it be anything else? The following is fairly typical, from William McLeary in Burnside, New South Wales, in the 1950s:

> Our meals were taken at scrubbed tables with bench seats. The food was very spartan, consisting mostly of home-grown cabbage, broccoli, stringy marrow, broad beans and pumpkin. We also had mashed potato, and rice pudding and bread and butter pudding.

William remembered something that others recounted too, and which was vividly depicted in the 2002 movie, *The Magdalen Sisters*:

> Staff took their meals at the same time and sat at tables covered with crisp white starched tablecloths and napkins, silver cutlery and serviette rings. We would sit and drool at their food. They had chicken, meat, bacon and eggs, toast with real butter, scones with fresh cream and jam.

Sometimes food was eccentric, as recounted by Barry Cook, who was in the Victorian Children's Aid Society Home in Parkville:

> Breakfast consisted of either porridge or leftover 'piddle soup' from the night before. 'Piddle soup' (the mention of which was rewarded with oil of cloves) was in actuality pea and ham soup of a thick consistency left to cool over night and sliced into squares — which you were supposed to eat with your fingers.

And quite ordinary food could be a treat:

> An occasional treat was toast — but generally with twelve at each table there were four slices of bread for each table and a large tin of Monbulk jam — no butter but very, very occasionally dripping, over which there was always a fight to get the brown jelly at the bottom.

Mim McKew's memory of food in her many Victorian Homes, both state and non-state, is typical of many:

> They made us eat the most vile 'whatever' on earth. Stuff like vomit-inducing tripe with white lumpy sauce, gristly sausages, cereal porridge with a little cold milk and no sugar, lambs' brains and non-slurpable brothy soups. Another dietary food of the establishment was protein-moving Weeties, sometimes with warm milk, other times cold. They moved because of the weevils that inhabited them. No matter how much protein they thought we

required, weevils just could not cut it. Yet we were made to sit, and sit, and sit until we ate it, little worms and all.

There are many accounts of food practices which, as Kerry Geldard remarked, 'showed the degree of disregard with which we were treated'. She was in the Protestant Federation Girls' Home in Sydney:

> I have become a vegetarian as a result of often vomiting up meat that was off and we could smell was off before we ate it, but were forced to eat it anyway. I often recount with humour how as each child vomited another would be sent to clean up the mess of the child before. We soon learned that if you were going to be sick make it early, or you would have a very big mess to clean up at the end.

William McLeary added to his account (above) that, 'Friday was always tripe night, which I invariably vomited up and was force-fed my vomit.' Many people recount this as common practice in Homes. Margaret Turnbull, who was in Victorian Catholic Homes, remembers being either deprived of food as punishment, or force-fed both food and her own vomit. Leesa Stevans, force-fed as a little girl in Melbourne's Nazareth House, took action of her own, and would hide food up her nose if she could not eat it, to avoid having to eat her own vomit if she brought it up. It was her mother, on one of her infrequent visits, who complained of the smell; the nuns took her to a doctor, who discovered the source and removed the rotting food.

This also shows that children did attempt to exert some control over their environment — like the small child in my Home, called Tracy, whom I have never forgotten. She was not a permanent, but she spent many months there, from the age of about two and a half. Tracy would never eat the morning porridge, and as a result she had to stand in the corner in her nightie with a lump of porridge in her mouth. There she stayed all morning, or perhaps all

The youngest children at Methodist Dalmar in Sydney in their dining room with their 'nurses' supervising. Many of these children had older brothers and sisters, but they did not eat, sleep or play with them. There is no date on the photograph, but it looks to be c. 1940s.

day, and refused to swallow. I can still see her skinny little legs, blue with cold, her white nightie and fine pale hair curling over her head, and the dogged look on her face, as she stood there unmoved by slaps and harsh words, determined to remain true to herself.

In some Homes there was just not enough to go round. Douglas Mann, in Parkerville, Western Australia, in the 1950s, remembered that 'hunger pains were always with us. There was never enough food. I used to always offer to do the dishes so that I could scrape the pots and eat the scraps.' Many Homes were run on a shoestring, as I describe in the next chapter, and it might well have been difficult to feed the number of hungry mouths that had to be fed, without donations; and donations might not have been reliable. A lack of adequate food was not, however, always the result of inadequate resources. Mark Greenhalgh said in his submission that at the state's Westbrook Farm Home for Boys in Queensland in the 1950s, 'Even though we worked hard for our food, we were always kept near starvation point.' He continued:

> The animals that we raised — mostly cows and pigs — were better fed than us boys. Many of them won prizes at the Toowoomba Show. Sometimes we sneaked some of the animal fodder from the troughs, just to keep from starving.

The Home, the world

> The entire week was rostered and every moment of the day accounted for.
>
> Bette Formosa, in Methodist Dalmar, Sydney, in the 1950s

The major factor that made everyday life in a Children's Home different from everyday life in a family home was that sleep, play and work were carried out in the same place, under the same authority and, as Goffman says, 'cut off from the wider society'. 'The church was beside the orphanage and the school was inside it,' said Pearl Webster of her Catholic Home, and this was true for many Homes. Children in these places went outside the gates only very occasionally, for an outing or to go to church. It was quite common for large Homes to have their own primary schools — many Catholic Homes did, for example — and the Burnside Presbyterian Homes in Sydney also had their own hospital and farm. State Homes, such as the NSW Department's 'establishments', also often had schools on the premises. Where children went out to school, it did not lead to the sort of social activities which it might have for children with families, such as visiting schoolmates or inviting them back home. The authority of the Home accompanied children to school: they were identified there by their clothes (often different from the non-Home children's but similar within the group), by their food (lunch wrapped in newspaper, perhaps, or delivered specially to the school at lunchtime), and usually by their manner of travelling to and from school (walking in double file, for example). All these things showed quite clearly that they were the 'Home kids'.

When visitors came to the Home they stayed within the grounds, and with some exceptions, children did not leave the Home for overnight or weekend visits. Children living in an institution belonged to the institution, and it directed every moment of their lives. All activities were carried out in the company of a large batch of other children, all of them treated alike and required to do the same thing, in the same regimented way, together. Chrystal Lennox gave a typical account — this was Bidura, the NSW state receiving Home, in 1962:

> You had to get out of bed, line up. Open the door, line up with toothbrush. A grey locker, I had one dress and a school dress. Line up to go to the toilet, clean your teeth, get your uniform on, line up for breakfast, line up out of

breakfast. Out the back of the kitchen, way down the yard, the school. Line up, line up. Set times for TV, meals, then go to bed.

Alice Nanson, in a rural UPA Home in the late 1950s, recalled how 'you would get up, wash your face, there was a set routine — you couldn't deviate and wash your face at a different time'. David Forbes remembered that 'we even had a specific time that we had to go to the toilet in'. In most Homes there were also rules about when talking was allowed. Ralph Doughty described a typical, though extreme, and extremely administered, example of this in the Gill Salvation Army Home in the 1940s:

> The major rule in the orphanage was that you did not talk unless you were told that you could. However, in the playgrounds you could talk unless the boy was on a 'no talking' punishment. When the officer's whistle was blown all talking and movement had to stop immediately ...
>
> Under no circumstances were you allowed to talk in the dormitories, in the bathroom, in any toilet, in the chapel, in the 'library room', in the dining room, in the locker-room where your clothes were stored or when you were assembled in a group or standing in line. You did not talk from the night-time when you lined up to get ready for bed until the next morning when you had put your work clothes on and had moved to your work-place.

Many people recall being severely punished for breaking the 'no talking' rule, not only by being given 'a hiding', but also, for example, by having to spend hours standing in the dark outside the dormitory. No autonomous action or choice was possible or even thinkable.

School life generally was very regimented in these years, and children's behaviour was closely monitored by adults — at home as well as at school. But most children in family situations also had a great deal of unsupervised play, much more than is usual today, ironically. In Homes, children were denied all opportunity to explore possibilities, to test their own limits, to try out new things, push the boundaries a bit and see what would happen. This eventually creates people who are described as 'institutionalised', people who do not feel free to use their initiative, or, in the worst-case scenario, who do not even know that they can do so. The younger children are when they are institutionalised, the more profound this effect is, for older children have had some time to develop a sense of self — battered though it will be by the institutional environment.

I remember a book I read as a child, called *Island Magic*, by Elizabeth Goudge. There is one chapter that begins with the boy character leaping out of bed and running from his house down to the water, full of the joy of being alive and free in the early morning. I read that part once, then could never bear to read it again, and always skipped it. It wasn't only that he had the freedom to do that; it was that *he actually wanted to*. I would never have dared set foot outside the Home without permission, and — what I now see was worse — I did not want to; I would not have enjoyed it if I had, because the world outside seemed so frightening. I didn't know how to just *be*, and enjoy *being myself*. I think that is what hurt most in that passage, although I'm sure I did not understand that at the time.

One of the chief techniques for managing populations in a 'total institution' is surveillance. 'There were a lot of warders, like rats, running everywhere, and you were always being stopped and asked what you were doing, where you were going,' said Jack Fletcher of Royleston. 'I felt as though I was being watched at all times. I felt they were just waiting to dish out the next punishment,' said Pearl Webster of her Catholic Home. Another person remembered how the matron of her Home would stand at the door just watching the children: 'I could feel her through the back of my head,' she said. This kind of constant surveillance eventually makes inmates feel, in Goffman's words, 'inferior, weak, blameworthy, and guilty'. If you are being watched, you begin to believe that you must have done something wrong or unacceptable. In a Home, surveillance was intended to have that effect, to ensure that a child did not behave as an individual, but conformed to the norm and did exactly what was allowed and what everybody else did.

Work

> I often wonder who was looking after who.
>
> Nigel Shew, commenting on the amount of work done by the children in his Salvation Army Home in Queensland in the 1950s and 1960s

Work was an important part of the day for most inmates. For children in families, work is a way of being bound into family life, however much children might grumble about the chores they have to do. In a total institution, people work because they will be punished if they do not; they don't dare not work.

Many Children's Homes were in old mansions which had been sold off cheaply to churches, charities or state governments because they required servants to maintain them and so had outlived their era. A great many histories show that children commonly supplied the domestic labour necessary for keeping the Home clean and functioning even though this contravened the law. In all the Child Welfare Acts of the time there was a section devoted to the regulation of child labour. Their main concern was street trading and public performance, but what is obvious is that the employment of children was meant to be both limited and quite strictly regulated. Many Children's Homes, however, operated as if children's labour was merely an available resource. In

Ralph Doughty's rural Salvation Army Home, which housed over 100 children, 'the boys did all the work,' he said, with no outside help brought in. He was there for 10 years, from 1941 — until long after the war years, with their restricted availability of labour.

So it was in many Homes. Sally Fenton, in a Catholic Home on Sydney's Central Coast for 10 years from 1947, remembers how 'we had to do all the work'. This consisted of 'cooking, the lawns, scrubbing verandas, washing, starching nuns' habits, we cleaned fish and killed chooks, and one day,' she said, 'I nearly cut another child's hand off with an axe'. Bette Formosa, in Methodist Dalmar during the 1950s, gives a lengthy description which is typical of very many accounts, and which also shows the degree of regimentation involved:

> At eight years of age I was placed in the senior girls' cottage, and the senior girls at Dalmar performed and were responsible for all domestic duties and chores in this home of over 100 children. Senior boys were responsible for all outside work on the 67-acre property as well as the dairy. We worked seven days a week, arising at 5.45 am except on Sunday (6.30 am), and were expected to start our jobs by 6.15 am, lights out at 7.30 pm. The entire week was rostered, and every moment of the day accounted for.

Bette then described the work she did:

> Rostered jobs over the years ranged from working in the kitchen, laundry, washing wet bed sheets, scrubbing and polishing floors (at eight years I was using an industrial polisher), washing windows, lighting the furnace for hot water, dusting, serving breakfast or dinner, making school lunches (humiliatingly wrapped in newspaper), bathing children, polishing shoes, collecting pig slops, scraping and washing dishes, polishing silver, cleaning bathrooms, filling coke buckets, getting children ready for school, working in the babies' home, setting tables, working in the

> staff pantry, taking children to school, working in the isolation ward ... the list goes on and is seemingly endless.

Keeping children busy by making them work kept them under surveillance and under control. It ensured that they remained within the power of the adults running the Home rather than exploring their own childhood domain through unsupervised play. Work was corrective and disciplinary, which is why, apart from its cost-cutting purpose, it went far beyond 'doing chores'. Children from this background, so the reasoning went, from 'inadequate' families, needed to be kept on a tight rein even if some of the tasks were meaningless — at Burnside, Harry Baker had the job of sweeping the gum leaves off the roadway in front of the home every day. Marigold Kendall's recollections of Cooinoo (a small NSW Home run by the ladies' auxiliary of the local Church of England church), from 1946 to 1952 show the underlying agenda clearly: children were made to work even though there were staff:

> We hated Saturdays because we did more work — scrubbing out bathrooms and toilets, then matron's private bathroom, then the downstairs toilet. They'd have inspections. There was a big dining room floor had to be polished, and a lot of brass — bells, gongs, knobs — and big windows to be cleaned.

These tasks were a demonstration that objects such as brass bells, toilets, floors and windows were more important than children. Meaningless and demeaning chores, such as cleaning marble stairs with a toothbrush, were often used as a punishment in Homes, as they were in the state 'training schools'. This is all an example of what concentration camp survivor and writer Primo Levi called 'afflictive' work, 'useful only to break down current resistance and punish past resistance'.[12] It is interesting to read an account of a 'training' Home on the other side of the world, Canada, in the same period:

> [T]he task everyone tried to avoid was scrubbing the hallways on your hands and knees with a hand brush (this was also used as a from of punishment; but sometimes you were given a toothbrush instead of a hand brush).[13]

Labour was yet another of the techniques employed to alienate children from any sense of themselves as individuals, or even as human beings. They were part of an assembly line, as in a factory, cogs in a machine, ensuring the efficient operation of the Home, this being the highest priority of the total institution.

Children were also used as unpaid labour for commercial purposes. The extent of this is only now becoming known. Lorraine Davis related what happened when, in 1950, she was sent to a Magdalen laundry in Hobart, because she kept running away from the Launceston Girls' Home:

> I was only eight, but had to work every day in the laundry from after breakfast until 5 pm with a break for lunch. It was a huge laundry and we used to do the laundry for all the hotels, schools and hospitals in Hobart. I worked in the ironing room. Sometimes I would iron, but mostly I would fold and damp the laundry ready for the presses. They must have made heaps of money from doing all this laundry; also from the huge farm out the back where they grew everything.

'Bad girls do the best sheets' was how this labour was conceptualised at the time[14] — but how bad can an eight-year-old be? Or a 10-year-old like Jeanette Barnacle in the Convent of the Good Shepherd at Oakleigh, Victoria, who recalled how they made her a box to stand on so she could do the ironing: 'Just think of a child of 10 standing on a box all day ironing, and I did that for 4½ years.'[15] This is the story powerfully told in the 2002 film *The Magdalen Sisters*. It is set in Ireland in the 1960s and is based on the accounts of actual inmates, demonstrating how this was a universal experience for 'bad' Catholic girls. The laundries were run by the Good Shepherd order, and Sandra Pendergast, in the laundry of their convent in Ashfield, NSW, in the 1950s, described a similar environment to the one depicted in the movie, 'a *de facto* prison, totally enclosed by high stone walls (in some places topped by barbed wire) and all the doors locked', where the girls were incarcerated for 24 hours a day, seven days a week.

To the bleakness of eight-year-old Lorraine's life was added the separation, once again, from everything that was familiar. She said of the Tasmanian Magdalen Home, 'it was an awful place and very strange to me. I had never seen nuns before and … I felt really lonely, too, as I missed my sisters so much.' She was to have more bad experiences: at the age of 12, after going on strike at the laundry, she was sent to the Lachlan Park Asylum. As before, she was there to work, this time looking after the children living there:

> [babies and toddlers with encephalitis,] with their swollen heads just lying in their cots waiting to die, [other girls] who were just vegetables, [and] 25 little Down Syndrome children who would be taken out of their beds each morning and strapped onto potty chairs where they stayed all day until they were bathed in the afternoon and put back to bed. They weren't allowed to walk or run around.

Verneta Lohse talks of doing similar work, also when she was aged 12, when her Catholic orphanage, Mater Dei, run by the Good Samaritan nuns at Narellan in rural New South Wales, was turned into what she describes as 'a school for mentally retarded children' and it became her job to look after them. 'Can you imagine what this was like for a 12-year-old, to have all this responsibility so young?' asked Verneta. There was no more school for her after this, and fifth class is the last she remembers. Similarly, Lorraine Davis had no schooling between the ages of eight and 12. But she made her own efforts to remedy this:

> We had torn up newspapers for toilet paper, and as I loved to read, I would go to the toilet a lot so that I could read the pieces. Often I would try and find matching pieces so that I could finish whatever I was reading.

Education

These little girls, instead of attending school, were doing unpaid work for which the Catholic orders received payment. This both contravened state legislation and also defrauded the workers themselves — the children — of payment for their labour. The children, of course, could not be paid even had the order wished to do so (and there is no indication that they did), because this would have exposed the illegality of the operation. It is a tragic irony: 'charity' children working to enrich organisations which, as charities, were exempt from paying any taxes to the state whose child welfare legislation they were flaunting. The resulting lack of education in most cases condemned these children, as adults, to low-paid work and caused them embarrassment and shame.

It is obvious that it was not considered important that these children, by working, missed out on an education. In some Homes, and it might have been the majority, children did receive schooling. At the same time, in other Homes, while schooling was not actually deliberately withheld, there was what appears to have been a cavalier attitude towards children's education.

* * * * *

This had not always, apparently, been the case in Children's Homes.

In a 1994 paper called 'Orphanage education', Melbourne youth studies academic David Maunders reported on the results of a study he conducted with people who had spent all or part of their childhood in orphanages or other institutions of care in Victoria. In 19th century orphanages in Victoria, said Maunders, formal classroom education and practical training, even if at a rather basic level, were recognised as valuable elements in preparing Home children for life as adults, given that they had had little help from their family circumstances. Education was seen as a form of personal capital, he says, intended to provide children with 'literacy, sound morals and competence to enter the workforce': that is, to help ensure their economic survival. (On a broader level, it was also, of course, an investment in ensuring that children from 'deprived' families were turned into useful workers and citizens, rather than joining the 'criminal classes'.) Interested in testing the endurance of these beliefs, Maunders interviewed 81 people who had grown up in care about their education, looking at four different age groups and so covering a very long period, from 1914 to 1985. He concluded that by the time even the oldest of his interviewees had gone into care, round the start of World War I, 'the concept of education as capital [for Homes children] had been eroded', and that it did not resurface until the 1960s. The protective value of education therefore had little currency as a component of institutional care for most 20th century inmates of Homes, and this is obvious in probably the majority of care leavers' accounts of their schooling.

Muriel Dekker, a state ward in Queensland's Presbyterian WR Black Home, related how the matron had prevented them from studying, saying that they need not bother, since, 'You're nothing. You'll always be nothing. You're from the gutter. You'll end in the gutter.' And Lorraine Rodgers spoke for many when she said of her education, growing up in the Ballarat Orphanage in the 1940s and 1950s:

> The schooling was very poor, I did not get the EDUCATION that I should have, as the teachers could not care one little bit about our education, plus our school was on the grounds, which went to six grade, when I went to high school, which was the most terrible year in my life, because I did not know what the teachers were talking about. That got me in a lot of trouble, plus I had the DUNCE HAT put on my head a few times, while I was there. The other children would pick on me, laugh at me, or throw things at me. I just wanted to crawl into a HOLE.

Lorraine's reaction to this experience is typical of how many Home children reacted: 'I then just went around like a zombie, did everything I was told to do.'

When people relate their schooling histories, it is plain to see how profoundly the Home environment affected their learning, even when the opportunity to learn was there. Psychoanalyst Donald Winnicott, in an essay called 'Children learning', observes that when it comes to handing on to children 'beliefs that have meaning for yourself', or to your culture or religion:

> you will have success only in so far as the child has a *capacity to believe in anything at all*. The development of this capacity is not a matter of education ... It is a matter of the experience of the person as a developing baby and child in the matter of care.[16] (emphasis added)

Douglas Mann's experience in Perth in the early 1950s shows exactly what Winnicott is talking about:

> We attended school regularly and even if we were sick we still had to go. I was a bit of a dunce at school and had a real fear of the teachers. The beltings I got daily for wetting my bed made me really fearful of those in authority. I felt victimised at school and used to get the

> cuts a lot for getting sums wrong. I found it hard to learn and just remember trying so hard to be quiet and 'invisible' so that I would not get into trouble. I gained nothing from my schooling.

David Forbes' submission to the Inquiry is an extreme example of why children did not learn, but I think not an uncommon one. Removed by the NSW Department from an abusive and violent family home at the age of eight, suffering all the usual separations and losses that state children of the 1950s suffered (see Chapter 5), he was then subjected to profound and traumatic abuse of every description at the hands of staff in the NSW state institutions where he was placed. He became severely depressed and was eventually sent to Werrington Park, a NSW state Home for 'subnormal children'. There he received education at kindergarten level only, and so never learned to read and write. When he did eventually go to school, he said:

> I was there in body but not in soul. My constant abuse was so severe and my trauma so great it was like I was not there at all. I spent a lot of time in my own safe little world where I did learn the most important lesson in life — survival.

I wonder how many other children, profoundly emotionally disturbed by the 'care' they had been subjected to, were also labelled 'subnormal', and assigned from then on to a 'subnormal' life. David did eventually learn to read and write, at the age of 50.

Religion

Along with work, religion was also a large consumer of children's time — in some Homes it took up the entire Sunday as well as substantial periods on weekdays. Since the majority of Children's Homes were run by religious organisations or orders, religious observance as a feature of Home routine is hardly surprising. But even in the wider society, for many people, religion – even if only the outward observance of it — was regarded as one of the essential components of a child's 'training'. Failure to provide it would have been seen as a failure of responsibility on the part of the Home organisation, particularly in a society far more religiously observant, in daily life, than today.[17] Elizabeth Miller, in the Protestant Federation Girls' Home, recalled:

> Sunday of course was church day and we marched off morning, afternoon and night to church. We also went to Sunday school. In winter we wore brown dresses, with brown hats, shoes and gloves. We looked like little old ladies with baby faces.

Catholic children, like Sally Fenton in St Catherine's at Brooklyn, NSW, had 'mass every morning and three times on Sunday, benediction at midday, rosary of an afternoon, all day in church on Good Friday. Catechism in school of the morning.' Other children marched through the main street of town to church, sometimes with a band, as in rural Salvation Army Homes. In Cooinoo, in Sydney, Sunday school and church took up the entire day. As Marigold Kendall remembered:

> [O]n Sundays we not allowed to make a noise, call out or play loudly. To this day my sister hates the cooing of doves — it reminds her of Sunday afternoons in the Home, when you couldn't do anything.

The major function of religion, however, was to rationalise and justify the punishment of children, as I discussed in Chapter 2.

Punishment

The infliction of corporal punishment is one of the most characteristic features of life in a Home. It is a recurrent theme in almost all histories of growing up in institutional care. When people say about this era, 'times were different then', they are often referring to the fact that attitudes to corporal punishment were different from those of today. Corporal punishment was certainly standard practice in families and in schools, to a degree, at times, which today would be described as abuse. The following vivid example, which sums up standard teaching practice at this time, comes from Britain, but it applies equally to Australia because the Australian educational system, like so many aspects of Australian society and culture until the last 30 or so years, was largely modelled on the British one.[18] This is an account by Sheila Francis, a primary school pupil in England in 1950:

> Talking in class earned you the cane, girls and boys alike, and the headmaster was the most feared man in the village. Today, he would have been gaoled; but in those days he was held in the highest esteem ... [——] got into terrific rages when he would literally throw pupils across the room or drag them by the hair. He had a bamboo cane about ten feet long with which he could reach the class from his desk, and he certainly used it. No parents ever came to school to complain.[19]

'No parents ever came to the school to complain', and the headmaster was 'held in the highest esteem'. Clearly, parents also believed that the infliction of pain and humiliation was necessary to their children's upbringing. Corporal punishment was so usual as to be unremarkable, which gave certain adults ample scope for the exercise of extreme behaviours with little risk of being brought to account. However, we can probably assume that parents would have complained had their children received broken limbs or black eyes.

There were no such limits in Homes, where there were no parents around who were likely to complain, or who might be told to take their children away if they did. Bruce Randle, in the Sydney City Mission's Mt Gibraltar Boys' Home in Bowral in 1954, said that the manager of his Home 'assaulted and victimised the kids; he treated them with utter contempt', and Bruce still has scars on his face where a hose fitting was slammed into his head and he had to be taken to hospital — with a warning from the manager: 'Don't you dare say anything.' Bruce described the manager's behaviour to the children as treating them with 'contempt', but this kind of treatment was common in that era; it was standard disciplinary practice. However, calling it 'contempt' is perhaps anachronistic — it was not so much contempt as a reflection of the invisibility of children as people with feelings of their own, and with intentions and motivations different from what adults assumed about them. It was 'normal' practice to treat children as if they had no feelings except those that adults allowed them; this was so usual that it was unnoticeable.

Beating children, then, was regarded as necessary 'discipline', and not only for boys. Bette Formosa, in her submission, told of discipline in Methodist Dalmar in the 1950s:

> punishment could mean extra duties, a good talking to, withdrawal of privileges or if the Superintendent was involved you could be in for a good beating, especially if he lost his temper. I recall two such beatings where he did lose his temper with me. The first, when I was punched directly in the face with a closed fist, after which I fell to the floor, hurting my shoulder. The second, after I ran away from the Home. When I was brought back the Superintendent, within the confines of his office, continually punched and hit me around the head and body in the presence of the Matron — who did not intervene, assist or help me anytime during or after the incident.

Bette's experience is absolutely typical of care leaver accounts; it occurred across all denominations of Homes, and in state Homes. The fear of certain and severe punishment — and, sometimes, having to wait for hours for it to be carried out — is yet another very effective method of containing large populations of inmates. Arbitrary punishment is another tool for curbing spontaneity, again because of the fear it engenders. When the matron in Sylvia Baker's Burnside Home asked, 'Who's been naughty?' Sylvia would always step forward to be strapped on the bottom, because she felt she must have been naughty, even if she could not think of anything she had done.

What stands out in Home accounts is not that there was corporal punishment, but that it was so often extreme — amounting to what would *even then* have been termed 'criminal assault' if done to an adult — and that it was often ritualised, deliberately humiliating, and sexualised. The total institution provided an opportunity for adults to use children for their own gratification, either sexually or by sadistically humiliating less powerful people who could not retaliate. It is obvious that corporal punishment in Homes was not always about enforcing order, but rather about catering to the emotional needs of adults. Geoff Price felt that the priests who ran his rural Church of England Home 'used to take pleasure in belting you for no reason'; this concurs with Ivor Knight's comment about the Christian Brothers institutions he lived in in Western Australia, at Clontarf, Castledare and Tardun. He noted:

> the obvious pleasure some Brothers had in handing out unjust, cruel and excessive punishments for minor transgressions; and in many instances for no other reason, I believe, than to relieve their own angers and sexual perversions.

Several inmates of the Gill Salvation Army Home at Goulburn describe how, as adolescent boys, waiting naked in the cold to shower, they were hit on the penis if they had an erection; or had a cane thrust up the anus. But girls also did not escape sexualised corporal punishment. Helena Dam recalled a beating in the Nazareth House orphanage in Brisbane when she was about nine years old. She was pulled out of line by a nun while on her way to bed, and taken into a room:

> Inside the middle of this room was a square-looking bench, much like a butcher's table. She closed the door behind us and removed my clothes from the waist down. I was forced to lean over the bench. Sister Padenciana then struck me very hard with the strap on my bare backside. The force of the strikes caused my backside to come up in welts and to bleed.

It was not only in religious institutions that this type of ritualised and sexualised punishment was employed, as Peter Brownbill's experience shows. He was a little boy in the NSW government Mittagong Homes in the 1950s:

> A common practice was polishing the floorboards of the building. Five or six boys, five or six years old, maybe more, would polish the front entrance hall. We would wear pyjama tops but no bottoms, we would polish the floors with a holly stoning action but with rags instead of stones.[20] Matron (I can't remember her name) would walk though the hall and smack bottoms with a wooden hair brush at random, sometimes almost absentmindedly.

When you read accounts of the type and degree of physical punishment in the majority of Homes, you might assume that this must have been facilitated by an absence of regulations or standards, but this is by no means the case. For example, section 56 of the *Child Welfare Act 1939* (NSW) spelled out quite explicitly the allowed range of punishments where an inmate was found guilty of an act of misconduct. These include corporal punishment 'not exceeding a maximum of three strokes on each hand' and 'isolated detention, but not for longer than 24 hours where the inmate is under 16, or 48 hours where s/he is over this age'. Isolated detention is reserved for 'exceptional cases', and 'every effort shall be made to enforce discipline without corporal punishment'. In fact there are over five pages of this Act devoted to specifying the conditions — including the type of cane to be used, approved by the Minister — under which punishment should be carried out. All these guidelines were designed to contain punishment and guard against the arbitrary misuse of power. This section of the Act, it is safe to say, was honoured more in the breach than in the observance. These regulations applied to the NSW Department's own institutions, but it was this Department which also licensed non-government Homes. It is extremely unlikely, however, that any government official inspecting the charitable Homes would have asked children about punishment routines, and staff made sure that children did not talk about them. Ralph Doughty said of the Gill Home that 'all punishments were supposed to be recorded in a book. Several times I have seen the "punishment book", but there are very few entries in the book.' The Senate Report (in Appendix IV) sets out the provisions from the relevant Acts (for several states) for the treatment of children in institutions, and concludes that comparison of what was legislatively permitted with what the Inquiry had revealed of actual practice indicates that 'laws were broken and actions were illegal at various times in many institutions across Australia'.

Cruelty

The feature of punishment which is most confronting in inmate accounts is the cruelty of adults to children. We can call this 'child abuse', but calling it cruelty puts it where it belongs, in the range of ordinary human behaviours. When we call it 'abuse' we can attribute it to people who do not behave 'normally', who are not 'people like us'. But the behaviour I am describing here is the behaviour of very many ordinary adults, men and women, towards the children for whom they had a duty of care. Consider this:

> I was there [the Victorian 'training' institution Winlaton] for about four weeks when I had my first encounter with Miss ——. She was the superintendent of Winlaton. We were eating our tea when she came in roaring like a bull. She singled me out, stood me against the wall, yelled and screamed, then for no reason she belted me across the face with a huge bunch of keys. My head hit a brick wall, I started to cry, she grabbed me by the hair, pulling me along the corridor to the toilet, pushed my head in the bowl and pressed the button.[21]

It is not an exaggeration to say that even in the times I am writing about, you would have been in trouble had you inflicted on an animal the degree and extent of beating and kicking which many children in Homes endured. The RSPCA would have stepped in and the animal would have been removed from your care, because somebody would have reported the howls of the animal in its misery. Nobody reported the misery of the children who were beaten and kicked in Children's Homes. Lynette Hyde, in St Joseph's, Bathurst, run by the Sisters of Mercy, related experiences common to many:

> [I spent] many a night exhausted from crying from the hurt of the hiding and the soreness of my body. My body never seemed to get a chance to recover; my body seemed to always have marks on it, which turned to bruises which I called rainbows when the colour came out.

Staff were not merely physically cruel; they were also emotionally cruel to children. Being locked in a cupboard or a small room, or made to stand in a dark corridor for hours, was a common punishment in Homes of all religious denominations and in state Homes. Shoe cupboards, the cupboard under the stairs, the strongroom, the cellar — all these small confined spaces were used. When 'girls' who were in the NSW government Home, Lynwood Hall, get together they often talk about the 'clink', 'a tiny, dark mosquito-infected cell'[22] with no window, where they were left in isolation for more than a day at a time. But other Homes had similar refinements. Lynette Hyde wrote in her submission of the 'many occasions I was locked up in the apron room under the stairs' in her rural Catholic Home:

> [T]here I would stay for days and nights, the only time I saw anyone was for food. I slept sitting up for days on end, no bath, no shower and the only place to go to the toilet was on the ground where I slept, and ate my food that was brought to me. When I was finally let out of the apron room my eyes had to adjust to the light.

Another cruelty visited on children by staff was taunting them about their isolated condition. Lorraine Rodgers related that:

> you were told that you were put in here because your parents did not love you, and you are not wanted by ANYONE.

And motherless Mary Gesch, was regularly told by the Matron of her Brisbane home that 'your father didn't want you, you'll end up in the gutter where you belong'.

Bed-wetting

A major opportunity to inflict punishment in Homes occurred around bed-wetting. Bed-wetting, or enuresis, is very common in accounts by Home children, which is hardly surprisingly, since it is a classic symptom of stress in young and not-so-young children. Children were not only beaten; they were also humiliated. Margery Chandler, in a Protestant Home in the 1950s, was stripped and 'belted' with a cane, then sent naked downstairs to a cold phenyl bath. Afterwards she was paraded, still naked, in front of all the other children at breakfast, as a 'dirty filthy creature' and the staff encouraged the other children to tease her. 'I used to think if I could only stay awake all night I wouldn't wet the bed, but of course I couldn't,' said Margery. Many people recount having their nose rubbed in the wet sheets, or having to stand with their wet sheets around their head, sometimes for hours. In Barry Cook's Victorian Children's Aid Society Home, 'You were made to wear a potty strapped around your rear end all day — thus disallowing you to sit for meals and [making sure you] became the brunt of much humour.' Other children were made to wear nappies to school, at the age of eight or nine. Ken Carter at the Salvation Army Boys' Home at Box Hill, Victoria, was one: 'I suppose there were always about 15 to 20 of us in nappies at school.' The Home could only do this, one would imagine, because the school was on the premises. Before going off to school in nappies, the bed-wetters — who slept in their own special 'wet section' — had already been punished for their crime:

> [We were pulled out of bed, and] those who had wet the bed got six of the best with a strap with little tacks at the end of it. They had the technique of trying to hit your fingers all the time, because that's where the pain was. Then we were grabbed and marched out of the dormitories into the assembly yard naked — and this was also in winter; it didn't matter what time of the year it was. Then we would have to walk perhaps 100 metres. Then we were sent into the cold showers. I used to nearly gasp for air it was that cold. If you didn't get under it, he'd turn the fire hydrant on you and stuff.

Lest we think that children 'get over' such treatment, here is Douglas Mann, in his submission to the Inquiry. He received similar treatment, as a little boy in the Parkerville Home in Western Australia in the late 1940s and 1950s:

> These beltings have had a profound effect on my life. To this day, I cannot have a cold shower and can't go swimming because I suffer from hypothermia. Also, right up to this day, almost every night I wake up and go to the toilet because of the fear of wetting the bed. This often takes me 10–15 minutes, as I don't really need to go.

Goffman describes these actions as control techniques that translate into moral terms behaviour over which the inmate has no control — so that wetting the bed, for example, becomes a failure of the child's character or will. This places the responsibility on the inmate, however young, to change, or to feel guilty if they can't change — like Margery Chandler, who blamed herself for wetting the bed and tried to stay awake all night.

Sexual use of children

> Enter the B———s, the next set of cottage parents; this is where the violation begins. I cannot begin to express what evil was about to unfold: a child sex offender and his wife, employed by the department to look after children.
>
> Elizabeth Behrendorf, state ward in Bunyarra Family Group Home, Victoria, in the early 1970s

> Naturally, there was also sexual abuse. It took place in the showers, mostly. Sometimes it was the warders who did it, other times it was the bigger, older boys who abused the smaller, younger ones. Oddly enough though, in a place so full of brutality, sexual abuse did not rank as highly as the other forms of abuse — such as mental and

emotional torture, lack of adequate clothing, shortage of food, and the strings of punishment that never seemed to end ... That sexual abuse was the least of our worries should tell you how bad things really were.

> Mark Greenhalgh, speaking of the state Westbrook Farm Home for Boys, in Toowoomba, Queensland, in the 1950s

[My submission] may not seem as horrendous to you as it does to me, as it leaves out stories of sexual exploitation which occurred but were not as meaningful as the emotional attacks,

> Kerry Geldard, Protestant Federation Girls' Home, Sydney, 1950s

Physical cruelty to children — what we now call abuse — is one of the most consistent features of all accounts of Home existence; along with sexual abuse, it is the feature of institutional care that is probably most familiar to the public. Sexual abuse tends to be discussed in narratives of traumatic childhoods in terms of the adult perpetrators, the perversity of the behaviour, and the significance of the abuse in the development of later disorders. But it is important to emphasise another dimension of both these forms of 'abuse': attacking a person's body is a way of invading their psyche, their sense of self. This is no less true for children than it is for adults. In fact it may well be even more traumatic for them, because the boundaries of self are still forming. Sociologist Jennifer Church points out that 'coming to be a person or a self and coming to own one's own body are not two different processes'; on the contrary, she says, they are two faces of the same process, 'a process whereby the psychological states of a body are simultaneously integrated *by* and integrated *into* an overall conception of self'.[23] How can you develop an 'overall conception of self' if your body can be acted upon violently by others, without your consent, throughout your childhood? It is vital to acknowledge this aspect of physical — and sexual — abuse if we are to understand how it affected Home inmates.

Sexual abuse, I think, can more accurately be described as 'sexual use'. Children in institutions were *used* by adults for their own sexual gratification. They were a commodity, they provided a service — to which they gave no consent — to any or all adults who wanted to avail themselves of that service. As Ivor Knight said of the Christian Brothers who ran his WA Home:

> Their commitment to 'save souls' was bastardised into a system whereby they 'stole our souls'; whereby they made us into mere ciphers, to be seized and used whenever the need for sexual gratification was upon them. We meant no more to them than the moment's pleasure.

It is very difficult to retain a sense of ownership of your body, and hence of your self, when somebody else can use it as they wish against your will. Can 'seize and use' you for 'the moment's pleasure'. Your body represents the visible boundaries of your self in the world. If the world, in the shape of your adult 'carers', can arbitrarily inflict pain and humiliation on your self as represented by your body, no sense of security is possible. Susan Brison, a writer who was violently attacked and raped as an adult, later wrote an essay to try to understand what it had made her feel about herself.[24] She talked of the 'undoing of self' which followed an unpredictable, violent physical assault and of how the very meaning of 'a self' was challenged by such an experience, even when, until that time, that self had been a stable and integrated one. How does a child — a self still in the process of developing — deal with this experience?

Submissions to the Inquiry, accounts in the 1999 Forde Report, and other accounts of institutional care all feature the sexual violation and use of children. The quotes at the head of this section indicate two important aspects of the sexual use of children in Homes. First, the extreme vulnerability of children in institutions — even in smaller ones, such as a Family Group Home; and second, the way that, for children, it was only one of a catalogue of horrors. There is also a third aspect: older children would victimise younger ones, so passing the abuse down the line. Sexual abuse is always highlighted as if it is the 'worst' abuse; this is an adult-centred perspective, focusing on the criminality and the 'unnaturalness' of the physical act itself. What gets lost here is that children were violated in every sense in an institution, and being used sexually was just one of those violations. This is how this kind of violation made Lynette Hyde feel:

> My first sexual knowledge came from a nun, and a priest who came to say Mass. This resulted in the loss of my childhood, a loss that I will always remember till I go to my grave.

I did not ask my interviewees about sexual use by staff; I left it to them to raise the subject, and several did. Sometimes it was presented simply as one item in the general catalogue of horrific situations they had learnt to expect as a part of their daily life, rather as Mark Greenhalgh had in his statement above. Viv Taylor, in a Tasmanian institution, wrote about how they used to see the gardener at her Home having sex with a goat: 'I think he knew we were watching, but at least he left us alone.' The follow-up came later, when she said that the superintendent of the Home 'took full advantage' of the girls living there. Unlike the gardener, he did not leave them alone.

We need to remember here that it was not only men who sexually molested the children in their care. In September 2002 a case in which five women were seeking compensation for alleged abuse at Nazareth House in the Brisbane suburb of Wynnum in the 1950s and 1960s made headlines. The women alleged they had frequently been assaulted by two nuns who worked in the institution. One form of assault was being raped with a broomstick.[25]

Sexual use of children, like physical assault, and emotional and verbal abuse, is hardly surprising in an environment where the inmates are so little valued and where there are so few external checks on their welfare. It can only be surprising if we believe that 'ordinary' adults (as opposed to 'perverts', psychopaths and 'bad apples') are incapable of such behaviours. Children who did not live with their families, whether they were in institutions or foster care, were vulnerable to being used in any way at all by their 'carers.' There is a powerful and shocking example of this vulnerability in one woman's submission to the Inquiry. She was placed in Goodwood Orphanage, Adelaide, in 1946, aged two and a half; at age six, she was fostered to strangers. Here she describes what happened to her in this placement:

> My bed where I slept was located at the back of the house in an enclosed verandah. They would have to pass my bed to go to the toilet. I remember the first time that I was woken up out of my sleep it was very dark. I could hardly breathe with fear. My bed was shaking and there was a groaning sound. I could just make out that it was the father. He had his hand pressing harder on my head. I then thought he had blown his nose all over my face and hair, but when I saw his hand go to his PJs, I thought he had weed on me. I … started to cry and he put his hand over my mouth.

The horror of this experience must have been increased for this little girl by her knowing that it could be repeated over and over — as it was — and that there was no way of avoiding it and no-one to turn to for help. 'Do you know what it is like to be continuously told that you have nobody?' asked Elizabeth Behrendorf. 'That you are alone and that nobody will ever believe you?' Elizabeth was sexually molested day after day by the 'cottage parent' in her Victorian Family Group Home, and like Dorothy, could do nothing about it. There was often a hierarchy of vulnerability in institutions. Ken Carter in his evidence to the Inquiry about his time in the Salvation Army Boys' Home at Box Hill, Victoria, explained it like this:

> These sadists, paedophiles — whatever you call them — aim for the ones they know never get visits because they know that the other kids will talk to their parents and that sort of thing. They were as cunning as foxes.[26]

But how many of the children who were violated in this way would have been believed, had they dared to speak up?

Divide and rule

> I was in extreme pain, which caused me to cry out. The other children in the dormitory could hear me and I could see them putting the blankets over their heads. I think the reason they did this was because this sort of treatment used to happen to all of us. I guess they were afraid that it was going to happen to them next.
>
> Helena Dam, being strapped on the bare bottom in bed as a little girl, she did not know why, at Nazareth House in Brisbane in the 1930s

In Helena's account you can see how fear diminished the possibility — and the comfort — of solidarity among children. But staff also employed deliberate tactics to weaken solidarity, tactics which I would describe as a variation of 'divide and rule': deliberately generating animosity among inmates so that they would turn on each other. Margaret Turnbull, at St Catherine's in Geelong, Victoria, in the 1950s and 1960s, described what was common practice in many Homes: 'If one child misbehaved all children were punished.' 'Misbehaviour' could be anything from stealing an object to not eating the prescribed meals, or breaking any of the numerous rules that characterised institutional life. Caroline Carroll, at the NSW state Home, Lynwood Hall, in the 1960s, recalled, for example, how all the children in her Home missed out on seeing their visitors when she was unable to eat the food at lunch on visiting day. The superintendent of this Home, Miss Davies, would also punish *all* the girls if she caught one of them talking at night by making them all get up, strip their beds, fold the blankets, turn the mattress and then make the bed again. This could be repeated all night. 'Girls would faint,' said Caroline, 'but she left them on the floor.' One of the most extreme examples of this type of tactic is described by Ralph Doughty, who was in the Salvation Army Gill Memorial Home. It was called 'running the gauntlet':

> This involved a large number of boys being drawn up into two lines facing inwards to each other and the boy or boys who were to be punished made to walk or run (as instructed) up the 'tunnel'. Each boy in the lines had to punch or kick the boy as he made his way towards the end. If any boy failed to strike the boy then this failure would mean that this boy, also, had to 'run the gauntlet'. The boy or boys suffering this punishment had to run the 'gauntlet' until the officer was satisfied.

Ralph also described how the officers would make a boy bash his own brother, under threat that he would bash both of them if the first boy refused. 'There were many terrible scenes with this event,' said Ralph. When he saw this happening, he said, 'I was glad that my little brother had been given away, even though I missed him.'

Where children were not separated from siblings because they were of the age and sex that would allow them to be together, there was always the danger that their kinship tie would be used against them in some way — to cause them pain, or to exploit their feelings. Margery Chandler told how, at age four and a half in a Catholic Home, because she was 'robust' and her older sister Jane was 'a frail and delicate type of child', she (Margery) used to have to take her sister's physical punishment — 'three cuts of the cane on each hand whilst kneeling on a heavy coir mat: result, sore hands and knees'. Franny Mason, aged about seven in Bidura in the mid-1940s, shared a bed with her younger sister Mary, 'who would often have incontinent bowels at night, from fear, and I would be forced to bath her in a bucket and wash her clothes and sheets in the middle of the night, in buckets out on the balconies'.

One of the worst experiences of my childhood was seeing my sister punished day in and day out, and doing nothing to prevent it. Almost every day I witnessed her being beaten and kicked by the woman I felt my survival depended on. As Helena Dam says, quoted above, I was afraid it was going to happen to me next, and if it did, I would be annihilated: if I lost the approval of Betty I would cease to exist. So I would watch and also be standing outside myself, watching myself watch, in a form of dissociation from the horror, torn between my terror of being abandoned by Betty if I spoke up, and shame and self-hatred for not doing so.

Kerry Geldard, in her submission, told of a similarly searing event in her life at the Protestant Federation Children's Home in Sydney in the 1950s. One of the 'nurses' declared one Saturday that Kerry had to have a Bible by the next day. Kerry's mother, who visited that afternoon, could not produce one on the spot, but promised it for the following weekend. Kerry related the sequel to this:

> On Sunday morning at breakfast I was told to stand up and explain that the reason I did not have a bible was because my mother was a sinner and that I rejected her sinful way of life and that she was a liar. I refused and was put into Coventry until I would stand up and say it.

> All of my friends were forbidden to speak to me on fear of punishment and they left me alone for a week. I ate my meals on my own with my head bent and was not allowed to look at anyone ...
>
> Finally I relented and stood on the table and told the world that my mother was a liar and have never recovered from the guilt of having betrayed her.

This is a fine example of something Goffman describes as a feature of institutions where all the inmates have already been stereotyped as deficient: the staff problem is 'to find a crime that will fit the punishment'. Children in such an environment are always caught in a no-win situation.

Another classic technique of control he describes as 'looping'. This occurs when one person creates a defensive response in another, then takes that response as the target of the next attack. This was a very common way of dealing with children in Homes — adults would set them up as unable ever to be 'right', regardless of the behaviour of the adults concerned. Crying in response to punishment, for example, might result in a new threat — 'Be quiet or I'll give you something to cry for' — which also delivered the confusing information to the child that they did not already have a reason to cry. Any response which would serve a healthy self-esteem, like standing up for yourself, or even explaining your actions, could be used to further denigrate a child; it was evidence of 'cheek' or even 'wickedness'. This way of dealing with children also occurred outside Homes, of course: in families and particularly in schools. What made it worse in Homes was the totalitarian aspect: Home children had no opportunity to test the derogatory judgments made about them in other environments, environments where control of them was not the ultimate goal. For some children, as Margaret Saunders observed to me in her interview, 'it became a self-fulfilling prophecy — we had all the goodness abused out of us and became ratbags'. My own response, also reported by other care leavers, was, as I have related, to give up all effort to be authentic and simply conform to whatever was required, in order to avoid punishment or, worse, further abandonment.

The other dimension of all these experiences is that they give you a very bleak and pessimistic view of what you can expect from other people in the future. All children generalise from their own situation until, as part of growing older, they can begin to compare, contrast and re-evaluate it against other, different, situations. To be a child in a situation where adults are arbitrarily violent gives you a skewed view initially of what you can expect from the world; this becomes entrenched when most of your formative years are spent within a highly restricted institutional environment and you have few opportunities for comparison. You carry what you learn in the Home — trust nobody, everyone is out to get you, the world is a dangerous place — unreflectively into your adult life.

Words as weapons

Language was one of the most formidable weapons used against children in care. It was used in two ways. One was the actual words used to describe children: incorrigible, devil's spawn, wicked, bad, delinquent, no good, bad blood, poor stock, poor type, no-hoper, stupid, dumb, mentally retarded, low-grade (or high-grade) mental defective, slut — the list goes on. The other way was more insidious and is an example of Miller's 'poisonous pedagogy' — no matter what was done to children, it was described in terms of *their* needs and requirements and as in *their* own best interests (see Chapter 5). Public language, says writer Don Watson, is the language of power, which 'has its origins in the subjection or control of one by another'.[27] In a totalitarian state it is used to recast people in the mould that the state requires. It is particularly effective, if not irresistible, where the subjects are already vulnerable and powerless, as children are.

Children had little or no chance of challenging the repeated assertions by staff that they deserved punishment because they were 'bad', that they were engaging in deliberately wicked behaviour when, for example, they wet the bed, or that they were incorrigible, wayward and insolent rather than unhappy, abused, lonely and homesick when they ran away from Homes. As psychoanalyst RD Laing says, 'in many respects a child is taught what he is by being told what his actions "mean"', and 'there are endless ways in which a person can be trained to mistrust his own sense'.[28]

This sort of upbringing very severely affects the development of children's sense of who they are. They end up as adults with a collection of other people's self-serving judgments about themselves instead of an authentic sense of self that has developed through the gradual growth of self-knowledge out of experience, and reflection on that experience. Jilly Marsh made a comment that summed up what, in many different ways, care leavers often say: 'By the time that you've grown up and you've realised you're not normal, it's too late to do anything about it — you don't know how to be normal.' 'Normal' meaning being able to function in a way that furthers, rather than hinders, a robust sense of self and realistic life objectives — something denied to so many of us from this background.

Conclusion: The penal effect

> Throughout the twentieth century there were two penal systems. One was for adults, the other was for children. While prisons were regulated and subject to public scrutiny, convents were answerable to no one.
>
> Catherine Brown, an Australian who grew up in a Catholic convent/orphanage in Scotland in the 1940s and 1950s, reflecting on her experience there[29]

After I had collected the 90 interviews in my thesis sample, I was particularly struck by the impression that these children — we Home children — living in residential Homes that were not 'juvenile detention centres' were a deviant population. It seemed we deserved to be treated in a certain way, just as prisoners are subjected to a set of regimes which are seen to be appropriate because they have violated the norms of society in some way. Like prisoners, we must have violated some social norm. George Jackson said of the NSW boys' receiving Home, Royleston, where he lived from the age of 11 to 13 (1941–43), that there was barbed wire all round the Home, and since the school was on the premises, you never went out. 'I didn't even know why I was there,' he said. 'I didn't come from a criminal background but I ended up in a place with barbed wire around it.'

Care leavers from all decades described their Homes as 'one step away from gaol', or 'more like a gaol than anything'. The hundreds more accounts I have heard or read subsequently only confirm this feeling. Some care leavers compared their treatment with that meted out to the convict settlers of Australia. But, perhaps not surprisingly given that the people concerned are now middle-aged and older, the analogy with Nazi Germany and with concentration camps is the one most frequently drawn by people who grew up in the worst of these institutions. A CLAN member, Rona, raised in Queensland orphanages, began her letter to CLAN with 'thank you for all the newsletters of children and their lives in the Australian Nazi horror orphanages'.[30] The images of the Nazi camps, familiar from our childhood, are the ones that spell out most clearly the limits of human atrocity, in an analogy that is an emotional — rather than a historically accurate — one. For many children, the Home felt like a place of psychic death, of the murder of the self. Brian Cronin, speaking of his Catholic Home in Victoria, run by the Sisters of Nazareth, said:

> The orphanage ... was like being held captive by the Third Reich of Nazi Germany. We were led to our slaughter by these pathetic poor excuses of human savages. That also let the minders of a weekend nearly bash us to death, and death/or near death experience I do mean. And wreak his own form of punishment for his own sadistic fun and amusement. That brought our emotional death. And I guess the wish that we were.

Whatever the motives for setting up Children's Homes — and motivations were almost certainly benevolent within contemporary meanings of that term — what they most closely resemble is the description of the prison of the early 19th century quoted by Foucault in his work, *Discipline and Punish*: 'complete and austere institutions'. The prison, says Foucault, is 'an exhaustive disciplinary apparatus' which assumes responsibility for all aspects of the individual — 'his physical training, his aptitude to work, his everyday conduct, his moral attitude, his state of mind'. Indeed it must 'act on the individual as a form of unceasing discipline'.[31] Which is just what institutions did, and why the children living within them felt, as one interviewee expressed it, that 'we were punished for being children'.

Chapter 4

A window on the Homes

I thank individually and collectively the many church and other organisations for the cooperation and assistance they render to my Department in an honorary capacity. Throughout this State, thousands of excellent citizens, in many varied organisations, are doing outstanding work without thought of payment, for the benefit of the community ... Those who assist in this noble honorary work have a wide scope for their efforts, and the knowledge that everything they do to make better citizens of the less fortunate of our children is a valuable contribution towards the improvement of our society and our democratic and Christian way of life.

FH Hawkins, NSW Minister for Child Welfare
& Social Welfare, 1956

The Homes: who did the care?

The preceding chapter gives some idea, through the names of the Homes, of the church agencies and charitable organisations which every state other than New South Wales relied on to provide accommodation for their state wards, and which also housed 'voluntary' admissions, the children placed privately by relatives. In this chapter, my intention is not to discuss the histories of care providers or how various operations differed from each other. Institutional care providers have often commissioned their own official histories,[1] so there are accounts available of the genesis and operation of many institutions. These indeed have been almost the only source of what we know about how institutional care was delivered (though they are accounts which are necessarily one-dimensional, since they are written from the perspective of the organisation, not the inmates). Here, what I want to do is give an overview of the provision of institutional care, focusing on aspects which might help explain why it had the character it did.

The past providers of institutional care were mostly mainstream churches: the Church of England (now the Anglican Church), the Methodist, Congregational and Presbyterian churches (now the Uniting Church), the Baptists, the Churches of Christ, and several Roman Catholic orders, along with the Salvation Army and Barnardos, an organisation established in the United Kingdom in the 19th century for the sole purpose of providing care for children in need. A few Homes were run by the Red Cross, others by committees set up for the purpose, such as the Ballarat and the Melbourne orphanages. Some, like the Parkerville Children's Home in Western Australia, began as the project of individuals: it was set up by Sister Kate Clutterbuck in 1909, with a small group of Anglican sisters, under the name Parkerville Waifs' Home. In New South Wales, in 1938, a Christian couple established the

United Protestant Association (UPA) 'to meet human need in the community'.[2] By 1941, the UPA had set up a Home called Rathgar to cater for Protestant children in its area, Grafton, this was the first of 12 Homes across the state.

Older charities ran Homes too — the Sydney City Mission and the Melbourne City Mission, the Victorian Children's Aid Society and the Sydney Rescue Work Society, for example. Organisations such as the Sydney City Mission (founded in 1862 to 'improve the lives of Sydney's poor'[3]) give a clue to the 19th-century Christian philanthropic tradition which underpinned much voluntary 'child welfare' work well into the 20th century. There were also individual Homes, such as Hopewood (see Chapter 2), and those run by Christian sects, such as Silky Oaks Haven for Children (Open Brethren Assembly) in Toowong, Queensland, and Lutanda in Sydney, run by a similar Christian sect. This is by no means an exhaustive list. There might have been other Homes like mine, run as businesses under state licence, but there were possibly not many, since as far as I am aware, there are no reports so far from care leavers who had been in them.

How many Homes?

Even the Senate Inquiry did not attempt to come up with a definitive list of Homes across Australia; establishing exactly how many Children's Homes existed in any one period is an impossible task, so my figures are only approximate. Some Homes operated for a short period, others over a very long time, and some changed their names and occasionally their functions, which confuses estimations — they could end up being counted twice in any list. Occasionally at CLAN we hear of a Home that does not appear to exist in any records or histories. Demand varied over time, of course, as can be seen in the tables in the NSW

Department's annual reports. In particular, these show graphically how the need for out-of-home care increased sharply throughout the two to three decades following World War II. The number of licensed Homes, starting at 100 in 1940, climbed to 129 by 1952, and had more than doubled the following year to 288, and continued to increase, reaching a high of 383 in 1958. After this, the figure slowly declines, but in 1963 there were still 315 non-government Children's Homes in New South Wales alone.

None of the other states had anything like this number of private-sector Homes. For example, the first complete survey of non-government Children's Homes in Victoria, conducted over 1962 to 1964, shows a total of 63 Homes; however, this relatively small figure could be partly because there seems to have been a greater number of large Homes in Victoria than in New South Wales — that is, more children were accommodated in each Home. Queensland's 1999 Forde Report presented information, it said, about 'more than 150 orphanages and detention centres' operating in that state from 1911 onwards, but this figure includes Homes and hostels of every type, including until well past the institutional era. I would estimate that probably only 40 of this number would be 'orphanage' style institutions, either state or non-government. Other states, with smaller populations, had a correspondingly smaller number of Homes. An estimate mid-century would be that Tasmania had 12 Homes, Western Australia 20 and South Australia a similar number. This makes close to 450 Children's Homes mid-century in Australia, and that figure does not always include government Homes, of which in New South Wales alone there were 30. Nor does it always include special purpose Homes, such as for disabled children. We could assume, then, that in this period, there were around 500 Children's Homes in Australia delivering institutional care to children aged from under one year up to at least 16.

The administration of Homes

Management

It was religious organisations, by and large, that ran non-government Homes, but it was a fragmented enterprise. Child welfare work appears in all denominations to have been not so much an expression of overall organisational policy or philosophy as an aspect of pastoral care that was left to those who chose, for whatever reason, to take it up. Orphanages in the 19th century were often run by committees of volunteers, and this practice continued into the next century. For example, the large Homes complex in Sydney, Burnside, established and endowed in 1911 by the businessman and philanthropist James Burns, of the shipping line Burns Philp,[4] was run by an honorary board of high-profile citizens with connections to the Presbyterian Church. Voluntary service is an integral feature of the philanthropic Christian tradition, and Children's Homes provided a worthy cause for people with service to donate. A colleague of Sir Irving Benson, appointed superintendent of Wesley Central Mission in Melbourne in 1933, expressed just this:

> [Benson] was a great one for the voluntary principle. He believed ... the idea that a Christian service was a service that you gave, not for what you could get out of it, but what you put into it.[5]

This essentially Victorian tradition of 'good works' is quite clearly demonstrated in a Home described by one interviewee, a Home which was, in effect, the hobby of the ladies' auxiliary of the local Church of England church. Marigold Kendall, with her younger sister, was in Cooinoo from 1946 to 1952, from age seven. The full name of the Home indicates its lineage: the Cooinoo Home for Destitute Children. Cooinoo accommodated around

25 girls in a gracious 19th-century mansion, and was run by a committee of ladies from the Church of England church in Enfield, an inner-western suburb of Sydney. It was managed by two unmarried elderly ladies, 'Matron', who was a trained nurse, and her sister, Miss B——. They were from a 'good' country family and, in Marigold's words, were 'very strict, bigoted. We had a Victorian upbringing: children must be seen and not heard.' From Marigold's observations, the Misses B—— might well have been just as satisfied with some form of small business, like a boarding house or 'residential', but of course this would not have provided them with the high status that came with benevolence, with helping some of society's 'unfortunates'. The Home provided Matron and her sister with employment appropriate to their sex and their status, and which could be seen as part of the traditional practice of Christian charity. Marigold's memory is that 'every nationality under the sun was in the Home — migrants, refugees, German, Polish, Lithuanian, English, Scottish, Greek, Aboriginal, South Sea Islander' — and that many had no visitors and seemed to be without immediate family. Although these are not the destitute children of 19th-century orphanage histories, there is a sense in which, as dependants on this type of charitable benevolence, their position echoes this tradition.

Cooinoo was connected with its local church; other Church of England Homes were run by the dioceses of their areas and appeared to have little to do with those of other dioceses. There was no child welfare arm of the Church of England, with the task of supervising and coordinating all such activities. For example, the Church of England Boys' Home in Burwood, also in the inner-west of Sydney, and its related Girls' Home, were under the control of 'a group of citizens, who come from suburbs throughout the metropolitan area', according to one of the few files on non-government Homes I found in the NSW Department's archives. But these Homes had no connection at all with the administration of any of the other Church of England Homes in Sydney, according to the file. Similarly, it appears that the orders that ran Catholic Children's Homes were each very much a law unto themselves, which helps explain, for example, how the Christian Brothers could operate a reign of terror, now well documented, at their Homes in Western Australia: Bindoon, Castledare, Clontarf and Tardun.[6]

A great many of the Children's Homes in Australia were run by the Catholic Church. *A Piece of the Story*, the national directory of records published by the Catholic Church in 1999, lists 40 Catholic organisations that ran a total of 130 Homes in Australia — though not always concurrently, since the period covered is 160 years. But even a large and powerful religious organisation like the Catholic Church had no department — either state or federal — responsible for child welfare. Catholic Homes, like Catholic schools, were run by certain religious congregations or orders, each operating autonomously. Some orders were never associated with 'child welfare', while others specialised in it. Since the Sisters of Mercy operated the greatest number of Homes — more than 30 Homes altogether, in all states except Tasmania — it is not surprising that this order features in so many care leaver accounts, too often under the regrettable name given by former inmates, the 'Sisters of No Mercy'. Other prominent players were the Christian Brothers, the Daughters of Charity, the Good Samaritan Sisters, the Good Shepherd Sisters, the Sisters of Nazareth and the Sisters of St Joseph. A survey of NSW Catholic Homes in 1975 found that even at the end of the institutional era, as newer ideas began to influence practice, the Catholic Family Welfare Bureau, which had been set up in that state specifically to deal with welfare matters, apparently had little authority over standards or procedures; all it did was arrange admissions. The orders running individual Homes strenuously preserved their autonomy, resisting any outside involvement even from their own church agency.[7]

Deirdre McCourt, one of my interviewees and a child migrant from Britain, captured the atmosphere conveyed by many other accounts when describing her Catholic Home, St Joseph's Neerkol, Queensland, as it was in the early 1950s. The Home was run by the Sisters of Mercy in isolated bushland some 15 kilometres from Rockhampton, which was then just a small coastal town:

> The nuns were migrants too, originally Irish, some very young and maybe orphanage kids originally too. They used twigs, sticks, the lash, and we lived in fear of whipping. I guess they were just so frustrated. The Church was run by men. I can remember being met [on arrival from Britain] by the Archbishop of Brisbane, who seemed kindly, but nobody seemed to know the internal side of these orphanages. They were so softly spoken, so nice. They left it entirely to the nuns. No government officers came to check. If kids ran away, no official asked why.

Accountability

St Joseph's Neerkol — subsequently notorious through the Forde Inquiry and many care leaver accounts — is an extreme, although certainly not isolated, example, but we can see from this description how each charitable or church Home was, in effect, an institutional island. There were few external checks other than what were supposed to be the routine inspections by the Department responsible for child welfare — and such checks were by no means always carried out. Each institution operated as a private domain, the territory of either a particular religious order or diocese, or of local citizens who had taken it on as a benevolent interest, often through their church affiliation. One historian has commented that the 19th-century committees that ran Homes 'were largely free of government supervision or intervention and so could set their own rules and regulations'.[8] This aspect of the institutional tradition appears to have continued unchanged into the 20th century.

It is important to understand the type of administrative relationship between the Homes and the state, and the absence of any external, independent standards, when we are looking for reasons for the lack of transparency and accountability in the operation of Children's Homes. Where environments are closed, have little interaction generally with the wider community, and are seen as benevolent enterprises, they may operate as they choose; this means that inmates depend not on acknowledged and monitored practice standards but on the goodwill — or otherwise — of those charged with their care. This is one reason why abuses were invisible, and why so little was known at all about what went on in Children's Homes. The Home was regarded as an act of charity, a generous and even selfless contribution by those who had undertaken it, so there was little room for criticism. As one writer describes it, 'staff were, by definition, benevolent ... the child was positioned to be grateful'.[9] The fact that work is voluntary (Home administration, for instance), or ill-paid (workers in the Home, for instance), may pre-empt regulation and accountability; certainly in the case of Children's Homes this appears to have been the case.

It is impossible to say how much day-to-day interest the upper echelons of any church hierarchy took in Homes conducted in their name, and how much was left entirely to the management of Homes — whether secular or religious — to deal with. There might well have been an assumption that it was the responsibility of the state Department, not the church, to ensure that appropriate standards of care were maintained. This would be ironic, since, as the Forde Report noted of Queensland, where religious organisations ran Homes, state Departments tended to assume that the care provided would be above reproach.[10] Each then could leave responsibility to the other. There are multiple examples of the dire consequences of this for the children involved, in submissions to the Inquiry, indeed in the entire history of the operation of Children's Homes. The lack of transparency, and the acceptance of it, is difficult even to conceive of today. Its effects were exacerbated by the isolationism of the state and the charitable sectors which I describe below.

The relationship between the state and the non-government sector

> What is the welfare system? I have never seen it. I spent 10 years in that joint and never saw any of those people. I never saw a dentist and the only time I ever saw a doctor was when I poisoned myself eating wild pears and when they gave us the needle in the arm for polio. That is all in 10 years, mate. Nobody gave us anything in that place.
>
> Douglas Mann, who was in Parkerville, WA, from 1947 until 1957[11]

Most states relied significantly on the charitable sector to house their state wards, and to provide institutional care for 'voluntary' placements. Legislative requirements in relation to Homes varied from state to state, but it would be fair to say that regardless of the state, governments had little to say about Homes: they licensed them, monitored physical standards through inspections, and sometimes enacted regulations about payment for this care. The extent to which Homes were inspected by Departments across the country is difficult to determine. Ivor Knight, who was in the Christian Brothers institutions at Clontarf, Castledare and Tardun in Western Australia in the 1940s, said in his submission:

> The Child Welfare Department of the day contributed to this abuse and neglect by its own carelessness in never

properly examining the moral and psychological conditions under which its charges were incarcerated. They may have examined the physical aspects, perhaps even the health (though doubtful) aspects; never to my knowledge did they ever question any of their wards, in private, or for that matter even in the presence of the Brothers, about the moral actuality of their (for many) miserable existence.

In New South Wales, Homes were meant to be inspected a minimum of four times per year, and visits were meant to be unannounced and unpredictable. But as one field officer I interviewed said, 'Some were visited more often and others so regularly that the Home could predict the officer's visit.' In other situations, there was a very 'cosy' relationship between the Department and the Home. As Jim Fairmont, a staff interviewee, said, while a Department officer would visit monthly to inspect and sign the register at the Methodist Home Dalmar, physical inspections were minimal, since 'the past record and integrity of the Home seemed sufficient to satisfy the visiting officers'.

Where inspections did occur, what the inspectors were looking for is described in the following passage from the WA Department's 1956 annual report:

> The accommodation, bedding, ablution facilities, etc. are inspected and if, in the opinion of the Inspectors, improvements are considered necessary, representations are made to the controlling authorities and invariably matters are immediately rectified.

Some of the tension in my Home was generated by anxiety about 'Welfare' visits — my memory is that they were usually unannounced and so were one aspect of life that could not be controlled. These inspections had, I think, a powerful influence on my own perception of things, because time and again they passed and even praised the Home — which of course completely negated the validity of my own feelings, so there was obviously something wrong with me. As well, my sense that I had to be strictly vigilant of my own behaviour was confirmed by the way the women, especially the younger one, seemed to regard these inspections as judgments on them: this reinforced their teaching that it was an outside authority that told you how you should behave.

The memory of inspections occurring is not common among care leavers. Of my 90 interviewees, only one other person recalled inspections, and the 2004 Senate Report, *Forgotten Australians*, like the 1999 Forde Report before it, makes the point that a comparison of care leaver accounts with the legislation shows evidence of numerous breaches of the law in this respect. The authors of the 1975 survey of NSW Catholic Homes cited above were disturbed not only by the absence of agreed practice standards in Catholic Homes, but also by the apparent absence of any ongoing checks on children's welfare, deploring the fact that the government Department which was supposed to be responsible for all dependent children in out-of-home care appeared to have nothing to say about the quality of care provided, which meant that standards of care were left to the discretion of Home staff.

The Forde Report noted of the Queensland Department that its performance appeared to have fallen 'far short' of its obligations under the relevant Act, since inspections had been irregular or non-existent, according to former residents, when they should have been at least quarterly, and children were not encouraged to talk to inspectors. The attitude of the inspectors, said this report, 'appears to have been that the staff were performing worthy work in extremely difficult circumstances and that their endeavours ought not to be scrutinised or questioned'.[12] This attitude was certainly not confined to Queensland.

The indifference of the state to the operations of the charitable child welfare sector is particularly visible in Victoria. It was not until the 1950s, with the passing of the *Children's Welfare Act 1954* (Vic.), that the government even had the statutory authority to regulate and enforce standards of care in such Homes. Even the Victorian Government — in its submission to the Senate Inquiry — admitted that until then the system rested on a flawed assumption: that state wards would be placed in foster care and that charitable Children's Homes would only accommodate children placed there voluntarily by their parents. Hence there was no Departmental supervision of charitable institutions — parents, in placing their children, for payment, in a non-government Home, were making a private arrangement in which the state had no role and no responsibility. The government was only responsible where children were state wards. In fact, since the percentage of state wards who were fostered in Victoria was quite low, the majority of Victorian state wards were in fact placed in the charitable Children's Homes; and since the government subsidised state wards living in such Homes, it must have been well aware of this fact every time it made such a payment.

After the Children's Welfare Act was passed, Victorian non-government children's institutions, like those in New South Wales, were required to be registered with the Children's Welfare Department, to maintain adequate standards of care and be subject to Departmental inspection.[13] However, in 1976, a report into the Victorian care system (the Norgard Report) expressed concern that there was still no recognised code of standards for approving a Children's Home or for monitoring its operations. A code had been drawn up in 1970 in a joint state/voluntary initiative, but it had never been either formally recognised or made obligatory.[14]

The 1999 Forde Report contains a summary of the nature of the relationship between the state and the charitable sector in Queensland which could be applied, I think, to all other states (except New South Wales, where the state/voluntary sector relationship was different [see below]):

The levels of funding on which almost all of the denominational institutions operated were patently insufficient to allow the provision of proper individual care. Yet the Department continued to place children in those institutions because they provided a cheap means of lodging children for whose care it was responsible, and it was able to use as justification the fact that the children were, after all, in Christian care. The churches, for their part, acquiesced in this undiscriminating placement of children because of their perceived obligation to provide refuge to homeless children, however inadequate their resources might be. *By doing so, they acquired an ascendancy over the Department; it was most unlikely that the Department would jeopardise its access to those placements by subjecting the institutions to scrutiny of the kind necessary to ensure that children were being cared for properly.*[15] (emphasis added)

As the report observes, recognising this relationship 'is essential to an understanding of how institutional care could fail children in so many respects without intervention from the Department'.[16]

The situation in New South Wales

New South Wales is the one state which avoided wherever possible using the voluntary sector to accommodate its state wards. The NSW Department, according to one of my interviewees who worked in it, always held up the state system as a salutary contrast to the charitable system, and, by extension, to the child welfare practice of all other states. In effect, the NSW Department 'disapproved' of institutional care. According to this field officer, in New South Wales:

> The state tried to do as much of the work as they could get; the state did not want the charitable Homes. You

> wouldn't place a child in a church Home if you could get him into a government Home. The policy would be to avoid that like the plague.

The extent of this antipathy, he said, could be seen in the fact that at the height of the baby boom, in the late 1950s and early 1960s — 'when Departmental homes were bursting at the seams' — there was still no attempt to place children in the non-government sector. This occasionally happened, he said, but it was rare.[17]

Nevertheless, despite 'disapproving' of institutional care, the Department took no steps to eliminate it in the non-government sector. In an article written in 1960, the NSW Director of Child Welfare, RH Hicks, commented that 'it is rather difficult to understand why the private associations [i.e. the churches and charities] have not taken more resolute steps to introduce foster home programs'.[18] Hicks's statement seems to indicate that the Department did not appear to believe that it had either an obligation or the right to exert pressure on the charitable sector to change its mode of care — institutionalisation — in favour of the foster care which the Department insisted was preferable. It appears, then, that even though the Department believed institutionalisation to be bad for children, it accepted that the agencies had the right to run things their own way — which means that the autonomy of the agencies which made up the charitable sector was given precedence over the welfare of children. This is particularly interesting when we realise that in this state, the number of children cared for in charitable institutions was very similar to the number cared for by the state — in 1961, for example, it was estimated that both sectors cared for close to 4000 children.[19]

What Hicks is spelling out here is the clear demarcation of authority between the state and the charitable sector. 'Regular supervision by the field staff,' says the NSW Department's 1956 annual report, 'ensures that the children receive proper care and attention and that the conditions imposed by the licences are being observed.' These were the limits of the Department's concern and of its perceived responsibility for the wellbeing of children other than state wards. It also, incidentally, gave no funding to the private sector Homes (see below). All of this means that New South Wales failed children in institutional care just as badly as did the states that used the charitable sector openly. I shall discuss the NSW Department in the following chapter, but it needs to be said here that this Department, despite 'disapproving' of institutionalisation, ran 30 Homes of its own.

People applying for licences to run Children's Homes in New South Wales followed a procedure specified in the regulations of its 1939 Child Welfare Act. A licence was only required if the Home took children under the age of seven, which meant that Homes with older children were unregulated. Applicants had to provide a certificate signed by one of the following: a justice of the peace, medical practitioner, minister of religion, member of the police force or 'other responsible person'. This certificate, in the words of the Act, attests to 'the fitness of the applicant for the rearing of children, and the respectability of the applicant, her husband, her family and her home'. Note here the assumption that the applicant will be a woman, reflecting the gender division of labour which was characteristic of this period: women were the ones who looked after children.

Neither the Act nor the regulations refers to any additional personal or professional qualifications that are required of applicants. Respectability and fitness to rear children are measured by reference to others — who themselves are assumed to be respectable because of their position in society. The granting of a licence to a church or charity would, presumably, be a mere formality, provided their buildings met the physical requirements. Regulation 41 of the NSW Act specifies in minute detail the procedures that licensees have to follow with regard to the children in their care, right down to providing each one with 'a separate bed and a separate towel'. Everything in the regulations is about the *physical* care of children, reflecting concerns and attitudes that are typical of the earliest decades of the century.

The location of Homes

> It was out in the middle of nowhere, which is where most of these places were — out in the middle of nowhere.
>
> Lewis Blayse, Salvation Army Home Indooroopilly, Queensland[20]

Photographs of standard Children's Homes usually show large, imposing buildings in extensive grounds; seeing a building like this certainly contributed to a child's fear and unease on arriving there to be 'cared' for. Large institutions required large houses, and since, as the 20th century unfolded, servants became an anachronism, many large houses were available — and possibly cheap to buy. They were also cheap to run: as I noted in the previous chapter, they provided more than usual scope for the employment of children, thus enabling them to be kept both gainfully occupied as well as under surveillance.

'Mr. Bailey always went after the very best locations, sites and buildings', says the biographer of the founder of the NSW Home Hopewood,[21] and in this he was united with the NSW Department, which in its purchase of historic old homes became, according to one historian, 'one of the most significant forces for conservation of the heritage of New South Wales'.[22] Bidura, the Department's 'depot' or receiving Home in Glebe, Sydney, for example, had been the family home of Edmund Blacket, architect of the main quadrangle of Sydney University and other notable city buildings, while the nucleus of Werrington Park, the

Departmental Home for 'subnormal' boys in Sydney's west, was Frogmore House, which had belonged to Governor Bligh.[23] The Department's purpose with these purchases, it claimed, was to give the children 'the best possible surroundings', with 'fine homes, beautiful furnishings, good food and clothing'.[24] Note the emphasis here on the material not the emotional environment, and the assumption that improved surroundings would have an elevating and remedial effect on the character and attitude of the young inmates. In these 'superior' surroundings, children 'had lessons in personal habits such as hygiene and table manners to enable them to fit more readily into their foster homes', to quote a 1955 NSW Department document, *Historic Houses for State Wards*. At the Department's Lynwood Hall the girls were taught manners, so that every girl could 'wait on a table, [and] bring up afternoon tea for the director', according to Miss Davies, its superintendent; exposing inadvertently the fact that it was domestic and service work that girls in the care of the Department were destined for.

As Bailey did with Hopewood, so other non-government organisations also used old mansions to house their charges; some older orphanages, however, would have been purpose built. Care leavers often speak of how intimidating the physical features of their Homes were. A memory common to many people is of the long driveway up to the front entrance — an interminable distance to a child walking away from everything familiar and into everything unknown. It would be hard to find a more eloquent description than Frank Golding's, in his submission to the Inquiry:

> It was a terrifying experience to be dragged to the doorway of this huge, two-storeyed institution, 'Orphan Asylum' in large letters outside and 200 other orphans inside. I remember it was my brother Bob's fourth birthday so I must have been two and a half. Bill, our half-brother, was a little older.

> I snatched at each shaft of the iron fence as the policeman pulled us towards the great double gate. The gravel crunched under our feet as we drew near the dark-red building. Looking up to the balcony on the second floor, Billy read to us the cast iron words 'ORPHAN ASYLUM 1865'. This was a grim place, this Ballarat Orphanage. Solid, like a fortress.

There were orphanages in many cities, but it was also common for Children's Homes, as Lewis Blayse says, to be located 'out in the middle of nowhere'. This is partly explained by the belief that a change of physical environment could make a major contribution to changing character. This belief in the restorative properties of a country environment and the contaminating effects of the city has a long history in the West in relation to children from disadvantaged or 'dysfunctional' families. In the United States, for example, between 1854 and 1929 the New York Children's Aid Society sent 150,000 'orphans' on trains from cities in the East to foster homes in the rural Midwest. The program was aimed at 'giving deprived youngsters a fresh start in what was viewed as a more wholesome atmosphere'.[25] Few were orphans; most were the children of poor, extremely disadvantaged families, and they became a ready source of cheap labour for the farms they were sent to. This history was later repeated in another part of the world, with the export of children from the United Kingdom under the Child Migrant Scheme, and many of those children, too, ended up as cheap labour on farms (like my interviewee Ray Lennox, in Chapter 2).

In 20th-century child welfare thinking, then, rural locations were also regarded as an antidote to the corruption of city living: 'work with animals in a pleasant, peaceful environment suits disturbed young men much better than city work', as the NSW Department put it in 1955. Several states ran farm homes for boys with 'problems'. The 1956 annual report for the WA Department comments that the Presbyterian Home Benmore for older boys is a farming property and, like Burnbrae (for girls and younger boys), 'is in a rural setting well away from the city'. This statement is not added to, so apparently its meaning is assumed to be obvious to readers. Similarly, Bailey made it quite clear that his motive in settling 'his' children in the country, at Hopewood, was to provide a life away from the moral and physical pollution of city living.

There is, of course, nothing inherently wrong with bringing children up in the country; it is the prioritising of physical environment *over all else* as the creator, shaper and renovator of character which creates the problem. Not only is it a simplistic, mechanistic response to a complex human problem, but part of its objective here — even if this is not often as obvious as it was in the 'orphan trains' program — is to erase the child's own 'defective' family.

There were several side effects of the isolation of Children's Homes. First, it lessened the possibility of contact for children with their families; visiting was very difficult, particularly for parents already struggling financially. Second, children who ran away found it much more difficult to disappear. And third, what went on in these institutions was also much easier to conceal from public view; this last is what Lewis Blayse is alluding to in his statement at the start of this section.

Size of Homes

Children's Homes varied considerably in size. The impoverished orphanage of the 19th century, with its meagre dinners, huge dormitories, threadbare clothes and no shoes, and too few nuns or other staff toiling for long hours to care for far too many children, features in some accounts: from Homes such as St John's Goulburn, NSW, St Joseph's Neerkol and St Vincent's Nudgee in Queensland, and the Ballarat Orphanage in Victoria. Catholic

The archetypal orphanage building — monumental in size, forbidding in aspect, a place to strike fear into the heart of any child who entered it. This one is Ballarat Orphanage, established in 1865.

Homes commonly had large numbers of children, up to 200, but so did Salvation Army homes, and also Barnardos Homes.

A survey in New South Wales in 1961[26] showed that there were seven Homes which each took more than 100 children, while 12 had between 60 and 100 children, and 22 had between 30 and 60 residents. This is only a small proportion of the total number of NSW Homes, in that year (319), which indicates that in New South Wales, the majority of Homes tended to take fewer than 30 children. This partly accounts for why, even allowing for its greater population, there were so many more Homes in this state compared with others. The survey of non-government Children's Homes in Victoria 1962 to 1964 (above), showed that the state's 63 Homes consisted of 12 babies' Homes, 10 girls' Homes, 17 boys' Homes and 24 mixed Homes (Homes which took both boys and girls, and thus were required to have separate dwellings for each [see Chapter 6]). There were nine Victorian Homes accommodating 100 or more children, the largest number being 175 at Nazareth Boys'. A further 18 Homes had between five and 92 children — including two of the Babies' Homes — and the remainder had around 50 each, although there was one with only six children.[27] The Forde Report noted that in Queensland, overcrowding and understaffing were a common problem in a number of orphanages, right up until the late 1960s. At St Joseph's Neerkol, for example, there were between 300 and 500 children — with only 10 to 15 nuns looking after them. This was obviously a contributing factor in the appalling standards of care in this Home, documented in two inquiries and numerous care leaver accounts. But a poor staff-to-child ratio within the context of very restricted resources occurred in other states too; it was a significant contributor to the systems abuse that characterised the 'care' of this era.

Beginning in the 1960s, 'cottage' and 'family group' Homes began to replace 'barracks' or dormitory-style accommodation, although change was uneven. A few Homes had always had cottage type care: the Parkerville Home in Perth, for instance, and Burnside in Sydney, a large Homes complex established in 1911.[28] These 'cottages' were large, however, with 30 children in each, grouped according to age and sex, with couples looking after boys, and women alone looking after girls. The theory behind cottage Homes was that while children may not do well in large institutional settings, they are bound to flourish in smaller settings because they receive more attention from carers.

There is a false assumption here about the quality of the attention — a smaller setting does not necessarily guarantee a different institutional culture from that which prevailed in large Homes, if the staff attitudes to children are the same. In a large institution a child might get little attention, but in a smaller setting, staff could still be indifferent to children; alternatively, children could get too much unwelcome attention. The experience of Bruce Randle in Mount Gibraltar, the Sydney City Mission's NSW Home, from 1958 to 1966, is characteristic, in that although this Home took only about 30 boys, and was run by a couple and paid help, 'you had to fight for what you wanted', Bruce said, and the manager was a bully; Bruce was hospitalised on one occasion after being assaulted by him.

My impression is that although poor practice was undoubtedly exacerbated by chronic understaffing combined with large numbers of children and a lack of resources, the size of the Home had little to do with the quality of children's experiences unless it was accompanied by a different philosophy of care. For example, one of my interviewees was in the Church of England Girls' Home at Burwood, New South Wales, in the 1970s, when changes in attitude and practice were starting to have an effect. Yet in her 'cottage', in which there were no more than 20 girls, the inflexible regimen was little different from that described by interviewees who were in this Home 30 years' earlier, when the accommodation was more in the 'barracks' style. The atmosphere was 'unsympathetic' and punitive, she said, with 'no love, and harsh discipline'. Conversely, while the two Barnardos Homes in my sample were large, people who had lived in them in the 1950s spoke positively of them because they were treated humanely; John Brown describes his Victorian Methodist Home, Tally Ho, in the 1930s, the same way (see below).

There is even a case for saying that where Homes were very large and older children helped look after younger ones, there was sometimes the opportunity for personal relating which was otherwise so absent in institutional care. Liz Morton, in the huge barracks-like Ballarat Orphanage for much of her childhood in the 1950s, spoke affectionately of the 'toddies' (toddlers) that the older girls looked after. And Frank Golding, in the same orphanage somewhat earlier, recalls that although separated from his brothers, 'we were thrust together with hordes of other children and some became almost as close friends as brothers'.

Were all Homes the same?

'Better' Homes

In the previous chapter I described the institutional regime and culture that was typical of Children's Homes across Australia. Were there any Homes that were different in some way from the institutional norm? The answer is 'not really', but there were some variations. Hopewood, at Bowral, New South Wales, is a one-off, certainly unlike any other Home in its experimental purpose and in the manner in which children were 'collected' by Bailey in pursuit of his purpose. However, Hopewood was conducted along similar lines to other big Homes, whereas there were some Homes which appeared to attempt to provide a 'better' environment for the children living in them.

One was the Isabella Lazarus Home for Jewish Children in Sydney, where Rebecca Feinstein spent several years from 1957, aged nearly six until 1964, aged 13. An only child, she was sent there, as I related in Chapter 2, because 'my parents were divorcing and they couldn't look after me'. As far as Rebecca knew, this was the only Jewish Home in Sydney, located adjacent to the Jewish Montefiore Home for the Aged at Hunters Hill. There were 20 to 30 children in the Isabella Lazarus, boys and girls aged from about five to about 17, with two housemothers to care for them. The Home obviously made an effort to embed children in both the Jewish community and wider society, and to keep them connected to their own families. They went to synagogue on Friday night and Saturday morning, and on Friday nights shared the Shabbat meal with the old people in the Montefiore Home. On Saturday afternoons the children went for bushwalks, and they attended the local schools. They had television, and music lessons were available. Furthermore, contact with parents, although not frequent, was more regular than in many, if not most, Homes. As Rebecca recalled:

> We were allowed to go home one weekend in four. Our parents rang us on a Wednesday night, the next weekend we stayed in, the next weekend our parents would come on a Sunday to visit and the next Sunday we were taken out on a picnic by the Jewish community.

Rebecca's account is the only one I have heard where parents were allowed to telephone their children. Rebecca wrote about this contact routine in both her letters to me, which I took as an indication of how important this memory was for her. Loneliness was a major feature of the Home experience, and children felt most acutely the isolation of Homes from 'normal' contact and relationships with other people, particularly family.

Two interviewees who were in Barnardos Homes described

institutions which, although large, appeared to have some empathy with children. At Greenwood, in Normanhurst, New South Wales, although Barnardos were not allowed to accommodate boys and girls under the same roof (see Chapter 6), the children all ate together and the Home was run by a couple, who were called Uncle and Aunt by the children. Children went to local schools but not all to the same ones, to avoid their stigmatisation as 'Homies' or 'Home kids'. There were some other major differences from other Homes, according to Judith, who was there in the mid-1950s: children were not obliged to do the housework, they were treated as if they were all part of one family, and, she said, they received individual attention. Every child celebrated their birthday with a special dinner, presents and a cake, and they had pocket money, and money for school excursions. Children were taken into the city to choose their Sunday clothes and summer hats, and Judith remembered particularly how the girls 'had patent leather court shoes and stockings when old enough'. According to her, the children felt that if they ever had a problem they could take it to the house parents to discuss it, and they would be heard; she had fond memories of this couple and had kept in touch with them over the years.

Another positive account from even earlier can be found in John Brown's submission, in which he describes the Tally Ho Boys' Home where he lived from 1939, aged 9½, until the age of 14. Tally Ho was run by the Wesley Central Mission in East Burwood, Victoria, as a 'training' school for boys considered likely to 'get into trouble' (through truancy, for example).[29] John had lived in institutions all his life, beginning with the hospital in which he had been born — out of wedlock. It is interesting to see that the sort of routine that in other Homes could be sheer drudgery appears to take on a different meaning in John's account. He said, 'at Tally Ho they taught you to make your bed, wash your clothes, and we shared laundry duties, farm duties, cooking, separating milk, harvesting' — using words not often found in accounts of institutional life: 'taught' and 'shared'. The clue seems to be in the manager of Tally Ho, Edgar Derrick, the son of the Wesley Mission's founding secretary, who had been appointed superintendent of Tally Ho in 1931. An opponent of institutional life as 'a cheap way of dealing with boys en masse with staff ill equipped to meet their needs',[30] Derrick was influenced by both his reading in the developing area of child psychology and the ideas of the American, Homer Lane, who advocated 'the creative power of love' in place of detention and punishment as the most effective agent for reforming boys.

Tally Ho had a picture theatre and a boxing ring for boys to spar in (under supervision), and Derrick taught the boys how to handle money by having them make boiled lollies, which they bought with the tin money they were given. John wet the bed for 18 months until he settled down in the Home but was never punished. And, he says, he 'never witnessed beatings', although he knew they occurred elsewhere:

> Kids in other Homes that came to Tally Ho used to talk about the beatings they used to get at the other Homes. From memory they came from Salvation Army Boys' Homes and some Catholic Homes.

John was one of the 'privileged' boys, and so he may have had a better experience than somebody else would recount. However, it seems, from what he said, that it was possible to run a large institution on a humane system, where there was the will to do so.

The Roslyn Hall Children's Home, in Rockdale, a southern suburb of Sydney, also offers a decided contrast to the usual run of Homes. This was where Else Ferguson lived with her younger sister for five years — from age nine, in 1963 — after her parents separated. In this Home, the children were allowed to visit school friends, run messages to the local shops and, when older, go to the local pictures. They, like others with family available, went home fortnightly, and their mother 'popped in for visits, and would take us down the road for a milkshake'. There were usually about 30 children there altogether, and Else was not separated from her sister. This Home also was once a mansion, but the children, although they had chores, did not do the work of running the Home since there was a cook, a laundry woman, and two or three child-care assistants and a married couple who managed the Home. The children went across the road to the local school, returning to the Home for lunch. Physical punishment was rare, and the children were taken for outings. Else and her sister were also allowed to spend weekends with the family who had lived next door to them before they entered the Home, and to go away with them for holidays. Contrast this with David Walshe's experience in the Salvation Army Gill Memorial Home in the 1970s, where, he says, it was only in his last year there, as an older teenager, that he was allowed to visit his grandmother on weekends, even though she lived in the same town.

Else observed that 'you got Christianity rammed down your throat a bit much, but that doesn't hurt'. In fact, Roslyn Hall was run by the Sydney Rescue Work Society, a non-denominational organisation founded in 1890 on the principles of the New Testament.[31] In Else's time there, the Society had a 'Department of Evangelism' and ran many community services besides the Children's Home, which had started as a Babies' Home in 1894, when it took in 'foundlings'. What I find particularly interesting about Roslyn Hall is that here is a Home activated by strong evangelical Christian principles, yet which is in distinct contrast to most other evangelically inspired Homes, such as those run by the Salvation Army. Since I had only the one interviewee from this Home, however, I cannot say whether it had always been run along these lines.

'Worse' Homes

There were also Homes that were at the extreme end of punitive. All the 'training schools' (see Chapter 5), and the Catholic Homes run as laundries, fit this description, but that was their intention: their purpose was to punish children for 'waywardness' and to break their spirit. Among these are some where the cruelty and inhumanity seem a direct link back to our convict past — state institutions at Hay and Tamworth in New South Wales and Westbrook and the Wilson Youth Hospital in Queensland, for example, which I touch on briefly in the next chapter.

Here I am concerned with the residential Homes, the ones intended simply for the care, not the punishment, of children. Of these, the ones that, from inmate accounts, were most savagely repressive of children, were institutions run by the most fundamentalist expressions of the religious life: particularly repressive, and many would say distorted, versions of Christianity whose adherents passed down to children the inhumanity of the practices imposed on themselves. Among these are the Homes of some Catholic orders, the Protestant sect Homes, and many of the Salvation Army Homes. The Christian Brothers' Homes in Western Australia, at Bindoon, and at Castledare, Clontarf and Tardun — which I mentioned above — are notable, as are many Homes run by the Sisters of Mercy. This order, as I have said, ran by far the largest number of Homes in Australia of any Catholic order, more than 30 in all. Christian Wolmar, in *Forgotten Children*, says of these sisters:

> Perhaps the key to the awfulness of the regime lies in the strict emphasis on obedience which led to an iron discipline that not only oppressed the children but also any of the nuns who were concerned at the ill-treatment of the residents.[32]

The Sisters of Mercy had exported what Wolmar describes as 'their brand of institutional terror' from Ireland, where they ran two-thirds of the children's institutions. Wolmar quotes from a 1970s report on St Joseph's, the Home they ran for 90 years in Neerkol, Queensland:

> Madness, ruthless and sadistic madness, on the part of at least some of the nuns, and a depthless depravity on the part of some of the men who inhabited the place, are the defining characteristics of some of those who ran the orphanage.[33]

Among the Salvation Army Homes, one which recurs as a template for inhumanity is the Gill Memorial Home at Goulburn, New South Wales. I had a couple of interviewees who had been in this Home (one told me they called it the Gill Memorial Junior Gaol), but it was only through CLAN and then the Senate Inquiry that I heard enough accounts of it — stretching over years — to realise that this Home, because of its brutality, mindless discipline and sheer cruelty to children, was among the worst. The rituals and routines of institutional life which I described in the previous chapter were here intensified into a regime which appears designed purely to oppress the spirit, break the will and destroy the hope of any boy who lived there. Ralph Doughty, now aged 71, said in his submission:

> At times, memories of many of the happenings in that orphanage, have nearly tipped me over but to date I have not succumbed ... This agony stays closer to you than can your wife or your children or little grandchildren.

This Home had not even the 'excuse' that it was a 'training' school: it was simply a Home for dependent children whose families were unable to care for them, young boys like Ralph, and James Luthy, and David Walshe, whom I have quoted previously. Ralph, however, says that the Gill Home *was* a training school: 'a training institution for young male Salvation Army officers. They learnt the basic art of torture and small unprotected boys were their raw material.' The boys who lived there had their own song, sung to the tune of *The Road to Gundagai*:

> There's a gaol on a hill
> and they call it the Gill
> along the road to Goulburn High.
> You can hear the Sallies singing
> and hear the stockwhip ringing
> beneath the Goulburn sky.
> When my mummy and daddy are thinking of me
> I'm in the Sallies' office copping six, four and three.
> There's a gaol on the hill
> and they call it the Gill
> along the road to Goulburn High.

'We used to sing this song on the way to school and after school,' says John Hepton, who was in the Gill for nine years, from the age of seven in 1948, 'anywhere we could, just so long as the officers didn't hear it, because we were well aware of the consequences.' Even in the most horrendous of circumstances, children did try to hold on to their right to exist and have their own view of what was done to them.

Staffing in Homes

How were staff recruited?

Barry Coldrey, in his recent paper on staffing in traditional Catholic residential care, summed up its inherent problems in the title of the paper, calling it *The Devoted, the Dull, the Desperate and the Deviant*.[34] He notes that the 1946 UK Curtis Committee had deplored the shortage of 'the right kind of staff' for Children's Homes, attributing it to poor salaries, poor accommodation, unsocial hours and the isolation of institutions, plus the fact that residential care was perceived as low-status work, not least because of the low social status of the residents — that is, the children.[35] These observations about staffing standards and attitudes, from the evidence of the hundreds of accounts now available, can be applied equally to Australia — and not only to the Catholic institutions that are Coldrey's particular focus — probably until almost the end of the era of institutional care.

Cheryl Hannaford, an interviewee who was in the Protestant Federation Girls' Home, Sydney, in the mid-1950s, spoke for many people when she gave me her impression of the staff in her Home:

> You were lucky if you got the time of day from the staff. They were just women, none of them married, who applied for the position of giving care, if you can call it that. Some of them were hopeless, some tried to make up for the shortcomings of our being there. There were some very sadistic ones. A lot of these women, when you think of how they said things, and what they said, were a bit crackers.

Staff were 'just women', said Cheryl, but who were these women? In Else Ferguson's Baptist Home, they were 'Christian women, attached to the church. The pay was not good, and most were rather young.' Else added that 'maybe women do it because it's a refuge, until they get something better' — which is exactly what she did herself, working there for a while once she ceased to be an inmate. Much of what I learned about how Homes were staffed came from people who answered my advertisements: 10 in all, who had been employed in Children's Homes from the 1930s to the 1960s.[36] The gender division appeared to be that women were matrons or domestics and men were superintendents or managers. Kath Emmett, whose working life had until 1960 been spent in offices, got her job at Methodist Dalmar when she was in her early twenties by writing to ask if there were any positions available, because, she said, 'if you were affiliated with the Methodist church, you were pretty well assured of a job'. She thought that most of the others there had come through church connections, and all the carers in her time were single women, even in the boys' Homes. Matron, she said, was a trained nurse, unmarried and in her sixties, with 'Christian principles which she lived up to strictly'. Daphne Calhoun was told of the job at the NSW government Home Weroona by her Sunday School superintendent, because he knew that she 'loved working with the children'. Daphne said:

> I was very young, but they seemed to be desperate for staff at the time so I was given the position. I was given no training at all but I was told what I was required to do: mostly supervision.

Burnside, the NSW Presbyterian complex of Homes, used to advertise for staff in Christian magazines, and it is instructive to note the change in the tone of its advertisements over the years. In 1950 a position for 'sub-matrons' is described as 'an opportunity for you to secure a congenial, well-paid position and at the same time do a really worthwhile job in caring for the children'. By 1964, the 'opportunity', while still presented as the chance to take part 'in a very worthwhile social work', specified that 'the first requirement is a definite love for children and a desire and ability to live with them'.[37]

Rural church Homes might approach locals, even those without any particular qualifications, or accept people who approached them, according to Jim Rodgers, who helped set up a UPA Home in Wagga Wagga, NSW, in the 1950s. Another male staff member, Jim Fairmont, had come from a career in trade and commerce but had a strong interest in church youth activities, he said, and 'a desire to perhaps make some social contribution'. At the age of 32 he applied for a position with the Central

Methodist Mission at Dalmar, and was eventually appointed assistant superintendent. He had no training in child welfare, but then, as he said, specific training for childcare workers was not available in Australia in the late 1940s and 1950s. According to a child welfare executive I interviewed:

> there was no award and no training for childcare workers [throughout most of the period of institutional care], and agencies weren't keen on an award because costs would go up. Staff didn't organise either, because of the charitable aura about the work — you were supposed to be doing it out of love for children, as a 'good work', if you were religious.[38]

There was, in any case, little awareness that you needed any sort of training to look after children. The major emphasis in 'child welfare', whether state or charitable, was on administration. For women, nursing training was apparently regarded as an appropriate — even the *most* appropriate — background for 'child welfare'. This reflects the earlier 20th-century preoccupation with the health and mortality of children, but beyond this understandable concern, it also indicates that care of children was conceptualised primarily as care of their bodies. When I asked Bunty Randall, matron of a church Home outside Sydney in the 1950s, what sort of training she had had, she answered, 'double-certificated registered nurse, trained for the overseas mission field in the Church of Christ Bible College'. There was an obvious connection in her mind between nursing training and caring for children — religious 'training' was an added bonus. Beryl Sawyer, matron first of a Church Home and then superintendent of the NSW Department's receiving depot, Bidura, in the 1960s, had a similar background.

All female managers of Homes appeared to have been called 'matron' even if they had no nursing training, and their staff were often called 'nurse' or 'sister', titles which conferred the authority associated with the superior knowledge and status of medical training. Janet Maxwell, a Barnardos inmate, described her matron as 'exactly what you imagine a matron [to be] like — big, stern, with a white uniform'. A 1954 promotional brochure for Dalmar has a photograph of the matron 'relaxing with some of the sisters', around a tea table, with matron wearing a full starched nurse's headdress. Matron had 'recently been awarded a Coronation Medal for her long and devoted service for the children'.

The Curtis Report, as I said above, had noted the difficulties of finding and keeping 'the right kind of staff', and many Homes did appear to have had a high staff turnover. Where good staff were hard to both attract and to keep, for whatever reasons, it was likely that those who remained did so because they had few other options, or because it suited an agenda of their own to stay. Frank Golding, in the Ballarat Orphanage in the 1940s and 1950s, recalled:

> A hard core of staff stayed forever, but otherwise there was a high turnover and constant shortages of staff. Anyone with any humanity couldn't bear to stay after they saw what the Orphanage was like and what they were expected to do to keep the children under control.

Coldrey claims that these difficulties in recruiting staff led to, among other things, 'a mindset that encouraged abuse and provided a cover for abusive carers'. It is the mindset of the martyr, carrying out work that is considered unattractive and unrewarding and that nobody else wants to do — 'sacrificing so much for the deprived children'.[39] It was the 'deprived children' who were the real sacrifice — Sylvia Baker said of her Home, Burnside:

> The Matron would have you lined up for evening prayer, and she'd rant and rave about how you'd all been dragged out of the gutter and you should be grateful. But what thanks do the staff get for all their work, etc. etc.

And Mim McKew said this about the staff of her Victorian Catholic Home:

> The nuns made sure to tell us often that we were there because nobody wanted us, and that they looked after us because they had to, as that was their work. 'We're not paid enough to look after these brats,' we'd hear them say to one another. And to us they'd say, 'Whatever treatment you get from us, you should be thankful for, because we're giving it out of the kindness of our hearts.'

This is emotionally abusive of children whose feelings of self-worth were already low, but there is an even darker side:

> The darker side covered inappropriate behaviour by staff members, which could be rationalised, and excused, by the fact that 'their work was so hard, their hours so long and their contribution to the cause so great' that unsatisfactory behaviour was trivial by comparison.[40]

With this martyr self-perception, concludes Coldrey, 'it was not far to more sinister attitudes of excusing destructive behaviour and illegality in their own and in their colleagues' conduct'. Coldrey also notes the tendency of Catholic orders to place their least qualified members on the staff of Children's Homes, including former orphanage residents. There was a clear prioritising here, he says, particularly where orders ran schools as well as Homes. Schools would get the better-educated staff; anyone would do for a Children's Home. He quotes a 1951 internal report by a Christian Brothers inspector of that order's institution at Bindoon in Western Australia, an institution subsequently notorious for its abuse of the children in its care, under the brutal Brother Keaney.[41] 'This has a staff of oddities,' wrote the inspector, 'and if they knew I was writing this they would not much care.'[42]

Donella Jaggs, a former inspector of residential care in Victoria, once said that 'the staff I observed were often almost as deprived as the children for whom they were trying to care'.[43] Certainly, when you read care leaver histories, you cannot help but wonder just what sort of childhood experiences some of the people who ended up working in Children's Homes had had. And it is difficult to avoid the conclusion that some Homes' staff, as well as being 'deprived', may have been psychologically disturbed: the nuns in Helena Dam's Brisbane Home, for example, who, on finding she was terrified of frogs, would regularly place some on her desk and force her to sit there with them, and the Salvation Army officers who enacted torture rituals for hours on end with the boys in their care at the Gill Home in Goulburn, NSW. And it was not only in religious Homes that apparently disturbed staff operated. Caroline Carroll, in Lynwood Hall, NSW, in the 1950s, described Miss Davies, superintendent for many years of this institution, and a highly regarded, very senior employee of the NSW Department:

> She hit, kicked punched, dragged you around by the hair. She would get so angry she would spit all over you as she screamed the foulest language. Most of us had never heard the words she came out with, but after living there a while we could all put any sailor to shame.

It is a characteristic of closed regimes that their functionaries — in this case, Home staff — have the power to make the lives of inmates bearable or not. The previous chapter showed the effect of staff members on their charges, and in submissions to the Inquiry, some names occur over and over, remembered by inmates as particularly terrifying or sadistic (or, very occasionally, the opposite, like Edgar Derrick in John Brown's Home, Tally-Ho, above). The staff I interviewed had apparently answered my advertisements out of interest in my research, and some claimed they had found their work with children 'fulfilling'. Nevertheless, they showed little or no empathy with what children in institutional care might have been feeling. The remarks by Kath Emmett, about her time at Methodist Dalmar during 1960–61, were typical:

> I don't think those children really felt they were hard done by. They were really nice places they lived in ... if they had problems they didn't show it. As long as Mum turned up on visiting day with a few sweets and took a bit of notice of them, that was all they wanted. I can't remember any being too upset when parents left.

When I asked Norma Arrowsmith, who, with her husband, had been in charge of a NSW church Home from 1960 to 1965, if the staff had made an effort to get to know individual children, she said that 'it didn't take much effort to get to know them' and that 'we counted ourselves fortunate that we never had any real bad girls'. Similarly, when I asked Daphne Davies, described above, about the histories of the girls who had come into her care as superintendent of Lynwood Hall, she said, 'Oh, you can't waste your time looking into their backgrounds, I didn't have time for all that.' Staff seemed to regard the children in their care as almost interchangeable, differentiated only by how 'good' or how 'bad' they were; this attitude is very familiar to me from my own childhood. Joy Hill, transferred to Lynwood in 1956, described Daphne Davies as 'an ogre' who 'continually destroy[ed] our self-esteem'. I have heard many accounts through reunions at Lynwood Hall which all support this view of Miss Davies. I had in fact interviewed her for my thesis, after Joy Hill took me to meet her: Joy had kept in touch with her because, she said, although 'I hated her when I was there, she was the closest I had to a mother'.

Davies had in fact run the Training School for Girls, Parramatta, until 1943; her transfer to Lynwood Hall undoubtedly signalled the NSW Department's belief that the girls in this Home required the same aggressive handling as the hardened 'delinquents' of the training school. Davies was almost a textbook example — on the far end of punitive — of the attitudes to children which I described in Chapter 2. 'If you give children everything they want, they just want more,' she said, 'so you make them earn what they get, and take it away if they misbehave.' There is a particularly sad irony in this statement: these children had almost nothing of what they wanted, such as parents, their siblings, love, or anyone to take a personal interest in them. Davies was extremely derisive about 'psychological' approaches and said that when, as sometimes happened, staff turned up at Lynwood Hall who said they would treat the girls as equals, she said to them, 'Well, I don't want you if you're only as intelligent as them.' Lack of intelligence in her charges was taken for granted. 'I always got the deadbeats,' she said, in front of Joy, who had been one of her charges.

At Lynwood Hall, girls had only two days of schooling per week; the rest of the time was spent on laundry, cooking and sewing, and Davies scoffed at the idea that some girls, given a chance, might have been revealed as bright. The proper, 'natural' female role, according to the norms of this period, was that of housewife and mother, so this type of training could be seen as an attempt to fit girls for their appropriate role in life. This ideology, however, also coalesced with other assumptions of this period, ones clearly held by staff of children's institutions, whether government or charitable: that lower socio-economic status was linked with low intelligence. Girls in Lynwood Hall were assumed, *merely because they were there*, to be of 'mediocre' intelligence and therefore only suitable for, and capable of, domestic labour. According to the NSW Department's 1956 annual report, while males committed to institutions were of normal or above intelligence, 'the average I.Q. of females committed is in the middle 80s', and 'the typical girl to be dealt with in the Training School [is] usually of a "dull-normal" intelligence, aggressive in outlook ...'

Norma Arrowsmith (quoted above), concluded her remarks with, 'During my stay in the Home I was respected and that was very satisfying.' The issue of respect was important to this generation of child welfare staff, in the sense that Beryl Sawyer meant: speaking of the children who went from Bidura into foster care, she said, 'You generally knew if a kid would be returned, from their attitudes and behaviour, for example disrespect to elders.' Sawyer added that in her opinion, 'everything was done that needed to be done for children' who came under the care of the NSW Department. And when children were fostered out, she said:

> They were very good with them, the government. Every time a child went to a foster home they gave them a suitcase with all new clothes. Often it was hocked and the girl would get on a bus and go somewhere. They didn't appreciate it; they were beautiful clothes.

The public and the private face of the Homes

How Home managements described their work ...

One of the unifying threads in care leaver histories is the discrepancy between how children experienced their lives in care and the apparent intentions of Home managements, as stated in their promotional literature. Parents who believed what the Homes said about their care arrangements could have been forgiven for thinking that they were putting their children into hands that were not only safe, but also loving. Compare the account of the Gill Memorial Home, for example, with these words in a Salvation Army promotional pamphlet in the 1950s:

> Children who have been robbed of their rights and are as a result woefully handicapped in the race of life, are the Army's first care in these fine Homes where they are mothered, educated and trained under ideal conditions.[44]

The annual reports of Homes usually give some insight into how managements regarded their work. The Burnside annual reports of the 1950s, for example, always had what would now be called 'mission statements', and the attitudes found in these reports could be generalised to almost any institution for children of the time.

Burnside's 1954 annual report has a story called 'Burnside is my home ...' purportedly written by Susan, aged almost 11, who had been at the Home for three years after her 'Daddy went away' and 'Mummy and I had nowhere to live'. She catalogues all her activities, including hiking and physical culture, marching with the pipe band and the garden she is 'proud of'. She was 'lucky enough to go to the Royal Easter Show, where 'we all took an interest in the displays'. With the other children she went to wave at the Queen and the Duke at a local venue — 'I have never seen so many other children in my life'. 'Everyone is very nice to us at Burnside ... I think I will be sorry to leave my Home,' she concludes. There is no mention of her parents at all, even in the context of visiting days. The piece reads as if it were written by an adult (as it probably was). It is an adult's version of what children 'need', presented in pseudo-childlike language, an idealised version of 'life' which prioritises amusement and physical activities over feelings. And yet there *appears* to be an awareness of children's feelings. The 1958 report, for example, says that:

> behind all the lovely innocence of childhood there lies a vast experience of sorrow, tragedy, pain, loneliness and struggle. Through the circumstances of human travail, these children at Burnside have been denied the advantages of their natural home!

So what is being done for 'these little children'?

> Fundamentally, the work is the endeavour to provide what every child is entitled to — the warmth and love

and discipline of a responsible home. The policy of
Burnside is activated on compassionate grounds —
Christian love — wherein the children's welfare is
paramount ... Strict attention is paid to the total needs
of the children. Our care for them is expressed in a
three-wise dimension — in body, in education, in
religion. This administration is given to the children with
careful understanding.

Although the Homes pay 'strict attention' to the 'total needs of children', feelings are apparently not part of this — or perhaps feelings are dealt with through religion, an irony indeed when we know through inmates' accounts that the primary purpose of religion in Children's Homes was to justify punishment and to remind children of their low status. The use of the word 'administration' here is telling; it is as if children can be dosed with whatever they 'need', as with medicine. And 'the advantages of their natural home' are not described as if they are connected to feelings for specific people, such as their own parents, brothers and sisters. Children are objects of concern and grateful receptacles for adult benevolence — not living beings with feelings as intense and deep as any adult's. The report is lavishly illustrated with photographs of either apparently carefree or pensive children, along with florid musings on the child's world which emphasise 'wonder' as the special province of childhood. Here we see adults making the sort of assumptions about children which satisfy *their* needs: to believe that children are 'innocent' and naive, contemplating nothing more challenging than the 'wonder' of the outside world rather than the pain of separation and loss. This perspective could never recognise that what children actually wondered was why they were there and why their parents did not come and rescue them. Underneath one such photograph is written:

with time and kindness, the sharp, ugly mountains of a
child's fear and the hurt of hollow-aching loneliness

> become dusted over with the blue powder of distance ...
> and then there is laughter, silver shimmering, sunlit
> laughter ... the laughter of children. This is our work at
> Burnside.

This sort of sentimental language depersonalises and objectifies children. It is the language of colonialism, describing happy, carefree 'natives' who do not have feelings like us because they are 'other' — simple and primitive and easily pleased. There is no recognition that the fear and the loneliness might arise from loss of family — including the loss of their brothers and sisters within that actual Home — and from the experience of living in a sterile institutional environment where kindness was arbitrary. These attitudes appear to have been difficult to change. Norma Parker, head of social work training at Sydney University, remarked in 1957 that 'the way many of these institutions function indicates that they have remained relatively untouched by modern thinking on the psychological needs of children'.[45]

'Hollow-aching loneliness' is a very good description of the feelings recalled by former Home children. Because of their multiple and fundamental losses, which no staff member ever tried to help them deal with, children in Homes could never feel at home *in themselves*. Sylvia Baker, who lived at Burnside for 10 years, from 1938 to 1948, said of her childhood there:

> You never felt loved. When you're a child you don't even
> voice those things, you just feel them. Sometimes I felt so
> depressed I'd just cry and cry, and when they asked me
> why I was crying, I'd say, 'I don't know', and I didn't.

There is also not a little self-congratulation underlying the words of the annual reports of Homes generally, for the Home is fulfilling a responsibility that the parent has reneged on. Parents did not have much credibility with the managements of Homes. The very fact that they needed the Home was proof that they had failed in their responsibilities. The Burnside Arrears of Maintenance register for the years 1950–64 exemplifies these attitudes; they are found in all child welfare literature of the era. While some allowance is made for illness, accidents and 'unfortunate' circumstances as factors in non-payment, the terms used to describe parents make it clear that arrears are almost always and almost entirely attributable to character deficiencies. Mothers are described as 'unsatisfactory', 'a neurotic type', 'incorrigible', 'hopeless', 'irresponsible', 'very irrational', 'very erratic' and 'a mental case'. Fathers are 'a hopeless type', 'always an unsatisfactory person to handle' and 'a hopeless drunkard' — one is described as 'a widower but a very poor type'. These attitudes resonate with those of the previous century, with Dr Barnardo's comment, for example, that in his 'child-saving' enterprise, parents 'are my chief difficulty everywhere; so are relatives ... because I have to take from a very low class'.[46]

... and what they did

Total institutions, says Goffman, usually present themselves to the public as 'rational organisations' which have a conscious design aimed at 'producing officially declared and approved ends'.[47] In a Children's Home, this would be the production of healthy, educated, functioning young citizens, who have been 'mothered, educated and trained under ideal conditions', in the words of the Salvation Army pamphlet quoted above. Nevertheless, says Goffman, most of the time, total institutions 'seem to function merely as storage dumps for inmates', and the 'contradiction between what the institution does and what its officials must say it does, forms the basic context of the staff's daily activity'.[48]

That orphanages were in reality 'storage dumps for inmates', whatever their managements professed — and even believed — can be seen in the fact that institutions often had a very different public face, for visitors and child welfare authorities, from the one seen by their inmates. This surely indicates that managements knew that something else was expected of them, and that they wished others to believe that those expectations were being fulfilled. This was the hidden agenda when Elizabeth Miller was taken by her mother to the Protestant Federation Girls' Home at Dulwich Hill in 1954, aged 10:

> I chose a bed I wanted in the dormitory called 'Cosy Cottage', right next to a window. All the beds had cotton quilts on them and everything was very neat and clean. In reality, after my mother left, I was taken to another dormitory and told which bed I was to have.

Obviously this management thought that it would look better if they pretended that children had a choice. The Forde Report, noting the repeated failure of the Queensland Department to carry out its legislated inspection obligations, pointed out that where inspections did happen, they were expected and prepared for by the addition of embellishments not usually available, such as toys for the children, quilts on the beds, and tablecloths. Mary Gesch said this of the Presbyterian WR Black Home for Girls in Chelmer, Brisbane:

> There was a playroom with toys and a dolls' house. The toys we took to the Home were put in that room. We didn't get to play there; it was just for show. We hardly knew what play was.

Other people related how they had different food when there were visitors (it was 'the only time we saw an egg', said one interviewee), or being dressed up in better clothes and told to smile — that is, being conscripted into the presentation of a public face which the management knew was false.

I saw the same thing on a daily basis in my Home. When taking in children from their parents for 'holidays', Betty would talk about the enjoyable and interesting things they would be doing and how they would have 'a lovely time'. She knew that this was what parents expected and she also, apparently, knew what would normally be provided for children. But the Home in fact was much closer to Goffman's 'storage dump'. Betty's major objective was to return children, at the end of their stay (whether long or short) who were not visibly injured, sunburnt, bitten by mosquitoes or exhibiting any other blemishes, and who were wearing spotlessly clean, beautifully ironed clothes — anything else would reflect badly on her. In reality, they were all treated as interchangeable with the other items in the storage dump during their stay; their movements were restricted and they were under constant surveillance. A further discrepancy occurred in what I heard her say to parents about punishment ('I don't think a little tap now and then hurts — children do need discipline') and what she actually did to children.

It is obvious from other inmate accounts that staff knew that much of what they did to children was not acceptable. Ken Carter, at the Salvation Army Boys' Home in Box Hill, Victoria, in the 1950s, records how 'the monster' (as he describes the officer in charge) would warn the boys about saying anything when 'the Welfare' came:

> S ... said to each and every one of us, 'If any of you kids say anything about how I'm running this organisation ... I'll know about it, because the reports come back to me.' So I thought to myself, well, there would be a lot of the kids that would not even say anything.

It should also be said, however, that the presentation of a 'sanitised' public face was probably not true of all Homes; in some, parents were made to feel that they were lucky to have anywhere for the children they were so feckless as to be unable to look after.

The economy of Children's Homes

Jim Fairmont, one of the staff I interviewed who became assistant superintendent of Dalmar, the Methodist Home at Carlingford, New South Wales, remarked that up to World War II:

> Homes for children had changed little from the 19th century orphan asylum system where 'charity' was dispensed with prime regard to providing food, shelter and clothing for which the child should be eternally grateful.

'Elements of this concept persisted,' he said, 'long after they should have been abandoned.' He thought that some Homes were simply 'reluctant to change the status quo', but also that some could not afford to make alterations to their practices. The continued existence of the majority of Homes was dependent, as it had been for similar institutions in the 19th century, on bequests, donations and private endowments, supplemented by whatever parents could pay. Added to this was whatever governments contributed; this varied from state to state.[49] If we look at it in a broader perspective, however, we would also have to say that it was obviously not a priority, with either established churches and charities, or with state governments, to invest funds in establishing out-of-home care for children on more enlightened principles than institutionalisation.

State financial support of non-state Homes

It is difficult to work out just how much state governments funded charitable Homes, or on what basis, over and above the subsidy paid for each state ward. The 1956 annual report of the WA Department says that, 'All institutions are subsidised on a per capita basis by the government', but few annual reports state the situation as clearly as does the Queensland Government's 1956 annual report:

> Besides paying £1.5s. per child per week to each denominational Home for state wards, plus school requisites, the Government pays 50 per cent of the cost of additions, renovations and repairs to buildings.

It seems obvious, though, that Homes in all states were funded in an inadequate and piecemeal fashion by the government — where they were funded at all — and that Homes knew that ultimately they had to depend on their own resources. Institutions appeared to regard government subsidy more as a gift than an entitlement: that is, the institutions themselves seemed to agree with the state view that they were private enterprises that were only minimally responsible to government and not necessarily *entitled* to its support. The Salvation Army Boys' Home in Hobart, for example, notes in its 1956 annual report, its 'gratitude' to the state government for its 'unstinted support' of the recent construction of a new wing to the Home — to which the government had contributed somewhat less than half the total cost. The Launceston Girls' Home says, in 1956, 'we had no Government grant this year' — this implies that government support was not a predictable occurrence. This Home took the step of employing an appeal organiser to boost their finances, and 'an intensive canvass … realised the magnificent total of more than £1,000 — most of it promised as a renewable annual contribution'.[50]

The Clarendon Children's Home at Kingston, Tasmania, in its 1956 annual report, outlined just what it cost it to keep each child, and where that money came from. For each state ward they received £2 per week from the government, plus 10 shillings. Commonwealth child endowment, which was payable also for the children who were 'voluntary placements'. The parents of these latter children were also required to pay £2, but overall, payments for this group fell under the £2 mark — as there were parents who could not or would not pay — and so some children were wholly maintained by the Home. Since the average cost of maintaining each child was £4 per week, there was always a considerable shortfall to be met by voluntary contributions.

In New South Wales, as I have said, since the government avoided using the charitable sector to house state children, the state contributed nothing to the running of the charitable Homes.[51] The only government contribution to the charitable-sector NSW Homes, until 1960, came through the Commonwealth, in the form of child endowment. In Western Australia, the Department, in addition to a subsidy for each ward in an institution, also arranged for the Lotteries Commission to pay seven shillings and sixpence per week per child to the institution to assist with maintenance costs. Where the institution declined this assistance — presumably because of a religious prohibition against gambling — the government matched this amount. In Victoria, there was a long-running dispute — beginning in the 1920s — between the charitable Homes and the government about the rate of pay for accommodating state wards in charitable institutions: the charities found it increasingly inadequate.[52] As the Forde Report notes, lack of funding and resources is 'one of the most obvious causes' of systems abuse,[53] yet it was a feature of institutional care in all states.

How did Homes manage financially?

All Homes, across Australia, operated, to a greater or lesser extent, as charitable enterprises. Although a large Homes complex like Burnside had its own farm and hospital and was also well endowed, and Hopewood was subsidised by the sale of women's underwear, many Homes depended on charitable donations not only of money, but also of provisions. A NSW Department district officer commenting on the Burwood Church of England Boys' Home in 1950 noted that 'the Home depend[s] considerably on gifts for supply of fruit and green vegetables' but that biscuits were always plentiful, being donated by Arnott's. The file on Our Children's Home, which in late 1950 was investigated by the NSW Department for alleged neglect of the children, reveals a Home which was quite obviously under-resourced, judging by the meagre diet, the inadequate supply of clothing for the children and the generally very poor condition of the Home's premises and its lack of amenities. The superintendent, Mr Ardill, was most resentful of the implication that he was not doing the best for his charges — as perhaps he was, given the resources available. Some of the resentment here may well have been caused by the charitable sector's perception that while the Department did not fund non-state Homes at all, it nevertheless felt it had the right to criticise them.

Cheryl Hannaford, in the Protestant Federation Girls' Home in Sydney in the 1950s, remembered how at harvest festival time, 'we'd be dispensed to various churches to pick up whatever harvest produce was available and take it back to the Home to help stretch provisions'. The only meat they ever had on sandwiches was 'when the butcher donated a roll of Devon — I can't stand it to this day'. The ladies' auxiliary of the local Church of England church raised the money to support Cooinoo, but Margery Kendall said that some local businessmen also took an interest in the Home and helped out with necessities, and even gifts for the children. One supplied the children with a Christmas present, another 'was a bachelor and used to come regularly to the Home and bring gifts — sweets, biscuits and chocolates ... but he contributed a lot in other ways, with linen and things'.

Bunty Randall said that to keep her NSW Churches of Christ Home running, as well as the annual appeal 'a whole team of ladies from the various churches used to make up clothes, knit, sew, and do mending and repairs'. The Dalmar Homes, said Jim Fairmont, were required to be self-funding, and could not look to the Central Methodist Mission for financial support; this meant, he said, a lot of time spent on fundraising. The Methodist Church hierarchy — and here it was no different from the other churches — did not appear to regard the Home as a social investment; it was rather an enterprise that would not continue unless it could pay its way. It was the same for the Catholic Church. Berreen and Tyrell's 1975 study of the NSW Catholic Homes noted that in that year, private donations, bequests and fundraising appeals were the *major* source of income for most of these institutions, even an important factor in their survival, since the diocese itself rarely funded Homes. Homes with more 'emotional' appeal drew better public donations — those for babies attracted funds, those for 'delinquent' girls attracted none.

Coldrey (2003) claims that Catholic Homes were in general financially much worse off than Protestant and state Homes. The Catholic communities, he says, were in the main 'communities of poor people trying to provide educational and social services which paralleled those of the state' — and thus to keep Catholics firmly within their own faith community. The only possible means of doing this was to rely on what Coldrey describes as 'the unstinting work of the men and women in the religious congregations, supported by voluntary lay assistance'. It is not difficult to see that standards might be considered a luxury in this situation. In some Catholic Homes, children were drawn into the enterprise of adding to the finances of the Home. Susan Fitzgerald recalled how in her first year at St Joseph's Lane Cove, New South Wales, 1967, she was sat on the median strip at the traffic lights outside the Home to collect money, with a huge sign, saying 'I'm from St Joseph's'. Bernard Brady, in another St Joseph's, in Surrey Hills, Victoria, said:

> The only shame and humiliation of being an orphan was the reaction of people and other children in the 'outside world' when they saw us doing our Sunday walk with our escorting nun accepting donations from passersby and us boys hoping that instead of giving the nun money, that they would buy us all a penny ice-cream instead.

Brady was a repatriation (Commonwealth) ward, and pointed out that the war orphan pension paid for wards such as him 'must have been a boon', since it provided a supplement to 'the general orphanage funding pool'.

The Tasmanian Department attached to its own 1956 annual report several of the annual reports of the Tasmanian private institutions — as the charitable-sector Homes were called in that state — and these illuminate many of the standard features of the economy of Children's Homes. All such reports record appreciation for the members of the various committees which ensure that the Homes function — the auxiliary, the mothers' union, the ladies' guild, the gardens' committee, the building committee, and so on. Legacies and bequests are noted, as are the contributions of various community organisations, such as the Rotary and Apex Clubs. The Clarendon Children's Home noted how the Master Ladies Hairdressers' Guild had visited the Home at regular intervals to cut the children's hair. The Launceston Girls' Home and the Northern Tasmanian Home for Boys listed the benefactors who had helped with repairs and painting bees, and supplied, among other things, firewood, gravel, newspapers, clothing, material, pears and apples, potatoes, meat and wool — along with knitters who turned it into garments for the children. Stalls and button days were held, and in the early part of December 1955, Ampol donated one penny from the sale of every gallon of petrol, each penny matched by the company itself, in a Children's Appeal Week that it conducted across Australia.

Children's Homes also depended on benevolent outside interests to provide variety and entertainment for the children. Goffman notes how every institution could be described as 'a kind of dead sea in which little islands of vivid, encapturing activity appear'[54] — but only occasionally. For children in Homes these were the picnics and outings provided by community organisations such as the Lions or Rotary, or 'some sort of charity thing called Toc-H' described by Alice Nanson and Jilly Marsh, in different NSW Homes, through which 'old men would come round and show movies'. In her account of Cooinoo, Marigold Kendall remembered how the highlights of life in the Home were treats provided by the same businessmen who provided useful goods. At Christmas time a lot of community groups came to the Home and gave parties for the children, and a group called the 'Jolly Revellers' would take them out on a bus for an excursion. On 'cracker night' ('Empire Day', 24 May) one of the businessmen brought fireworks and they had a big bonfire. Goffman regards these infrequent highlights of the institutional year as yet another important 'deprivational effect' of total institutions, for they expose the tedium of life at other times. As Alice Nanson said:

> Suddenly Christmas would come and you'd go to parties at this charity and that, people in town gave you presents. There'd be nothing, a desert, then it was overwhelming. I remember thinking, why don't they do more during the year?

Parents' contribution to the support of their children in Homes

Where children were state wards, they were subsidised by government; where they were 'voluntary' placements, parents, or near relatives, were expected by management to pay for their children's care in Homes. Some parents presumably paid regularly, but payment did not always occur as a matter of course. Among my interviewees, some had little idea of the payment arrangements while others were quite clear. Margery Chandler's father paid 10 shillings a week at the Protestant Dr Bill Mackey Home in Sydney in the 1940s. Rosemary Bartlett's mother paid £10 a week for her three children, at Sydney's Dalwood Home,[55] in the early 1960s, but only when she could. At the Salvation Army Bexley Boys' Home in Sydney, parents were expected to pay £2 per child per week in 1964. The Arrears of Maintenance file that the Burnside Homes kept seems to indicate that parents' obligations were fairly closely monitored, but there were many Homes which perforce accepted that payment varied according to the parents' ability to pay, or that parents did not pay at all. As Kerry Geldard, in the Protestant Federation Girls' Home in Sydney from 1949 to 1957, related, her mother 'paid money for me each week based on her income, and this fluctuated according to whether she was in work or not'. I suspect this was the case for many parents.

Beryl Sawyer said of the Church of England Home where she worked before running the NSW government receiving 'depot' Bidura, that some children were there because their parents 'couldn't afford to keep them', and a lot of parents did not pay, although they would be asked to give donations. In Catholic Homes, where children often came from large families, non-payment was undoubtedly common. Child endowment was paid directly to institutions[56] and must sometimes have been the only payment received for some children. The Burnside files for the years 1951 to 1962 indicate that the fee charged by the Home quite often was paid out of a court order, that is, a maintenance order for the children. Where parents ended up listed in the Burnside Arrears of Maintenance files, it was because they were poor, or in circumstances that did not permit them to pay debts

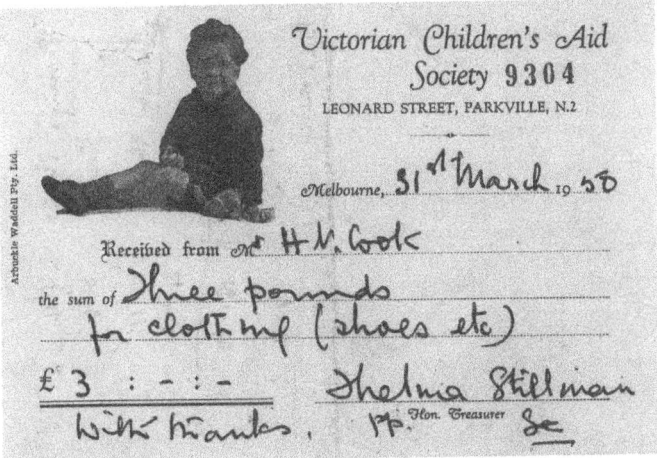

A parent's receipt for payment of his two boys' expenses in the Victorian Children's Aid Society Home in Parkville, Victoria. On the back of this receipt are recorded the items this amount covers: shoes at 24/11 and 23/11 (about $5, and slightly less) and socks at 5/6 and 4/6 (about $1, and slightly less).

— had become unemployed, for example. All such cases were pursued by an investigation officer, but the majority of the debts in the arrears file were written off.

Bette Formosa tells in her submission that as a condition of the children being accepted by Dalmar, the NSW Methodist Home, her mother had to retain financial responsibility for them by paying £5 per week; 'non-payment would be classified as abandonment', and Dalmar would then apply to have the children made wards of the state. 'This was my mother's greatest fear,' recalled Bette, and she witnessed over the following years:

> the many tears shed by my mother after coming out of the superintendent's office, several times being denied access to us children and being turned away from our fortnightly visits because she was unable to pay.

When this happened, the superintendent accused Bette's mother of being a liar, and of squandering her money on entertaining men and on wild parties. She was not 'a good moral person,' he said, 'let alone a good mother.' 'My child's heart was torn apart and broken,' concludes Bette, 'not only from our physical separation but to see my mother in such a powerless position.' This scenario was repeated numbers of times over the five years that Bette and her siblings lived there. The superintendent's attitude shows the prejudice against women on their own, but we can also see here the techniques employed by Homes to intimidate parents. Mim McKew, in Victoria, remembers a similar scenario, and how her mother's reaction to it increased the instability and uncertainty of her children's lives:

> A 'Fee for Care' was required to be paid by mother regularly to the institutions for our food, board & living expenses. Unfortunately, that didn't happen very often and mother was always arguing with the authorities. When the authorities threatened to take the matter to the

courts to force mother to hand us over to the state, she
would promptly pack us up out of there and hide out for
a while. When she managed to find another institution,
or sort out the problem with the previous one, she would
promptly dump us back.

The Homes that were run by religious organisations were part of their church's pastoral mission, and if parents could not pay, the church or charity assumed this obligation. The price was in fact paid by the children, in the type of status that this bestowed on them. And not only in religious Homes. My mother, also, often owed my Home for our maintenance. In fact from what I remember, she was always behind. It was during one of these crises perhaps that the carer offered to dispense with payment for me, which increased enormously the price that I paid for my existence there. What actually happened was that my mother ended up paying half-price for both her daughters, but it was described to me as a further reason for my gratitude — now they were looking after me for free.

Children as objects of charity

It is not difficult to see why children cared for within this ideology of charitable benevolence were regarded as fortunate to be cared for, rather than entitled to care as highly vulnerable, emotionally and socially disadvantaged, members of society. The only response permitted to the recipient of charity was, as it always has been, gratitude; indeed the child is required to be 'eternally grateful'. Children in Homes were 'charity cases', the offspring of families who were 'failures' or worse — otherwise, why would their children be in Homes? In exchange for their care — and undoubtedly, a great many people did give their time, labour and money — children were required to give up their attachment to parents, family and family identity and, above all, their feelings about losing them. If they were well cared for physically, they had no right to be other than happy and 'good'. Where children were 'lucky' enough to live in beautiful surroundings, the obligation of gratitude was increased. My Home was on the waterfront in Sydney and I was often told how fortunate I was to live in such a lovely spot — one which I now cannot bear to visit.

Sylvia Baker, after an emotional interview with me which conveyed poignantly the extreme desolation of her Home childhood, suddenly said, towards the end of the interview: 'Saying all this now, you feel so ungrateful — they tried to do their best.' The belief that good physical care is the single most important marker of a 'good' childhood is a powerful one, especially when it is internalised at such an impressionable and vulnerable time as early childhood. It also feeds into the already poor self-image of children who feel abandoned and valueless. This is a significant contributing factor to the difficulty of speaking out about the reality of the Home experience.

Charity always confers a stigmatised identity, and it made us invisible as anything other than objects of somebody else's 'goodness'. The inability to comprehend any other view of the situation can be seen in this report on a Home by a state child welfare inspector in Queensland to his Department:

> These children in —— are members of an extremely happy family and it can safely be said that they have far more enjoyment than any other child in their own home and although State children are placed in employment and as foster children in excellent homes, they could never be as well off or feel as happy as those accommodated at ——.[57]

The 1999 Forde Inquiry into the abuse of children in Queensland institutions identified certain risk factors for institutional abuse. These occur in the context of a discussion of a particular institution, the Petford Training Farm, but the factors existed in many, if not most Homes of this period. They are:

- geographical isolation;
- absence of proper human resource management in addition to high staff turnover;
- absence of attention to basic management and accountability;
- a lack of adherence to practice standards;
- inadequate monitoring mechanisms; and
- poor physical facilities.[58]

I would add to this list as a risk factor the charitable status of Children's Homes, and the fact that the children living in them were regarded as objects of charity. This was one of the major reasons that Children's Homes were so dangerous to the wellbeing of children. In presenting the 1956 annual report of the NSW Department, the Minister for Child Welfare & Social Welfare, FH Hawkins, made the following fulsome tribute to the voluntary sector:

> I thank individually and collectively the many church and other organisations for the co-operation and assistance they render to my Department in an honorary capacity. Throughout this State, thousands of excellent citizens, in many varied organisations, are doing outstanding work without thought of payment, for the benefit of the community ... Those who assist in this noble honorary work have a wide scope for their efforts, and the knowledge that everything they do to make better citizens of the less fortunate of our children is a valuable contribution towards the improvement of our society and our democratic and Christian way of life.

All the factors that made institutional care such a high-risk environment for children are here. And within this view of the operation of Homes, there is absolutely no possibility of either transparency or accountability. Excellent citizens doing noble, honorary and outstanding work without thought of payment for the benefit of the community, that is, labouring selflessly to make better citizens of the less fortunate of our children, are above criticism. This is even more the case when their valuable contribution aids in the *improvement of our society* — this last is particularly worrying, since it implies that without this effort, these children will have a detrimental effect on society. And all of this within a Christian ideology which, within such an unequal power relationship, could be horribly distorted, as we have seen, to rationalise the most palpable cruelty.

Chapter 5

'The Welfare': what happened when the state got involved?

When I look back over my chequered life I don't blame any individuals for any misery caused, but the welfare system itself was very hard on kids and on parents too.

Joy Hill, NSW state ward 1944–61

I have one thing to say after I read my welfare file — that is, being a ward of the state was a cruel joke and my guardians ought to be charged with gross neglect of their duties for I was never protected, and in fact was placed in danger.

Rachel Anne Smith, who was in state 'training' Homes in NSW and Victoria in the early 1960s

I spent 8 years of my life as a ward of the state and quite honestly I can't imagine how you can fix that.

Kerry Snell[1]

In the previous chapter I related what happened when families themselves had to place their children in a Home. What happened when the state stepped in, or parents had to call on 'the Welfare' for help? The short answer is that in all states except New South Wales, children ended up in the same institutions into which parents 'voluntarily' placed their children.

When the state removed 'neglected' children from their parents and made them state wards, it processed them through a state receiving Home or 'depot' and then, except in New South Wales, placed most of them in one of the Homes run by the charitable sector. Some children were fostered: the percentage was small in every state except New South Wales. In that state, children taken into state care were more likely to be fostered than institutionalised, but if they 'failed' at fostering, or were considered unsuitable from the outset, they would be placed in a state institution, known as an 'establishment'. The number of institutions run by the government varied from state to state, but all states had one or more receiving Homes as well as one or more 'training' schools, which were for the 'reform' of 'delinquent' children and young people.

My interest, and the focus of my discussion here, is in the attitudes underpinning the way statutory 'child welfare' was conceived and carried out. What follows is a very general sketch of the child welfare 'system' across Australia in the period in which institutional care was the norm — it is here in order to give a statutory context to that care. To call it a system is in fact misleading — child welfare was a state responsibility and every state had its own legislation and its own policies and practices. However, apart from the occasional significant variation in practice, such as the high rate of foster care in New South Wales, there was not a great deal of difference between the states in attitude, policy or legislation.[2]

In their 1981 survey of Australian child welfare, authors Cliff

Picton and Peter Boss observe that in Australia, child welfare services developed 'pragmatically, piecemeal, erratically':

> [In the 19th century,] Australian governments were never particularly enthusiastic about becoming unduly involved in child welfare ... They were far more in favour of leaving such matters to the care of private charitable organisations.[3]

This attitude continued well into the 20th century — state governments left the charitable sector more or less alone to do the work of institutional care. It was only in New South Wales that this attitude existed alongside its opposite: a system of statutory care characterised by extremely interventionist practices. There is a passage in the WA government's submission to the Senate Inquiry which I think could be generalised to all states. Reflecting on attitudes to child welfare, the submission quotes the 1979 annual report of the Department:

> A basic theme for government officials and legislators has been that the care of children should be left in the hands of ordinary citizens and religious bodies, with the minimum of government interference. The government has provided subsidies of various kinds, and has gradually been called on to increase its regulatory activity as the State has developed. The fear that too much government meddling would lead to a regimentation against the best interests of the children has kept the activities of the public servants concerned in the background, a position they still prefer to maintain.

It is clear from the annual reports of child welfare Departments that where the state did get involved, it was a reluctant parent, concerned more with balancing the budget than with children's welfare. The Forde Report notes that Queensland Departmental officers routinely tried to dissuade parents from making their children state wards, 'more, it would seem, from concern about the financial burden placed on the State than from any belief in the value of the family':[4] in the Queensland Department's 1956 annual report, the director observed that the Department 'has to cope with the problem of selfish parents who wish to pass the responsibility of caring for their children to the State'. Officers of the Department, he says, 'spend not a little time in endeavouring to sort out the genuine cases'.

State governments everywhere expected the parents of state wards to contribute towards their children's maintenance in state care — even where the state had removed the children. Maintenance and custody, then as now, did not necessarily go together. The Northern Territory's 1958–60 Child Welfare Ordinance spells out these obligations very clearly: the near relatives of a child, it states, 'are liable to pay for or to contribute towards the maintenance of a State child in accordance with their ability'. Near relatives were then listed in a hierarchy of responsibility — the father, the mother, the stepfather and the stepmother — each becoming liable if the one before was unable to pay or reneged on their obligation. Non-payers could be summonsed before a court by the Director of Child Welfare and forced to pay; penalties for non-compliance were not specified. There are similar obligations spelled out in the legislation of other states or in Departments' annual reports. The Tasmanian government, according to the Department's 1956 annual report, expected parents or near relatives to contribute, where possible, to the maintenance of wards *wherever* they had been placed — in Departmental institutions, foster care, or charitable institutions. In Queensland in 1956 the state collected just over £21,000 for this purpose from parents. It made 'every effort to locate defaulting debtors and compel them, if necessary, by Court action to maintain their offspring', and the Department's annual report expressed surprise at 'the number who desert their children entirely'.

'Welfare' attitudes towards children in need of care

> Deprived children, whether in their own homes or out of them, are a source of social infection as real and serious as are carriers of diphtheria and typhoid.
>
> RJ Heffron,
> NSW Deputy Premier, Minister for Education, 1956

One of the most paradoxical aspects of child welfare in this era is the contrast between the stated and published beliefs of state governments and the way children were actually treated. This is not just the gap that occurs when coalface workers lack the necessary training, skills or empathy to carry out the policies their organisation promotes. This is a gaping discrepancy between what was said in policy statements and what was done by workers *because it was the usual practice*. Five minutes listening to the history of any state ward in any state — or reading their submissions to the Senate Inquiry — is enough to show a contrast so huge as to totally discredit the Department concerned. As one submission to the Inquiry baldly expressed it: 'If I was sent there for my own good, then why did they treat me so bad?'[5]

Annual reports of all state Departments in this period speak with apparent compassion for the children who come under their care. The Queensland Department's 1956 annual report, for example, lists among its functions to 'protect young life' and 'particularly to see that children of tender years are not permitted to be placed in undesirable and unsavoury surroundings'. It is difficult, however, to imagine more 'undesirable and unsavoury surroundings' than some of the institutions described by their inmates to the Forde Inquiry of 1999 and the Senate Inquiry of 2003–04. Similarly, the young girls who were sent to the NSW Training School for Girls, Parramatta (see below), because they were judged to be 'in moral danger', were placed into much more dangerous surroundings than they were ever likely to encounter outside the walls of that institution. The actual experiences of children in care in the institutional era suggest that all state governments were in breach of their own child welfare Acts on many levels, and particularly with regard to punishment (see *Forgotten Australians*, Appendix IV, for extracts from the relevant Acts in several states which demonstrate this conclusively).

A further discrepancy can be seen in the way that Departments often spoke of the superiority of fostering, and yet left the majority of state children in institutional care. This is not to say that children who were fostered necessarily had better care experiences than children in institutions. The point is that other governments (as well as New South Wales) asserted the superiority of foster care, yet did little to ensure that it was a real alternative to institutional care. And the Victorian government, at least, was well aware of the deficiencies of institutionalisation: this is what it said about its recently established Family Group Homes in its 1956–57 annual report:

> Reference has been made to the importance of children being placed, where possible, where they will share in the common life of a small group of people in a homely environment. Many of the Department's wards are members of families ... Having suffered emotionally by removal from their parents by court order, it is supremely important that they do not suffer again by being separated from one another.

Yet even by 1964 these Family Group Homes accommodated a mere 96 children; 3755 other children were still living in non-government Children's Homes, large-scale institutions with a far from 'homely environment', where siblings were not housed together.[6]

The status of 'Welfare' children

How do we explain this discrepancy? There are obviously no simple answers, but some factors do suggest themselves. First, there are the beliefs about and attitudes to children generally, which I described in Chapter 2; in the 'care' domain, unmediated by kinship ties or love, these took on a particularly punitive expression. Another is the judgmental view of such children and their families that I referred to in the previous chapter; this conferred a particularly suspect status on children who came to the attention of 'the Welfare'. In Chapter 1, I quoted Kate Gaffney's statement in her submission to the Inquiry: 'to say that a child should be treated differently on the basis of his or her parents or socio-economic circumstances at birth should be abhorrent'. This is a contemporary view. In the decades covered by this work, it was considered not just acceptable, but appropriate, to treat some children as second-class citizens. State wards experienced it as a part of daily life:

> I remember being disappointed to hear the woman telling everyone outside church how 'she [I] was a ward of the state who needed discipline, she wasn't very bright but what could you expect when who knows who or where she came from'.
>
> Caroline Carroll, NSW state ward, in 1961, aged eight

Barry Coldrey has observed that when institutions for children were originally established, 'their first priority was not the welfare of children, though this was important to some, but the protection of respectable society from the depredations of certain classes of children'.[7] This perception of the children of the poor or unfortunate as a potential threat persisted well into the 20th century. There is little to distinguish attitudes to the children who became state wards in the 20th century from attitudes to the visibly disadvantaged children ('street arabs') of 19th-century cities who were the focus of the 'child rescue' movement, where the objective was to reclaim such children from the streets and turn them into useful members of society. Donella Jaggs, the historian of Victoria's child welfare legislation, notes that the Juvenile Delinquency Advisory Committee, which was set up in 1955 in Victoria to advise government on an appropriate response to what was regarded as an increasingly pressing social problem, 'offered a definition of juvenile delinquency virtually identical with the categories of "dangerous" and perishing" classes proposed by Mary Carpenter a century earlier'.[8] Carpenter, one of the leaders of the 19th century 'child rescue' movement in Britain, had categorised children in 'need' of reclamation as 'dangerous' (actually living by criminal activity) or 'perishing' (without criminal conviction, but living in circumstances in which they might fall into crime 'if a helping hand be not extended to raise them').[9] This helping hand was usually an institution: reformatories for the 'dangerous', industrial schools for the 'perishing'.

This attitude underpinned all state child welfare interventions of the institutional era, whether they focused on children who simply lacked (or appeared to lack) adequate parental care, or children who had actually committed some crime. Just as it was in the previous century, the line between 'neglected' and 'delinquent', 'deprived' and 'depraved', was one that was easily blurred, in the way that Kerry Carrington in her 1993 study of 'offending girls' in New South Wales in the late 1970s, describes. Carrington's study shows that all children who came before the courts were homogenised 'into a unitary category of maladjusted youth in need of prescribed treatment of one kind or another'. Within such a discourse, she says, 'the delinquent and neglected child are symptomatic of the same problem — a dysfunctional family which has failed to adequately rear, care and educate their offspring'.[10] So a century after Mary Carpenter, we find in the Victorian Department's 1956 annual report the following statement:

> Popular textbooks may divide children into categories and label them 'dependent', 'underprivileged', 'delinquent', but the line of demarcation becomes very blurred to the worker in the field. To that person the delinquent is just as under-privileged as the neglected child, and in both cases he feels it is a challenge he must accept to remedy the deficiency in the child's life.

Most boys and girls who are committed to care for 'living under conditions as indicate that the child or young person is lapsing or likely to lapse into a career of vice or crime', says the report, 'are delinquents in the same sense as those dealt with and committed to the department by the courts on precise offences'. No supporting evidence is offered for this statement. That children were simply unfortunate enough to have parents unable to look after them appeared to be forgotten once they were gathered into the state welfare system. This goes some way to explaining the punitive practices of the states' child welfare Departments — and also, I think, the punitive environment of children's institutions generally. It also explains the fact that, certainly in New South Wales, 'delinquents' and children who had committed no crime but who were regarded as 'uncontrollable' were accommodated together in the same institutions, even though this contravened the state's legislation and stated policy.[11]

'Neglect'

This set of beliefs underpins the definition of 'neglect' via which the majority of children were removed into state care. Definitions of neglect in all state child welfare jurisdictions of this era were both stringent and broad — they included standards for parental and for children's behaviour. The definition changes little from state to state, either in language or in the spectrum of behaviours it covers, over the years up to and often including the 1970s.

Some of the provisions are obvious and appropriate. Children are neglected if they are 'ill-treated or exposed' and without proper food, clothing or lodging or are destitute. Several submissions to the Senate Inquiry give vivid descriptions of children living in such conditions before the state stepped in. Other definitions reflect contemporary mores. Children are neglected if they are living in or associated with brothels, with thieves or 'common prostitutes', even if these people are their parents (which presumably means that a prostitute could be charged with neglect of her child by reason of her profession), or are in contact with opium smoking, or if they are tattooed without permission of a parent or guardian.

Other definitions are so vague as to allow intervention solely on the grounds of an unfavourable assessment of the family by a Departmental officer. The point here is not whether or not that happened, but that it could. A child was neglected, for example, when one parent was drunk, dead, insane, in prison or otherwise not exercising care of the child and the other parent was 'a drunkard'; or when the child was, in the opinion of the court, under incompetent or improper guardianship; or when the child's parents — or one parent if the other was missing or 'a drunkard' — were unfit to retain a child or young person in their care.

In the Northern Territory, children were neglected if they associated with persons who had been convicted of vagrancy or were 'known to the police as of bad repute'. In Queensland, if they were 'likely to fall into a life of vice or crime' (in ways not specified), or if they were 'without lawful excuse in a betting shop or billiards room'. In New South Wales, if found to be suffering from venereal disease — interesting in an era when 'sexual abuse' had not yet been identified as a category of offence against children.

The majority of these latter descriptions are subjective — 'lapsing or likely to lapse into a career of vice or crime', 'falling into bad associations', 'exposed to moral danger', under 'incompetent guardianship' or having a parent 'unfit to retain the child in their care' — but are embodied in law as if they need no explanation. Add to these the other charge that could be levelled at children, that of being 'uncontrollable', and you have a very wide discretion for intervention by the state. Here is section 29 of the *Child Welfare Act 1947* (WA):

> [A]ny officer of the Department authorised by the Minister and any police officer may, without warrant apprehend any child *appearing or suspected to be a destitute or neglected or incorrigible or uncontrollable child.*
> (emphasis added)

The Northern Territory Child Welfare Ordinance 1958–1960, section 31, repeats this almost word for word, a reminder that there was little difference across states and territories in how children in this situation were regarded. The term 'uncontrollable' is never defined in any of the Acts. Where a power relationship is not equal, as between an adult and a child, a vague definition in a context such as this one means that fair dealing depends disproportionately on the goodwill of the party with the power — on the person who could, alternatively, exploit this inequality for his or her own ends. A child who began to 'act out' by becoming aggressive or defiant, or who ran away from home or truanted from school, for example, could be labelled 'uncontrollable' and sent to an institution for 'retraining'. That there could be a child's perspective on this was inconceivable. It's likely that a majority of the girls who ended up in the NSW Training School for Girls at Parramatta, or in Victoria's Winlaton training school, came from family situations of sexual abuse, incest or domestic violence. When they ran away or otherwise expressed their despair, they were stigmatised as sexually promiscuous (why else would they be on the streets?) and charged with being 'in moral danger'; this then became the rationale for their incarceration.

It is important to remember that, as legal academic Richard Chisholm notes, the child welfare system is a vital factor not only in our *response* to problems such as poverty, unemployment, lack of family support services and so on, but also in our *definition* of them. The 'individualising tendency of the law', he says, may well obscure these broader aspects of the situation in its focus on the victim as the problem.[12] This is precisely what happened under child welfare legislation throughout this era.

The child alone as the target for intervention

In her 1975 analysis of Australian child welfare legislation, social analyst Lynne Foreman points out a very significant aspect of child welfare practice throughout the institutional era: where families did not conform to community standards, the children of the family would be the target for the state's intervention. Foreman suggests the following reasoning for this:

> The child is part of a family unit which ought to have been organised to protect itself and its members, and if it fails in the fulfilment of this objective then state intervention is justified to remove the child from the prevailing circumstances.[13]

Even in 1975, only South Australia had rewritten its legislation to conceptualise children as belonging within families and communities (*Community Welfare Act 1972* (SA)). When families broke down, the state paid little attention to the mix of family, social and economic circumstances that shaped the family's, and thus the children's, life. And once children were isolated from their family circumstances, they were dealt with as if their families were unimportant: here is a child of problem parents who will also become a problem without appropriate intervention, and since the parents are a problem, the child is better off without them.

It was always children themselves who were charged with neglect. Whatever the reason for this — it has been suggested to me that it was to accommodate the fact that parents were not always around to be charged — the effect on children was nothing short of terrifying. Mavis Devereaux-Dingwall, forcibly removed from her family home in Sydney in 1943 by police acting for the NSW Department, remembered the series of events clearly:

> After suffering the early morning trauma of being dragged away from my family, I was taken before the court, standing beside my brothers with the escort of police. We were charged with what? I can remember thinking, what have we done wrong? I looked at my mother, who was in tears, my grandfather with his head in his hands.

Children were of course deemed incompetent to participate in their own affairs. But, as Foreman says, the legislation extended this attitude to their parents, who were barred from participation and decision-making with respect to their own children.[14] The definition of 'neglect' in every child welfare Act of the period implicitly contains within it the exit papers for a child's family. Foreman (writing in 1975) makes the important point that 'it is difficult to discover from existing legislation just what the legal rights of children and parents are'.[15] How parents were to go about getting their children returned, for example, is not spelled out. Care leavers who obtain their files may discover what Lorraine Rodgers did — that her mother had tried to bring her children home from the Ballarat Orphanage 'but the Welfare refused her', with no explanation given.

When it came to carrying out their policies, Departments seemed untroubled by any doubts about their practices. The NSW Department's in-house literature, for example, demonstrates an apparently unassailable confidence in its district officers — even where their practice had no basis in law, as this extract from a 1972 NSW Department document quite explicitly states. Here is Alice Miller's 'poisonous pedagogy' (see Chapter 2) writ large:

> It is of interest that the District Officer has no statutory authority to undertake preventive work. There is no legislative provision giving him the right to enter such homes without a warrant, or to enforce the parent's compliance with his instructions regarding the improved care of the children. His statutory authority begins at the point where preventative work would seem to end — with the power to remove the child and take them before a Court as neglected ... but this power combined with casework techniques is all an experienced officer needs.
>
> The old argument that the authoritarian and the casework role are mutually exclusive is increasingly discredited among social workers generally. For the District Officer it never existed. Although in most situations legal authority is not required, the authoritarian approach, skilfully timed and handled, can on occasions be a most effective casework tool. The threat of removing the children may be the only means to motivate parents ... and where this fails, the actual removal of the child may provide the motivating force. This is shock treatment, but it can have dramatic results.[16]

This is the rationale for the traumatic events related in so many care leaver histories, where 'the Welfare' behaved in just the manner described above (see Lin's story, at the end of this section).

Poor care for 'poor' children

These are obviously children not worth a great deal of investment. One famous Australian put it this way:

> ... to say that the industrious and intelligent son of self-sacrificing and saving and forward-looking parents has the same social desserts and even material needs as the dull offspring of stupid and improvident parents is absurd.[17]

This is Sir Robert Menzies, Australian Prime Minister 1949–66, expressing in his 1942 'Forgotten People' speech views that presumably had popular appeal. Lack of intelligence and poverty are self-evidently linked, and there is no acknowledgment that people's lives are shaped by complex social and economic factors that are outside their control, or by misfortune. The child welfare literature of this period is littered with similar language. When state wards see their Departmental files they are often shocked by the judgmental statements they read in them about themselves and their family.

Services provided for children in the 19th century originated, as Picton and Boss observe, in 'highly moralistic and residualist notions of welfare'.[18] Attitudes such as those exemplified in Menzies' speech ensured that this description could be applied equally to care provision in the 20th century. 'Poor care for poor children' is another way of describing it, with the second 'poor' carrying the connotation 'poor value' as well as 'poverty', but with the other meaning of 'poor' — unfortunate — completely eclipsed. Peter Quinn, who worked for the NSW Department for over 40 years, told the Senate Inquiry that in New South Wales, 'the priority for both politicians and officials was not the wellbeing of children but cost cutting and economy',[19] and that this was partly because such children were regarded as being from a 'delinquent class', and 'not worth spending money on'. The continued existence of institutional care long after it was known to be damaging to children was also evidence of this, he said. Indeed, the head of social work training at Sydney University, Norma Parker, whom I quoted in the previous chapter, deplored — in 1957 — the fact that 'Australia still seems to have a great deal of confidence in the institutional method of caring for children in need.'[20]

Whatever the rhetoric of government policy statements, the actual practice of child welfare, for a large part of the 20th century, appeared to reflect a conviction that children 'of this type' were not worth investing in. Institutional care was cheap, especially when it was done by charities and churches, and it was good enough for these children.

The NSW Child Welfare Department

I referred above to the belief held by governments, and described in the WA submission to the Inquiry, that the care of children should involve 'the minimum of government interference', although government intervention certainly occurred where there was no alternative. New South Wales is the one state where this attitude existed alongside highly interventionist practices. 'Minimum government interference' was applied to institutional care conducted 'privately' by the charitable sector, even though, as I said previously (see Chapter 4), the charitable sector cared for a similar number of children as were in state care. It was a very different story when children became state wards. New South Wales makes an interesting study because the ways in which it was different from other states show just how systemically abusive — of both children and their families — state child welfare practice could be.

The Minister for Child Welfare & Social Welfare, FH Hawkins, boasted in 1959[21] that 'the work of the New South Wales

Department is quoted as an example in the field of child care not only in Australia but also abroad'. The Department particularly prided itself on the fact that in contrast to all other states, it fostered out the majority of its state wards — approximately three-quarters of the total. In 1956, for example, 76 per cent of NSW state wards were in foster care; this figure is typical over a long period. Compare this with the 1965 Queensland figure of 11 per cent, or with Victoria, which in 1963 had only 23 per cent of its wards in foster care. Even as late as 1976, 45 per cent of Victoria's almost 6000 state wards were still in institutions run by the private sector. This figure was only topped by Western Australia, which, in this same year, housed 60 per cent of its state wards in institutional care.[22]

Hendrick, the historian of British child welfare, notes how in the postwar democracies, the 'properly functioning family' was regarded as a 'therapeutic agent, the perfect environment for the healthy development of children'.[23] Rhetoric about the importance of 'the family' is common in the NSW Department's literature in the immediate postwar decades — here is its 1958 Field Manual for new recruits:

> The child is the product of the family and all the diverse schools of psychology agree that the family is one of the most effective of the influences that mould a child's life, for good or bad. They are unanimous that a good home is the most precious of jewels.[24]

Every effort is made, says the Department's 1956 annual report, to keep children in their own family. Where that is not possible, however, 'the best approximation under the circumstances is a foster home, and every endeavour is made to place each suitable child with foster parents'. The actual practice of fostering through the Department, however, showed the same indifference to children's feelings and kinship ties as did institutionalised care, so it was a matter of good luck rather than good practice if children matched well with the foster carers they were assigned to, and had good experiences with them. Despite the appeal to psychological knowledge, with its pseudo-scientific ring of authority, what is operating here is an idealised and conservative notion of 'the family' — 'family' is important only if it is the 'right' family. This automatically eliminated children's own birth family, already evaluated as deficient.

Family is not conceived of as a set of personal relationships involving emotional and kinship ties, in which children themselves have a subjective investment. It is more like a culture that, if correct, will grow the correct product. Care leaver histories show that children who were fostered through the NSW Department stood a very good chance of losing their birth families, sometimes forever. In the 1960 article by the Director of NSW Child Welfare, RH Hicks, which I quoted previously, Hicks said:

> Because children come into the care of private agencies almost entirely by means of applications made by or on behalf of their parents or guardians who pay for their maintenance, *the wishes of these people must thereafter be taken into account.* Because many of them wish to visit the children frequently, conveniently and at regular intervals, the institution has obvious advantages over the foster home.[25] (emphasis added)

It does not seem to occur to Hicks, or to other welfare authorities, that state intervention could be done differently, that the wishes of parents could be taken into account *even where the state had intervened*. That is a concept that belongs to a later period. It is obvious from Hicks's statement that parents of children in state care (such as foster care) may *not* 'visit their children frequently, conveniently and at regular intervals'.

Given its attitude to institutionalisation for children, it is an interesting paradox that New South Wales had by far the greatest number of state-run institutions, 30 in all, including 'an extensive system of Homes for the training of wayward children'[26] — 11 of these in all. The largest number of government Homes in any other state is six in South Australia, and one of those was conducted by a Roman Catholic order under state supervision. New South Wales had, to borrow Foucault's term, a highly evolved 'disciplinary apparatus'. The reason for this large number of Homes was the 'need' to cater for children who did not respond to, or were not initially considered eligible for, fostering, and who were then labelled according to specific categories of deficiency, and on that basis allocated to appropriate Homes, known as 'establishments'. In other states, these children might have been sent to charitable Homes when their foster placement broke down, but as I have noted, New South Wales avoided this as much as possible. This was perhaps not merely to distance itself from the charitable sector; it may also have been to further a particular agenda. As Hicks says in the same article:

> It should be remembered that wards are a selected segment of the juvenile population with a heavy bias towards emotional instability, mental retardation and inadequacies of character, the consequences of defective home environment in early childhood.[27]

The Department's 'establishments' provided different types of 'service', tailored to help their inmates remedy their 'inadequacies of character' and thus qualify for foster care — 'in many cases a period of treatment or training will remove obstacles to placement', one in-house field manual explained.[28] What we are seeing here is how newer, psychologically informed ideas melded with an older, entrenched set of beliefs about what children 'need', to create a system which was inherently oppressive of children. This is 'scientific' child welfare practice, grafted onto what Robert van Krieken describes, in his 1997 study of the NSW Department, as essentially a 19th-century view of human nature.[29] The NSW Department's literature in this period is a curious mix of psychological jargon and the fundamentalist, judgmental attitudes of 19th century individualism. In a 1966 Departmental publication called *Child Welfare in New South Wales*, the author discusses the first orphanage in Australia (founded by Governor King in 1800):

> Its purpose was to remove young girls 'from the vicious examples of their abandoned parents', and this concept of providing an asylum from vice and destitution was to pervade child welfare thinking for the next sixty years.

Sixty years takes us only up to 1860. Yet, although the language changes, this type of thinking appears to be alive and well in the attitudes and the practices of the Department well over a hundred years *after* 1860. The 1966 publication itself contains the following statements:

> Pre-disposing factors in delinquency are numerous. Unhealthy, weak and unrewarding relations with parents, inadequate moral teaching and poor example within the home ... all are factors leading to a drift into crime.

And the Victorian 'fallen woman' is vividly present in the following statement:

> While male delinquency is essentially crime, it would be unrealistic to regard 'female delinquency' as crime only ... the Department regards female delinquency as crime plus 'moral delinquency', the main component of the latter being sexual promiscuity, which is usually associated with general waywardness and irresponsibility.

As van Krieken points out, NSW Departmental thinking involved 'profoundly unscientific concepts like "goodness", "health", "cleanliness" and "pollution"',[30] so 'despite the lip service being paid to modernity and science, a major feature of the role of science, psychological or social, in child welfare was its minimal impact'.[31] However, although it is obvious, I think, that as van Krieken says, new ideas made little real impression on the thinking of the Department, the appeal to 'modernity' and 'science' did give it tools to oppress children even more effectively. The NSW Department ran a psychological counselling service, for example, but its purpose, as described in the 1966 manual, was to assess the personality and test the intelligence of state wards — not to give workers an insight into their family circumstances, social situation or emotional state. The purpose of the psychologist's report, says the manual, is to assist the institution 'to commence effective training immediately'. Although van Krieken's study finishes in 1940, it is obvious from care leavers' experiences that his observations about this Department apply equally to the decades following World War II. Indeed, the 1939 NSW Child Welfare Act — already little different from the 1923 Act — continued to serve the Department until 1987. Although it was substantially amended over this period, it was not rewritten to reflect a different philosophical approach.

If we put it in basic terms, we could say that in New South Wales, 'good' children were fostered, and 'difficult' children, the ones covered by Hicks's description above, were placed in state institutions, with institutional care becoming progressively more punitive as children became more 'wayward', 'uncontrollable' and 'delinquent' (or, from another perspective, more neglected and abused by the welfare system). A primary school-aged girl, for example, who was taken into care as 'neglected' would be sent first to the 'depot', Bidura, for processing and a court appearance, and then to a foster placement. If this did not work out, she might go back and forth between Bidura and further placements until she was sent to the King Edward Home in Newcastle (described in annual reports as a 'Home for girls who are considered to require some training to fit them for foster home placement'). If she did not 'adapt', or was 'insubordinate' or 'wayward' or ran away, she could graduate to Lynwood Hall, where girls received 'the kind of training which can only be given in a residential school'. If she ran away from the grim regime of Daphne Davies, the superintendent (see Chapter 4), she might be picked up and charged with being 'in moral danger' and the next stop would be the Training School for Girls at Parramatta, for the rehabilitation of female juvenile offenders, and, finally, as a last resort (from 1961) to the Institution for Girls, a closed juvenile prison at Hay in rural New South Wales. There was a similarly graduated chain of institutional correction for boys, culminating also in a closed juvenile prison, the Institution for Boys at Tamworth. Both the Hay and Tamworth institutions were located within former colonial gaols (see below).

Alternatively, as David Forbes' eloquent submission shows, a child could end up in an institution for 'subnormal' children, having 'failed' in all his previous ward Homes until he earned the label 'mentally defective'. David's 'failure' stemmed from his unremitting sexual abuse at the hands of his state 'carers'. Similarly, one of the most reflective of my interviewees, Marion Tucker, was in Brush Farm, a Home for 'subnormal' girls. She was placed there in response to her disruptive behaviour when she discovered at age nine that she was not really the child of the foster family who had cared for her from birth. Marion, once made a state ward, was processed through the Department's testing department — 'to see if I was all right in the head'. Her IQ results allocated her to Brush Farm. 'I was an odd jigsaw piece that didn't fit in any puzzle,' she said. The unexamined underlying belief operating here was characteristic of the period: when children do not behave as required, the reason lies either in their deficient character (similar to their parents') or in their intellectual capacity — but never in their circumstances.

New South Wales had three Homes for 'subnormal' children along with a 'special school' for truants — Anglewood, in rural New South Wales — as part of a highly bureaucratised system catering for all possible gradations of children's behaviour. This is the state that did not believe in institutional care and so did not fund charitable organisations to provide it. Its own institutions were rationalised within a different discourse: they offered specialised attention to the 'needs' of children handicapped in the ways that Hicks outlined. What the Department claimed to be doing *for* children in these institutions and what was actually done *to* them bore little relationship to each other. This is clearly demonstrated in the submission to the Inquiry by Lin, a NSW state ward whose story begins in 1968.

Lin's story

When 'the Welfare' got involved in Lin's family, her mother was raising her seven children alone; the children's father had deserted the family a year before. Her mother worked three jobs to support the family, which meant that Lin's older brother, aged 12, and oldest sister, aged 11, became the carers of the other children. One day in 1968 when her mother was at work, officers of the Department came to the house in Sydney and told the frightened children that they had to go with them. Lin was then aged nine. The children were taken to the state receiving depots in inner-city Glebe and separated — the girls went to Bidura, the two boys to Royleston. Lin and her sisters, after a court appearance, were made state wards. All this time, the children did not know where their mother was or when she would come to get them. 'Months turned into years before I would see her again,' said Lin. Her five-year-old sister went to foster parents, where she remained until she left their home as an adult. Lin's older sister left Bidura but

Lin has no idea where she went. She also has no idea what happened to her youngest brother, then only two years old. Lin's own experiences were of a series of state 'establishments'. She remained at Bidura until she was 11, when she was sent to one of the ward Homes at Mittagong, south of Sydney, and finally to Lynwood Hall. Lin's submission contains a series of questions which anybody reading it can only echo: 'Why was it done that way? Who was running these places in this way?'

> Why? Why? Why didn't anyone in the child welfare department ever feel that it would benefit these children if they knew why they were where they were? And for what reason.

All of this was made worse by the environments Lin found herself in. At Bidura, the 30 girls in the dormitory were locked in at night with night watchmen who offered them cigarettes in return for sexual favours. 'The place we were placed in for protection,' says Lin, 'was the most dangerous for any young girl':

> I remember night after night lying in my bed crying and wishing that I could see my mother, brother and sisters. Just anybody that could get me out of this scary place.

There was no sense of security possible, she says, because you didn't know from one day to the next where you would be, and 'just as you thought you had a friend, your friend would be moved to another home or foster parents':

> I was so frightened in Bidura. My sisters had gone, my baby brother had gone, I had nobody. When I asked where they were they told me I would see them soon. I remember the small babies in rows and rows of cots crying and obviously distressed and being ignored by staff. There had to be a better system than this for caring for abused and neglected children.

At the Mittagong Home, the house parents were 'abusive and cruel' and the regime was the one which I describe in Chapter 4, with the usual draconian punishments — yet this was a small 'cottage' Home for dependent wards, not 'delinquents'. At Lynwood Hall, it was 'sleeping with bars on the windows and having to line up to go to the dining room for your meals' and 'being treated as a number'. Now, at age 44, she prays to be able to bury her past, 'but no matter how hard I try, it just comes back to me and I feel a deep depression and great sadness for my family'. For, she concludes, 'we have never to this day been able to be a family again'.

One of Lin's statements about the state system goes the heart of the experience, and also explains, at least in part, why the people who lived it find it so difficult to come to terms with it. She said:

> We were children who had already been through tough times in our family homes, and then to be taken away and placed in institutions and abused physically, mentally and emotionally by people who were supposedly there to look after you is so very, very wrong.

It is hard to see how one could disagree with this statement, or with her conclusion that 'the system chose the worst possible way to treat these children'. Another NSW state ward summed it up this way: 'Reared by the child welfare as I was from about 1952 till 1965. As a consequence, I thought I was crazy.'[32]

I cannot conclude this section without referring to a court case in which the NSW Department was involved in the early 1960s, and which demonstrates the lengths to which it would go to assert, and defend, its authority. In November 1962 a man called William Neyens went to the Child Welfare Department in the ACT and asked them for help in looking after his nine-month-old son.[33] He had been living with the boy's mother — the two were not married to each other, for Neyens was already married, but separated from his wife — but they had parted acrimoniously and she had left the baby with him; he claimed that she had mistreated the child. Neyens was securely employed but could not look after the baby himself. He wanted temporary assistance only, for he was expecting to be reunited with his estranged wife, and she would help him care for his son. The Departmental officer assured him he would be able to reclaim the child when ready to, and after a court hearing in which the child was charged as 'destitute', the baby was made a state ward, transferred to the care of the NSW Department[34] and placed in a babies' Home. The next month, Mr Neyens was in fact reunited with his wife, and in January 1963 they approached the NSW Department and asked for his son back. The Department refused. After further efforts at recovery were unsuccessful, Mr Neyens applied to the Supreme Court of the ACT for an order giving him custody of his son. As Chisholm, reporting on the case, noted:

> The department did not argue about the welfare of the child. They argued about power. They said that the Child Welfare legislation gave them total power over the child since he was a state ward. Even the courts were not allowed to consider what was best for the child.[35]

The Supreme Court rejected this argument, saying that 'the father was a proper person to have the custody of the child, that his home and circumstances were such that it was *in the interests of the child that he should be with the respondent and his wife*' (emphasis added), having also determined that 'the mother of the child was not a fit and proper person to have the custody of the child'.[36] The NSW Department then appealed to the High Court, on the same argument, that the Supreme Court had no jurisdiction to hear the case. 'As it turned out,' observed Chisholm, 'the department knew more about its own power than about the child's welfare, because the high court upheld the appeal.' He concludes that the Neyens case shows the law allocating almost total power over some children's lives to a government department'.[37] But what is even more disturbing in this incident is the determination of the Department to assert that power — using public money — regardless of the effect on the child.

State-sanctioned rape

Caroline Carroll, a NSW state ward from babyhood, was sent back from her second foster placement because she had stolen money to buy lollies for the children at school to cultivate their friendship. Her first foster placement had been seven years with a violent and alcoholic family. She wrote in her submission of her return to the state receiving depot:

> On arrival back at Bidura I was given the standard vaginal tests — legs tied in stirrups. When I protested I was told they knew 'how quickly I would open my legs for a boy!' I was 9 years old! I had no idea what they were talking about. The pain was horrific. I was crying. The matron just pulled me off the table told me to 'shut up as I was nothing but a dirty stealing tramp'.

Here is the manifestation of the low status of children once they were outside their families, and the fear of contamination that I described in Chapter 3. The NSW 1939 Child Welfare Act stipulated that no ward should be boarded out (fostered) without being certified free of venereal disease. All children who came into the care of the Department were supposed to be routinely subjected to testing. Joy Hill remembers the venereal disease routine, and how they used to 'do a scrape or swab, no drapes, just on the couch, pants down'. Joy's file shows that she had been tested even at the age of 18 months, which appears to suggest that sexual abuse of even very young children was known of, but not openly acknowledged. One wonders what action would have been taken if a young child like Joy had been discovered to be suffering from a venereal disease. I have read no accounts by males of this sort of testing, but there are many accounts from women.

It also seems that girls were routinely tested for sexual activity. Nothing in Caroline's history suggested that she had been sexually active (at age nine!), but the 'misbehaviour' of girls was so sexualised by state discourses about girls that apparently it was considered appropriate to subject her to a vaginal examination. One of the NSW Department's field officers I interviewed gave a detailed account of this routine procedure. A girl picked up as neglected because 'exposed to moral danger', he said, would be subjected to a vaginal examination while on remand awaiting court appearance. If she objected, she 'got a whiff, an anaesthetic, and [was] put under'. The examination was used as evidence:

> When the matter came back before the court, the court would hear the evidence and it would have the medical report and the medical report would say virgo intacta or non virgo intacta. And very often the doctor would draw little marks alongside, like one two or three. You wouldn't pick that up, if you see these in the archives, you wouldn't know what they meant. But what they meant was: that's how many fingers you could insert into the vagina. Now the theory was that if you had three fingers, then you'd been highly promiscuous. Quite often the report would say things like 'appearances suggest frequent penetration' — that's a common phrase that you'll find on hundreds of reports.

He pointed out that this mode of assessment had absolutely no scientific basis at all, yet it was a — if not *the* — major feature of cases such as this, and could be used to consign a girl to a term in the closed correctional institution, the Training School for Girls,

Parramatta. The means of obtaining the 'evidence', as this officer commented, 'was just a straight assault, there's no doubt about it; it's a wonder somebody hasn't complained about being assaulted all those years ago'. However, he added, 'I don't think most people worried about it at all. It was completely routine. It was something that the court needed.' Little thought was given to the sensitivities of the girls, he said, 'because they were regarded as juvenile prostitutes'.

State wards were not supposed to be subjected to this routine, said this officer, but any girl who was regarded as having 'delinquent tendencies' could be examined, since it was an easy procedure to set in motion — even if the girl had done nothing and was not in the correction system. Caroline's story shows that girls other than those labelled 'juvenile prostitutes' were certainly subjected to this procedure, and hers is not an isolated account. Women who were NSW state wards often speak of being tested to see if they had been 'interfered with', and for 'promiscuity'; it appears likely that this was a test that was very often, and very indiscriminately, applied. Joy Hill suffered this routine more than once, in the 1950s, and it was always conducted by the same 'filthy, filthy doctor, a horrible man':

> The nurse would hold you down, because you were frightened, then whack, he'd stick his finger in and say — 'Yes, she's been penetrated' ['Yes, by him,' commented Joy], then he'd grin at you. He loved it. He was a creep and not very clean.

Most of the girls who ended up in the Training School for Girls, Parramatta, had been raped in this way more than once. Denise Dravine, speaking of her incarceration in this institution at age 17 in 1955, remembered:

> ... then the final abuse — sexual — by 'Dr Finger' as he was known to all the girls ... To identify this monster is

impossible. His face was hidden behind a white mask, white covering on his head and in the very dull light in the sick bay and wearing a white gown, on three occasions carried out digital examinations on me. No nurses were present. Two digital examinations I vividly remember took place after times allowed out of the home on day release. After this evil defilement of my body, I suffered great fear and nightmares. I was at the total mercy of whatever these so-called human beings perpetrated on me.

This practice was not confined to New South Wales, or to early decades of the institutional period. Girls entering the Winlaton 'training school' in Victoria were subjected to it, and girls who were placed in the Wilson Youth Hospital in Queensland (a remand, assessment and treatment centre, otherwise a 'correctional facility') suffered it even in the 1970s. Girls who refused were held down by male orderlies during the examinations, which, as in New South Wales, were carried out by male doctors. Beth Wilson-Szoredi, incarcerated in Wilson in 1976, said that the enforced gynaecological examination could require:

> up to four screws called 'training officers' to pin the young women in a position common for an internal examination. As many were virgins and knew this procedure was not only humiliating but unnecessary they fought and sustained vaginal cuts and injuries as well as broken hymens.

Beth's explanation for this treatment is that 'young women were particularly targeted in relation to their sexuality' — and her account shows that this attitude to girls who did not conform to a conservative female norm continued to be used to rationalise their incarceration until the very recent past. She observed of Queensland state practice:

> I've never known any boys to be locked up for being in moral danger, yet I've known dozens of girls who have had

that charge levelled against them. If the Department didn't like the place in which you lived or the person you were sharing with, if the Department deemed you as being promiscuous and in some cases if parents objected to their daughter's boyfriend or even friends, the girls were formally charged with being in moral danger. It was an outrageous and insulting charge that was gender specific.

State wards and the loss of family

The extreme irony of statutory child welfare in New South Wales is that the very practice which, in this state's view, put it streets ahead of other states — namely, a high rate of foster care — is precisely what made it much more likely that children in this state would lose their birth families. In other states, where a child was placed in an institution after removal by the state, parents or other relatives could at least visit them if they wanted to or were able to. Being placed in foster care, however, removed this possibility of continued contact with kin. As I have said previously, I think that at least in New South Wales, parents would 'voluntarily' put their children in Homes rather than risk the intervention of the Department, because if 'the Welfare' got involved, parents risked losing their children forever (as Joy Hill's history shows — see Chapter 2). Lin's story (above), which is typical of wards of the NSW Department, shows its indifference, as late as the late 1960s, to children's kinship ties, both to parents and siblings. Mothers, in particular, who came under Departmental surveillance were construed as 'bad' mothers in comparison with foster 'mothers', who were 'good', so that if they could not, for whatever reasons, care for their children, those children were automatically assigned to other women, women who fitted more closely the description of what children 'need' — they had husbands and a conventionally functioning domestic situation. This was not embodied in legislation or even articulated policy, but case files and care leaver histories reveal that it was usual practice.[38]

Once their children were in foster care, parents appear to have been — often quite actively — discouraged from contact if the *foster carers* did not want contact to occur, or if the district officer thought it would be 'better' for the children if it did not occur. The Department would then prohibit parents from contacting the foster parents, or refuse from the outset to give the parents the address of the foster carers. Children also often lost their siblings, as they were fostered separately, contrary to the Department's claimed intention to keep families together. Once a child was removed from their family, it seemed that they were expected to start on a different chapter of life, leaving the previous one behind. As Maggie Anderson, a NSW state ward from 1964 to 1971, said:

> You weren't supposed to have feelings or knowledge of parents. Whenever I asked, where's my mum, can I ring her? you'd be fobbed off with, 'you just forget that'.

In not one of her five foster placements did the Department arrange any contact with her parents. It was the foster mother in her final placement who, at Maggie's request, made contact with her natural mother so that they could meet.

In my research study, several of the interviewees who were NSW state wards had lost contact completely with their biological families, including all their siblings. George Murray, when he contacted me in 1992, had just been reunited with his sisters, who had been separated from him in 1948 by the Child Welfare Department. Even when George was an adult, the Department refused to disclose their last known whereabouts. Joy Hill had a similar experience: she was reunited with her sister Jan almost 30 years after they had last seen each other, and only after several years of 'begging letters' to the Department. Joy also discovered that the Department had withheld information about her family — for example, the fact that her mother had been killed when she, Joy, was 12 years old. Caroline Carroll, a NSW state ward, said in her submission:

> I realise my life may not have been ideal with my natural parents; I may not have survived, as two of my siblings didn't. What I don't understand is why the Department deemed it necessary to deny me any contact with any member of my family. When I read my file my sister and my parents had written asking for contact with me on several occasions.

In the late 1950s, at the age of 15, Caroline's unknown brother and parents visited her one day in Lynwood Hall — and she suddenly found out she was one of eight children. There was no warning and no explanation given by the Department: 'I was told to kiss them hello and go sit in the garden with them,' she remembers. But she did not know these people and, hardly surprisingly, her relationship with her parents was not successful — 'they were strangers'. Years later, she found out that her sister had been in an institution in a nearby suburb and that although 'she had written many letters to the Department asking about me, she never had a reply'. One of the most distressing experiences for care leavers is finding, when they get their state ward file, letters that family members had sent to them, but which had never been passed on.

Training schools

> I wonder what it was that they were training us for?
>
> David Forbes, NSW state ward

Many of the submissions to the Senate Inquiry are about the treatment of their writers in the institutions known as 'training schools'. While I said in Chapter 1 that this book was not the place to write the history of the juvenile 'correction' arm of child welfare, I will describe briefly here just what it meant for a child to be consigned to a 'training school', for it is in their operation that we see the fullest expression of the punitive character of attitudes in this era towards children without viable family. 'Training schools' were for children who had failed to conform: who, in the terminology of the day, were anti-social, maladjusted, incorrigible, hardened, wayward, uncontrollable and, ultimately, 'delinquent'. Or, alternatively, who had been failed or abused by every adult who had 'cared' for them and who were acting out their pain, fear and despair.

'Training schools' were conducted by the state governments and by the Salvation Army and certain Roman Catholic orders, with the mix varying according to state. In South Australia, for example, apart from a receiving Home, the several institutions which were run by the Department were predominantly 'training' Homes[39] and even the Catholic one run by the Good Shepherd Sisters at Plympton was under the control of the government. The Good Shepherd Sisters ran 'correctional' Homes in all states; these are the ones which appear in so many submissions as the site of 'remedial' laundry work for children sometimes as young as eight. The purpose of 'training schools' was largely as described in the Tasmanian Department's 1956 annual report, referring to its Ashley Home for Boys in Deloraine: this institution was 'to provide care and training for older wards, who, because of maladjustment and delinquency, require special institutional control'. This is a description which could apply to any of the 'training' Homes or schools in Australia.

In contrast to South Australia, in some other states it was the charitable sector which did the bulk of the work. For instance, although Victoria, from 1956, had the state's Winlaton at Nunawading to 'cater for' teenage girls, it otherwise used Homes such as the Salvation Army 'farm and vocational training centre' at Bayswater for boys, and three Catholic institutions. In Queensland also — as in Western Australia — both the Catholic Church and the Salvation Army ran the bulk of the 'training' institutions, although the state did conduct the notorious Westbrook 'industrial school and farm Home' for boys,[40] and the Wilson Youth Hospital (opened in 1961).

Wilson was both a corrective institution and a mental health facility. It could be described as the latter because it reinterpreted the misery and despair of children as either defects of character and socialisation, or the result of organic weaknesses for which medical solutions were required. Treatment in Wilson was based on the belief of the senior medical director that 'delinquency was primarily a psychiatric rather than a social problem'. In a letter to the director-general of Health in 1977, the director advised that between 50 per cent and 70 per cent (closer to the latter) of the children admitted to 'child welfare institutions' were suffering from psychiatric disorders.[41] Electroencephalograms were a standard diagnostic tool, and children, as well as being subjected to the extreme limits of regimented depersonalisation, were dosed with tranquillisers and anti-psychotic drugs, some of them not fully tested. A witness at the Forde Inquiry commented, 'It was called a hospital, but I don't know why; maybe you needed the hospital when they were finished.'[42] Reverend Dethlefs, who was chaplain at the Wilson Youth Hospital from 1973 to 1976, said this in his submission to the Inquiry:

> I must admit that I found it difficult to believe that our so-called civilised society could treat vulnerable young people in such a harrowing way. The only parallel situation which I had heard of was the psychiatric treatment of political prisoners in Siberia, by the government of the former Soviet Union. On many occasions, I was all but reduced to tears by the stories I heard from young people in Wilson.

Winlaton in Victoria inflicted on its inmates similarly inconceivable, if less sophisticated, treatment, as Rachel Ann Smith related in her submission. Removed at age six from her family, a habitual runaway from sexually abusive foster placements ('almost every home was Christian, almost every home I was sexually abused and often bashed'), Rachel arrived at Winlaton in 1961, aged 11. She was locked into a cell without a toilet, wearing only a singlet. She had to relieve herself on the floor. 'When the staff saw this,' she said, 'I was verbally abused and they stuck the hose in through the outside window and wet me and the cell. I had to sit on wet concrete all night.' The next day she was pinned down on the floor and given a tranquillising injection before being removed to Larundel Psychiatric Centre. Another Victorian state ward relates in her submission to the inquiry how, after beatings, food deprivation and six weeks of total isolation in a cell in Winlaton without even a bed or a toilet (as punishment for running away), she tried to kill herself with the pills she had saved from the daily ration handed out to tranquillise the girls. She was sixteen.[43]

Girls in New South Wales fared no better. New South Wales had 11 institutions for 'wayward' and 'delinquent' children. They included two 'special institutions': one for boys at Tamworth and, from 1961, one for girls at Hay. Both were located in former colonial gaols, both were in the country, and both were described in Departmental literature as 'closed' institutions. A graphic description of life first in the Training School for Girls, Parramatta, and then at Hay, appears in the submission of Wilma Robb, who spent 1962–65 in these two institutions. She had run away from home because her mother was chronically ill and her father very violent, and so came to the attention of 'the Welfare'. 'No questions asked why I ran,' she says. 'I was committed for 9 months for uncontrollable and exposed to moral danger.'

The Departmental assessment of girls like Wilma was 'bad beyond correction or reform'. Wilma describes being given Largactil (an antipsychotic drug) routinely at Parramatta. Once when she spat it out — 'I was sick of taking it all the time and being like a zombie' — she had her hands held behind her back and was gripped by the hair while her head was bashed repeatedly on the sinks in the shower block by two male officers. She lost teeth in this incident and was then put into isolation for 48 hours. During this period the officers would come in and amuse themselves by making her strip in front of them and stand under a cold shower for as long as they pleased. She was in solitary confinement for three weeks, in pain with black eyes and split lips. 'I just wanted to die,' said Wilma. When she was taken off Largactil she was given no help with the withdrawal symptoms. After this she tried to escape and was punished by being sent to the Hay Institution for Girls. 'The horror inhumane place it was, no one could ever comprehend,' said Wilma. 'We lost everything there. We lost our spirits. We lost our thinking and a lot lost their minds.'

Before being sent to Hay, girls had to be seen by a psychologist — 'to make sure you could handle the pressure at Hay,' said Wilma. This 'pressure' included having to always stand two metres (six feet) away from anyone else, with eyes down and no eye contact at all permitted, having only 10 minutes per day to talk, having always to move as if doing an army drill (march, click heels), being locked into a cell every day at 5.30 pm with no radio and no books except a Bible — and having no visitors. Initiation into Hay started with the cell: the cell was freshly painted, and all the paint had to be scrubbed off with a brick and a wire brush. 'Sleep wasn't even our time,' remembered Wilma: she was made to stand for hours at the end of her bed as punishment for sleeping with the blankets over her head. She received no education at Parramatta or at Hay, although she was aged 13 to 16 during her time there.

The Institution for Boys, Tamworth, was similar to Hay but, if possible, even more brutal. The 1956 NSW Department annual report said:

> [This institution] was established to provide more intensive discipline and training for habitual absconders and the more difficult and unresponsive delinquent, than that provided in the open situation ... In a closely controlled environment ... an excellent opportunity is given for the staff to help the maladjusted individual to develop his personality.

The experience of living in one of these institutions is described by Ben Smith (a pseudonym) in a submission to the Inquiry made by a prison officer (who was also a law student) who interviewed him about his experiences in the NSW care and juvenile justice system in the 1940s and 1950s. Ben had been at Tamworth around the time of the statement quoted above. Ben, said his interviewer, described the centre as 'the most unbelievably cruel, sick and sad place', comparing the conditions there 'to the conditions experienced by prisoners of war in the Changi prison camp in WWII'. The institution, he said, had been staffed mainly by former soldiers and run with the sort of rules that usually apply in institutions for hardened criminals or people regarded as enemies of the state. There were similar procedures to the ones Wilma described as typical at Hay, such as the prohibition of any physical contact with others, and of eye contact. The punishment for breaking the eye-contact rule was loss of meals for up to 48 hours, but habitual offenders were made to wear a cardboard cereal box that had two holes cut out for eyes — until it fell to pieces. Talking and moving were also subject to strict controls. Boys lived in cells with no furniture at all, only a mattress and some bedding on the floor, and solitary confinement with no meals could be imposed for up to 48 hours. Boys had to sleep in the 'corpse position', flat on their back, arms crossed over the chest with hands placed on each shoulder, their head and hands visible at all times. If a boy contravened this rule, 'a fire hose was pushed through the peephole of the cell and the boy and his bedding were soaked'.

Ben did have a visit, from his mother, and when she expressed concern at his appearance he told her of his treatment and of conditions in the institution. Upon her return to Sydney she made a complaint about the institution to the Department. Not long after this, all mail to Ben from his mother and older sister stopped, and a month or so later he was told that both his parents had been killed in a car accident, and his sister injured so badly that she was not expected to live. Ben can recall 'dragging' himself through the rest of his time at Tamworth until he was returned to complete his sentence at the 'training' institution, Mt Penang, from which he had been transferred originally. A fortnight later, on visiting day at Mt Penang, he fainted when he saw his mother among the crowd of visitors. Being told that his family were dead or injured was, said Ben, 'one of the many dark and dreadful ways in which the boys of Tamworth were treated'.

In her submission, Wilma Robb named her abusers, adding 'and anyone else that knew what was happening to us and never spoke out'. Peter Quinn, the former NSW Department official quoted previously, who has written a history of the NSW Department's juvenile correction system,[44] gave evidence at the Senate hearings that although there was meant to be an inquiry if anybody was caught assaulting a girl, 'unofficially, it was permitted as long as you made sure you did not do it in public' ('Abuse is okay, just don't get caught', as a newspaper headline put it[45]). Dr Quinn said that even though from 1905 there was a specific provision for it in the legislation, he had been unable to find a single instance of anybody being charged criminally with assaulting a child in the care of the state. Typically, if an episode became known, the perpetrator would be allowed to resign and no inquiry would be held.[46]

The language of child welfare

I quoted earlier Don Watson's comment that public language is the language of power, and 'has its origins in the subjection or control of one by another'. The public language of child welfare is a superb example of this, a type of double-speak that used pseudo-psychological jargon to present as benevolent what were actually programs of repression and coercion. This language is so prevalent in the literature that it takes on its own authority and it is only when we listen to accounts of the actual experiences of people exposed to child welfare interventions that we discover the duplicity hidden in the language. Ben's actual experience at Tamworth, for example, bears little resemblance to the intention of this institution as presented in the Department's description of it.

Annual reports of child welfare Departments speak without irony of how they are serving children's needs in providing periods of 'retraining'. The SA Department's 1956 report, describing the Home of the Good Shepherd in Plympton (a 'reformatory' for Catholic girls), asserts that the sisters who run it are 'devoted to the moral and social uplift of girls and women in need of specialised care'. 'Specialised care' presumably included unpaid labour in laundries operated for profit within such Catholic Homes. Similarly, the newly opened Winlaton institution in Victoria, said that Department's 1956 annual report, was for 'the *care* of teenage girls who *require* rehabilitation and training' (emphasis added). Speaking of the increase in the Department's field staff, this report said that the increase was in order to 'intensify the work of *social adjustment* with the older boys and girls who tend to be anti-social'. The word 'special', often attached to the names of institutions as if to indicate extra and individually tailored attention — as in 'special training school' — in fact indicated more severe treatment. The use of this word, as of the words 'need' and 'require' — indeed of the word 'care' itself — is specious. It attributes to the child what the authority itself requires. It would be more accurate for Departmental reports to say 'children who are regarded as potential threats to society are compelled to serve a term in a training institution until they have learned more acceptable behaviour'. That this was the true objective can be seen in the way that children were actually treated within such institutions.

This same annual report describes Winlaton as catering for 'seriously disturbed girls'. Anyone who spent time in Winlaton would tell you that if she was not disturbed on entering it, she was when she left. This is true for any of the 'training schools' across the country. It is abundantly clear from all the histories that are now available that the means of 'intensifying social adjustment' in all Departmental 'training schools' — and in the Salvation Army Homes or the Good Shepherd laundries — was a brutally repressive regime designed to break the spirit of the young persons subjected to it.

Chapter 6

'A terrible way to grow up ...'

I was an Aussie kid, sentenced to a childhood in hell by my fellow countrymen.

> Paul Bradshaw, WA state ward, on his life in Castledare and Clontarf under the Christian Brothers

Waking up day after day, year after year in that orphanage was always a struggle for me.

> Lynette Hyde, St Joseph's Orphanage, Bathurst, NSW

The overwhelming response as to treatment in care, even among those that made positive comments, was the lack of love, affection and nurturing.

> *Forgotten Australians* 2004

The denial of feelings

In Chapter 3 I described how most Children's Homes were run. In this chapter, people describe what it felt like to live day by day in an institution run in this way. Children in Homes existed in an isolation zone — 'twilight zone' might be a better term — a state of limbo where no normal life went on. By using a particular set of practices, Homes set up a barrier between themselves and the wider world. First, they separated siblings by age and/or gender upon entry. Second, they weakened children's ties with parents and relatives by making the rules for visits highly restrictive, and not allowing parents and relatives any other way to connect with the children. Third, there was often considerable physical isolation from the community and society outside. And fourth, they completely denied children's feelings, so that eventually children felt alienated from themselves.

Taken away

> Loss of a loved person is one of the most intensely painful experiences any human being can suffer.
>
> John Bowlby, *Loss, Sadness and Depression* (1980)[1]

Since children were only in Homes because, for whatever reason, their parents could no longer care for them, let us begin with the traumatic beginning event — being put into a Home, or removed by the state from your family. Here is William Anson, in the early 1970s, having lived for all of his few years in a violent family:

> One day I found myself being taken to a big house that had shiny wooden floors. And my mum telling me I was having a little holiday and mummy will be back soon. That was the start of more hell.

Two accounts, many years apart, show that being taken into state care was equally terrifying. 'It was in September 1943, when my brothers and myself were awakened to what only could be explained as a home invasion,' began Mavis Devereaux-Dingwall:

> I awoke that morning to the horrifying cries of my brother, Edwin, screaming, 'Quick Mamie, run, they've come to take us away.' I jumped out of bed with the thought of who has come to take us away, it was war years, was it the Japs, the Germans or who?
>
> My two brothers, who were in their pyjamas, were being tightly held by the scruff of their necks by two big men. I realise today they would have been policemen, although, when you are seven years of age that doesn't register. All I knew, at the time, they were strangers and they were holding my brothers against their will and I was in danger. I ran dodging a man in the hall only to run into the dead end of a bathroom, the only avenue open to me. I was a slim, agile child and I squeezed beside the bath and the wall-hung sink and held tightly to the rails on either side of the sink. One of these frightening big men came in and attempted to savagely pull me out. This fear has lived with me all through my life. I often have dreams where I am running and hiding from some man and I awake with a racing heart. I place this nightmare back to this early experience of my childhood.

This was the NSW Department in action; in Victoria, too, police were involved in child removal.[2] And 25 years later, in 1969, the experience in Victoria feels very similar. Elizabeth Behrendorf remembered being taken to the state receiving centre, Allambie, by van:

> There were other children in the van. Some were nasty. I was scared, I felt like an impounded dog, trapped and alienated, and I cried and no one cared. Never once did

anyone offer me any grief counselling. They had forgotten that my mother had died, or had they?

And then the arrival:

> Allambie was overflowing. There were the abused, the neglected, family violence, the babies for adoption, the disabled, some intellectually and some physically. You name it, they were there, the runaways, some petty thieves. What did we all have in common? A file and a number.

In Victoria, many Homes — including the Department's receiving depot at Royal Park — mixed children together regardless of whether they were 'delinquent', neglected or abused children taken in by the state, or children placed by their parents.[3]

Once inside the orphanage, things did not get any better. Bill Cremen, aged seven or eight, and his brother, three years younger, arrived at night at the Catholic St John's Boys' Home in Goulburn, NSW, in the mid-1940s, and was immediately separated from his brother:

> [The next morning] I was awakened by being dragged out of bed by a nun called Sister Genevieve and told to go and get some clothes. Another boy took me to a store room, Sister Genevieve threw some clothes at me. I tried to tell her we had our own clothes and I wanted warm jumpers, socks, long pants. I got a belt in the ear and was told to put on what was given to me: shorts, shirt, an old jumper and a pair of shoes. Then I was told to go down to breakfast; instead I went looking for my brother. I found him walking along the concrete verandah outside the laundry crying.
>
> We both missed breakfast that first morning.

Children placed in this situation felt — and were — powerless. This was the beginning of what is now described as post-traumatic stress disorder; many survivors live with its symptoms for their entire life. 'The screams as people tried to separate me from my mother still reverberated in my ears until I was forty-two, when I tried to get some therapy to deal with them,' said Kerry Geldard, aged four when left at the Protestant Federation Girls' Home in Sydney. 'You'd walk around like a zombie,' said Chrystal Lennox, living in Bidura, the NSW receiving depot. Like William Anson and the 'shiny wooden floors', many people have vivid recollections of details of 'the day'. 'I remember it was a rainy day and I could smell the pittosporums,' said Anne Martin-Smith, although she was only three at the time. 'I remember the day I was put there,' said Rebecca Feinstein, then five. 'Dad and I walked through the gate and there was a goat grazing there and I kept crying, saying, "Don't leave me."'

'Nobody had told me anything' — this statement is repeated over and over in care leaver histories. 'It's quite vivid, being taken,' said Joy Hewitt. 'I was never told where, for how long, nothing like that. At that age [six] you just have no conception of what's going on, time has no value.' 'We were just left there,' said Richard Miles, who was in several Homes in the late 1950s, 'and I'll always remember this little boy. He said, "Is my mummy coming to take me home?" The worker said, "No, she doesn't want you." He cried.' (Was Richard himself that little boy, perhaps?) 'The worst thing was that your family had deserted you,' said Harry Baker, aged 12 when he was placed in Sydney's Burnside, in 1950. 'The first week I remember being in a clothes cupboard and crying my eyes out. Why am I here? Why has this happened to me?'

William Anson, quoted above, had been placed in the Red Cross Home at Cronulla, a suburb of Sydney, and said, 'I had never been with so many kids in the same place.' This fact alone — being shut up, without any explanation, with dozens and dozens of strangers, all unhappy, bewildered and some visibly disturbed — was in itself deeply traumatising. 'The most traumatic thing was being put in the nursery at the [Launceston] girls' home when I was two and my sister was three,' Lorraine Davis told the Senate hearings in Perth:[4]

> There was so much crying because we missed our mother. Missing our mother was the worst ... I think removing a baby or a toddler from their mother is one of the cruellest things that can happen to a child.

Separation from siblings

Sudden, unexplained abandonment is traumatic, but as William Anson so memorably says, it was only 'the start of more hell'. Many children had already suffered distressing events daily, or devastating loss through the death or disappearance of one parent. Once in the Home, the one emotional anchor left to children, their brothers and sisters, was often, indeed usually, removed as well, unless by some lucky chance their ages coincided with the Home's arrangements.

In almost all Homes, both state and non-state, it was customary for children to be segregated by age and by sex, but I have never found any stated rationale for this. In late 1950, the NSW Department's district officer reported Our Children's Home in Sydney as unsatisfactory on several levels, one of the main faults being 'failure to segregate the sexes, during non-school periods'. This statement seems to imply that children of the opposite sex should not even be playing together. And when in 1954 the Barnardos organisation proposed to open Greenwood, its Children's Home at Normanhurst in Sydney, with separate dormitories for boys and girls but *under the same roof* — as if they were living in a family — it was thwarted, as a Sydney newspaper reported, by the NSW Department's 'strict regulations about the segregation of the sexes', which insisted on 'a separate roof above the boys from that which sheltered the girls'.[5]

My Home was licensed to take girls up to any age, but boys only up to four years and 11 months. To take boys older than this, the Home would have been required to have a separate bathroom and sleeping quarters. There appears to be a subtext operating here — children were not acknowledged as sexual beings, but the lengths authorities went to to segregate the sexes demonstrates not this belief but its opposite, and even an anxiety about this aspect of children. Care leavers often tell of being accused by Home staff of being 'wicked' and 'dirty' because they were suspected of sexual behaviour — when, for example they got into bed with other children for comfort. The religious foundation of most Homes, with its link between sex and sin and its denial of sexuality generally, obviously exaggerated this response.

Separate girls' and boys' Homes, therefore, were the norm across Australia. Jane Hamilton's experience at Burnside in the late 1940s, where the boys' and girls' Homes were separated by a road, was a common one. Jane only saw her brothers at the school which was part of the Home complex, but even there they were segregated, and 'you weren't encouraged to mix at all'. As an orphan, Jane had no visitors, and hearing other girls talking of mothers and grandmothers, she began to realise that she 'didn't have anybody'. 'The only thing that kept me going,' she said, 'was knowing I had my two brothers there. I used to wave, and blow kisses.'

Where Homes were large, even children of the *same* sex from one family could be separated because there was more than a certain number of years' difference between them. Alice Nanson, aged nine at the time, was in a rural United Protestant Association (UPA) Home in the 1950s. She remembered:

> There were two houses, one next to each other, and you weren't allowed to go from one house into the other. My sister was the youngest, about four, and she was in the other house. Even though we were both there, I can hardly remember seeing her, even once a day. We didn't live there as sisters.

Frank Golding relates how he and his brother Bob were together in one dormitory for a while, but only because there was 18 months between them; their other brother, Bill, was separated from them from the beginning, sleeping in a different section. Soon, however, they were all separated, and Frank, like Jane above, was reduced to glimpses only: 'If we chanced to see one another we waved across the playground.' Here we see in practice one of the defining features of Goffman's total institution: 'constant conflict between humane standards on the one hand and institutional efficiency on other'. It was considered easier to control groups of children of a similar age than of mixed ages; presumably on the basis that similar ages meant similar capacities.

Ralph Doughty's story shows what so often happened to siblings going into care. Ralph's mother had died, leaving six small children: 'My family was scattered,' he said. The two babies were 'given away', he and his little brother, aged three, went into the Salvation Army Gill Memorial Home for Boys in Goulburn, NSW, and his two little sisters were put into a Church of England orphanage in the same town. This is what it felt like for Ralph, who was still only a young boy:

> Only once were they brought from their orphanage to see me. Even now, I can see them; two little girls just standing there and looking at me. Here am I now, seventy years of age, and I still see them; standing there beside me, my two dear pretty little sisters. Wanda, the elder, gently ran her hand up and down my arm and sweet little Melba just standing in front of me and looking at my face. Little Melba had a faint fixed slight smile on her lips and her eyes had a soft frightened look in them. I see her face and the look in her eyes even as I sit here writing this. The incident reminds me of having seen a frightened baby fawn. Did she speak? No, only when leaving and she said, 'Good-bye Ralph' as she turned again to look at me as she was taken away to return to the orphanage.

Ralph saw his sisters only once in the 10 years he spent in the Gill. His younger brother, though entering the Home with him, also went out of his life with no explanation. Ralph was told one day to go and say goodbye to him, and then he disappeared. Ralph's interpretation of this was that he had 'been given away'.

That siblings yearned for and grieved for each other is clear from many accounts. This was one of the cruellest of the Homes practices and one of the greatest sources of heartbreak for children. Interviewees who by luck had their siblings with them, or were in Homes later, when this practice had changed, reported that it was their brothers and sisters who made the biggest difference to their lives. Sandra, in a bleak Anglican Home in the 1970s where 'you were never thought of as a person', remembers that what made it tolerable — and stopped her from running away — was that she was with her four sisters and brother: 'I had that security,' she said. Her brother used to steal from the cash-box and put money under her pillow and tell her the fairies had brought it.

'It didn't seem to occur to them that we might like to see our brothers,' said Sylvia Baker, in Burnside from age six. Close to 50 years later she wept as she recalled that, 'The only time I ever saw my brothers was when Dad came, and that was infrequent: once a month or sometimes fortnight.' Managements simply paid no attention to the quite obvious desire of siblings to remain together, and in fact children were often punished for trying to be with their brothers and sisters. Pippa Corbett, aged eight, in the Benevolent Society's Scarba House in Bondi, NSW, in 1957, recalls that her brother was in another area, with the other boys, and that she could only watch him lying in a cot from behind a glass window. 'He was never held or picked up,' she said, 'and I used to yell "Give me my brother" constantly.' She actually hid her little sister, and for her pains received 44 cuts on the legs. There were other ways of curbing this troublesome behaviour, however, as Mavis White recalled of her time in Burnside in 1935–36. 'I used to get into trouble because I wouldn't stay away from the boys' section, wanting to see my brother,' she said. The solution of the Home was to dress her in boys' clothes — 'I felt so humiliated I didn't do it again.'

There were these same segregations and separations in state Homes. Barry Cook, in the Victorian government's Royal Park, remembers 'being severely beaten for going up to the crèche area to visit my brother David'. To be with your brother or sister was a luxury. Barry recalled one specific fond memory:

> [I was] allowed to dress in 'new' clothes and spend the whole day with my brother and we spoke to Santa on the phone. I still possess a photo of this occasion.

In New South Wales these practices are particularly inexplicable: this was the state that made so much in its policy statements of attempting to foster children of the same family together. Yet Franny Mason, when in the girls' depot, Bidura, awaiting fostering, recalled climbing on a friend's back to look in the windows of the school for a glimpse of her elder sisters. And Jack Fletcher, in Royleston at Glebe (the boys' depot), recalled that about a year after entering the Home, he was smacked for stopping to talk to the sister he finally saw, after a year's separation, in the yard of Bidura — 'I didn't even know she was there.' The only chance brothers and sisters had to be together in a Home was on visiting day, when they could see their parent(s) at the same time. Often, however, this was not possible.

The consequences of prolonged separation can be seen in Hannah Brown's story. When Hannah was placed in the Church of England Girls' Home in inner-city Sydney, in the 1920s, her beloved little brother was sent to the Boys' Home in Carlingford, then on the far outskirts of Sydney. It was not until the Girls' Home moved to the same location, five years later, that she saw him again. 'I had left a four-year-old and now he was almost nine,' she recalls. 'I recognised him immediately but I doubt that he even remembered me.'

'Nobody told me anything'

State welfare authorities appeared to explain nothing to children, even such confronting and frightening events as court appearances. And once they were in the depot, children could come back from school and find brothers or sisters — the only links to their past and the only familiar persons in the present — gone: sent to foster placements, or to other institutions. There was never any warning of this, and no information was passed on to a remaining child about where their sibling(s) had been sent.

But parents, too, habitually deceived their children about what was about to happen to them. It was quite usual for children to be told that they were going on 'a little holiday', and that 'Mummy will be back soon.' Given that parents usually had no other options, and often felt not only pain but guilt at what they were forced to do, perhaps they could not afford to feel their children's grief, and had to deny it — 'children soon forget' and 'children get over things quickly'. Parents left children at Homes without any explanation and without any indication of the duration of the stay; and often, on the advice of staff, they left without saying goodbye. 'My mother would take us for a drive sometimes,' said Ellen Brown, 'and this was how she took me to Bidura the first time.' That is, her mother allowed her to wear her best dress for an 'outing', then left her at a government receiving Home with no explanation. Mary O'Halloran, placed in a Catholic Home in Goulburn when she was four, was not told it was because her mother had died, so she wondered why her mother did not visit. Jack Fletcher, who ended up with his brother in Royleston in the mid-1950s after his parents separated, said that 'we couldn't understand why our parents didn't come. Nobody told us anything. We didn't even know that our parents had split up, or why we were there.'

How this affected children can be seen in Kerry Geldard's submission. She was left at the Protestant Federation Girls' Home, her mother saying that it would only be for a short time, until she had found a suitable home for them all. 'This gave me hope,' said Kerry, 'something small children need and [that] enables them to put up with outrageous situations because they believe they will be coming to an end soon.' An older child eventually pointed out to Kerry, after she had been waiting six months, that this was what all mothers said to their children and that Kerry, like all the others, would be staying there indefinitely. Kerry said:

> The effect was like a bullet to my heart, a realisation that this girl was right and that there was no future for me. I believe it was from that point that depression, which was to dog me through my later life, descended. I examined the implications of what she said even though I was only five years old. I realised that I would have to adjust and accept the fact that my mother, who may have meant it at the time, was now lying to me. My dilemma was how to adjust to this revelation and like all young children my fears were greater than my resources and I clung even harder to the weekly, sometimes monthly visits my mother made on Saturday afternoons for 3 hours.

So all adults in this situation — parents, state welfare authorities and Home personnel — treated children as if they had no need or right to know anything about their own lives. This could only intensify children's feelings of hopelessness and powerlessness. 'We used to cry to Dad, to everybody, promise to be good if we could come home. I'll do this and that, we promised, if we could come home, but it didn't work,' said Cheryl Hannaford. Bruce Randle, institutionalised from age three to 16, recounted a common response from parents:

> One day I said to mum, why am I here? how long will I be here? She said this will be the last Home you go to I promise. But she never gave any time limit. The attitude was — you'll be right, just hang in there.

This does not mean that parents did not love or want their children. All these parents were operating under difficult circumstances. And even if parents had tried to explain what was happening, no explanation would have made the Home more acceptable to children who wanted to be with their parents. However, the standard approach did make an already traumatic situation much worse, because it forced children to deny and to doubt their own feelings. This strikes at the heart of healthy emotional development: as Alice Miller says, 'it is precisely because a child's feelings are so strong that they cannot be repressed without serious consequences'.[6] Parents who withheld information like this were little different from many parents in 'normal' families of the time, but children in families were not confronted with having to live in a Children's Home.

Another common practice of this era was to override children's feelings by telling them that they *ought* to feel differently. This meant that children eventually felt guilty about their quite natural reactions, and learned to mistrust their own responses. Alternatively, children would be told, as Bruce was, 'you'll be all right' when they quite patently did not feel 'all right'. Bruce's Home was so brutal that there was no possibility of any child's feeling 'all right' there.

The blindness of parents to their children's feelings could be devastating. Ellen Brown, the second of four children, was seven when her father died. Her mother gave up the two younger girls for adoption, and put Ellen (whose trip to Bidura is described above) and her brother into the care of the Department. 'The family disintegrated before my eyes,' she said. Her mother had decided to live in as a trainee nurse and so could not keep the children, and 'she tried to make it sound very nice — your sisters are going to be looked after for a little while by these very nice people who will give them everything they want ...' Ellen did not see her youngest sister again for 20 years. Note once again the mother's emphasis on providing the children with 'everything they want' — 'things', not feelings.

Children felt abandoned not only (in their own perception) by their parents, but by all adults, and although some tried to protest, the powerlessness of their position was so obvious to many that they made no attempt to even articulate their feelings. As Sally Fenton reflected:

> You never told anyone what it was like — you just thought that was part of what was supposed to happen. You had no way of thinking you could tell someone.

It is important to say here, though, that however much parents might have overlooked the emotional sterility of the institutional environment, it is most unlikely that they would have known just how brutal some Homes were, or how cruel the staff.

'Mum never visited'

> While growing up in the orphanage, I used to wish for our Mother to come and take us home, where we belonged, but she never came near the place. That sadden[ed] me, I would cry every Sunday, when the others had their parents to see, I would go in hiding, so no one would know that I was crying.
>
> Lorraine Rodgers, Ballarat Orphanage, 1950s

Although many parents did visit their children when they could — often with difficulty, given that many Homes were in isolated locations — it is also true that many parents never visited, or did so very infrequently. As Lorraine's statement shows, this intensified their child's feelings of abandonment. Ellen Brown, in the Church of England Girls' Home in Carlingford in the early 1960s, wrote letters to her mother every day. She wanted to write, 'come and get me', but wrote instead, 'I miss you, please visit', so that her letter would not be torn up by the 'nurses', as the other girls warned her would happen. But 'Mum never visited. I got one Easter card [which she still has] and once in a while she'd remember birthdays.' Peter wept as he told me that his mother came to his Salvation Army Home rarely, and 'another boy's mother gave me a biscuit and I always used to keep a bit for my mother, but she never came'. Although Janet Maxwell had some good memories of her Barnardos Home, what she remembered above all was 'being lonely' — although she thought of them constantly, her family did not keep in touch.

Sylvia Baker, in Burnside, had only her father's infrequent visits because he had quarrelled with her dead mother's side of the family and forbidden them to see the children. As in divorce, children could be used to punish other family members, with little or no regard for the children's own feelings.

'Don't say goodbye ...'

Norma Reading, who, like my mother, was deserted by her husband, placed her children in the Catholic Waitara Babies' Home and got a job there so that she could be near them. But things did not work out as she had planned. Once she began working there, she was deliberately separated from her children, because professional detachment had to take precedence over maternal feeling and she must not 'play favourites'. She was not allowed to see her three-year-old, Jennifer, for three weeks, but 'I could look over the windows and see how she was getting on,' she said. By the time Norma stopped working there and was able to visit her children, her daughter did not remember her at all and Norma had to convince her that she was her mother.[7] Norma also recalled a common practice of Homes, one which I observed many times in mine: she went to say goodbye to her son, who was only two:

> and they said, 'No, don't do that, it's better if you don't', and so I went away and just left him. But he suffered greatly for that because he felt that he'd been totally deserted. I didn't hear this until he was in his thirties.

Believing that a child's grief is short-lived is wishful thinking on the part of adults, but as Bowlby says, the classic response of children has also enabled that belief — after protesting, children eventually appear resigned and become quiet. This is the resignation of despair, better described as depression. Children do not forget their mothers, nor do they 'get over' missing them.[8] They grieve as deeply and intensely as adults, as post-Freudian writers have established — through, for example, the studies described in Bowlby's trilogy, *Attachment*, *Separation* and *Loss*. These are works which, as Penelope Leach observes, 'do more than any other single work to establish the importance of parental relationships to human development and mental health'.[9] 'From time immemorial,' says Bowlby, 'mothers and poets have been alive to the distress caused to a child by loss of his mother.' It is only in the last 50 years, however, he adds, 'that science has woken up to it'.[10] In an attempt to collect 'proof' of the assertion by psychoanalysts such as Bowlby, that separation from their mother can be not merely devastating but catastrophic for young children, James and Joyce Robertson, over a period of some 20 years (from 1952) filmed the reactions of children when experiencing this separation. The Robertsons wrote:

> It takes an exercise of imagination to sense the intensity of this distress. [A child] is as overwhelmed as any adult who has lost a beloved person by death. To the child of two, with his lack of understanding and complete inability to tolerate frustration, it is really as if his mother has died. He does not know death, but only absence; and if the only person who can satisfy his imperative need is absent, she might as well be dead, so overwhelming is his sense of loss.[11]

Norma's daughter Jennifer had forgotten the Waitara Home, but remembered how she had felt being placed in another Home later: 'I didn't even know we were going to stay. I cried and the sister [a nun] said, "It's only for a short time"' (which it was not). The effect of this accumulation of loss was ongoing and profound:

> most of the time I felt very, very lonely ... I remember one occasion, it was a beautiful spring day, I felt like I really wanted to be happy and yet I totally felt this complete emptiness inside. This was the first time I realised that. I must have been about seven.

The loss of family

Children suffered not only emotional devastation but also social dislocation when they lost their family. American scholar David Schneider, speaking of the enduring nature of kinship ties between blood relations, observes that:

> One expects diffuse solidarity and loyalty from one's own children. But if they turn mean, they cannot be taken to the local humane society to be 'put away'. They are yours and you stay with them as they stay with you.[12]

'You stay with them as they stay with you': through thick and thin, children and parents belong together. This does not mean that children should and must remain with abusive and neglectful parents, but it does mean that it is a tragedy when they cannot, and that that understanding must be built into the way children so unfortunate are treated by their substitute carers. When parents disappear from children's lives, the only way a child can interpret this is that the parent does not want them or care about them. Without their parents, children feel completely adrift in the world and the world becomes a dangerous place. Bunny Murphy, who grew up in an Irish orphanage of the same period but is now an Australian CLAN member, related an incident which shows this vividly:

> When I was around nine years old a stray cat came in and I needed something to love, so I hid it and collected food for it. She had kittens in my locker and when Sister Edna found out she was furious. She made me fill a bucket of water and she drowned those kittens one by one. They were only one week old. She said nobody wanted them. The look of power on her face was so scary and no amount of crying and pleading would change her mind.
>
> I told myself to be careful as she could do the same to me and no one would care. After all, we were unwanted and unloved too.[13]

In my case, extreme conformity was supposed to protect me from the harm I was certain would fall on me if I was not 'good'. I had no concept that my mother or my father might have some say if anything happened to me, because I could not comprehend them as people with any claim on me. This is one of the most disempowering aspects of being in a Home. Nobody who cared for you could possibly place you in this environment and then not come back to get you; therefore nobody cared for you. Being put in a Home *was* like being 'put away' — in the nearest receptacle that would have you — Goffman's 'storage dump for inmates', where you were, in effect, emotionally 'put down'.

'I used to fantasise about having a family,' said Sylvia Baker. 'If I saw a little girl come up to the Home looking lovely, I'd think, I could look like that if I had a mother.' Remembering a girl in her Home who 'had nobody', Alice Nanson said, 'She had a big fantasy about having a family, but we all fantasised; we had to, to exist — "Somebody will love me one day."' It was frequently the case that fantasy had to substitute for reality. Ralph Doughty describes how in the Salvation Army Gill Home, 'Everyone wanted to have a photograph of their mother so they could show it to the other boys and debate who had the prettiest mother.' Some of the boys, however, had 'no mother and no photograph'; they solved the problem by using photos of movie stars which were distributed by the local cinema. Having selected a photo which appealed, said Ralph:

> We would cut the lady's signature out of the photo and shape the photo to make it appear that it was a proper photo. This photo then became a photograph of your mother and you hid it — where you thought it was safe. It was funny at times, when a group of us would be comparing our 'mother's photo' that several boys would find that they had the same 'mother photo' and it would be necessary for one of them to acquire another 'mother'.

For state children, being fostered must have always offered this hope, and the NSW Department certainly presented it to children as a solution to their own 'inadequate' family. When it was not 'successful', it was always described as the child's fault, intensifying their sense of not being acceptable anywhere, of not being lovable. Children were sometimes picked out of a line at the Home to be fostered, something remembered by Peter Brownbill from his NSW Departmental 'establishment', Weroona, when he was nine or ten. 'These line-ups were emotionally expensive,' he said:

for selection for the line was sought after. Actually being picked was the dream, the fantasy, the way out. For one, the dream came true, for the others, another rejection, a reinforcement of that sense of despair that is only known by those who are totally abandoned, totally helpless and totally alone.

Peter was chosen at his final line-up by a couple who had come to support relatives in choosing a child, but he was not told. 'The first I knew of this "choice",' he said, 'was my arrival at their address several weeks later.' This way of doing things shows an indifference that is incomprehensible even by the standards of the time: it is as if children are inanimate objects. The same process was used when children were lined up so that the people who 'took an interest' in the Home could choose someone to take on holiday with them or for a weekend. Whatever the intention, and often it was well meaning, the effect of this practice on children was predominantly distressing, if not traumatic. 'People would walk through and say, "Can I take her out?"' said Janet Maxwell, in a Barnardos Home in Sydney; another felt that 'we were looked over like cattle'. Again, children who were not chosen could only feel even less lovable and less acceptable than they already did. And children who were chosen felt they were on trial, and often were uncertain how to behave. There can also be little doubt that this particular Home practice provided an open invitation to paedophiles. Ron Pritchard, who was in the St Joseph Orphanage at Largs Bay in South Australia as a child aged six to nine, recounts what was a common occurrence for many children in institutional care:

> The nun came up to me late on some Fridays and would say some people are taking you out for the weekend. Their name was not mentioned. When the people would pick me up they would sit me in the middle of them or on their lap on arrival at their home. It was dark on Friday. I would sleep in the lounge room, they would

> talk to me. On the Saturday the man and the woman performed sexual acts on me for their own pleasure. I was told if I said anything I would be punished. When I got back to the Home I complained to the head sister and told her what happened, as I was very sore by my ordeal, and I was taken down to the dungeon under the home where there is no windows just the dungeon and told by the sister the Devil is going to come and punish me. She then closed the door. It was pitch black. I could not see my hand in front of me. I was very frightened as I was waiting for the Devil to come, a terrible feeling came over me while I was down there a long time.

Ron described very vividly the effect on a young child of such prolonged terror:

> When the sister came and opened the door I was screaming and felt different as she took me up the stairs. I felt very rubbery and the light seemed to be different and I seemed to feel different.

What is terrible in this story is not only the acts perpetrated on Ron — by both the couples and the nun — but the completely impersonal way Ron is told his program for the weekend and then handed over like a parcel, a mere object. Is it surprising, then, that he was treated like an object by the people he was handed to?

Living in the Home

Visiting: 'Matron said we were spoilt'

Visiting was not regarded as a right of children or of parents, nor as an emotional necessity. In some Homes it was yet another form of control, and being deprived of a visit was a form of punishment. 'It was regarded as a privilege and they loved to take it from you for the slightest misdemeanour,' recalled Elizabeth Miller of the Protestant Federation Girls' Home in 1950s. Kerry Geldard, in this same Home, remembered that '[the] loss was not usually one week but one month or sometimes three months'.

Visiting procedures were designed to cause the least interference to the running of the Home. They bore no relation to the emotional needs of children or of parents and embodied a denial that blood ties were important and that people might long to see their family members. It was not usual practice to allow children to go home with parents for weekends, or even to go outside the Home itself. There is more than a suggestion in some accounts that visiting was even seen as a nuisance, since children would be unsettled afterwards and more difficult to 'manage', thus 'proving' that it was not good for them to see their parents or relatives. Lorraine Davis related how in the Launceston Children's Home where she lived from the age of nearly three in 1944 until 1950:

> My mother wasn't allowed to visit us at the home, as they thought it would upset us too much. This was really cruel. If she had of come, I would never have let her go. I missed her so much and if she could have visited, it would have made all the difference … The biggest memory I have at the Home was yearning for my mother because I was bonded with her. I vividly remember the nightmares I used to have about her — she would be at the end of a tunnel and I could never reach her.

Kath Emmett, working at Sydney's Dalmar, a Methodist Home, in the early 1960s, said that children did not go home to stay with parents except for a few who went at Christmas time. Going home for weekends was certainly not encouraged; perhaps, she said, because:

> they thought it would be too upsetting, and they were actually in the care of the church. To a certain extent the

matron didn't like them going because it wasn't fair to those who didn't go; she was concerned they all be treated the same.

NSW state ward Joy Hill's file shows that similar thinking underpinned state practices. Where foster parents complained that a natural parent's visit had 'upset' the child, both the foster parents and Departmental authorities decided that the parent's presence was therefore 'bad' for the child, rather than seeing the child's response as an expression of yearning for the parent and distress at another separation. The natural parent/s would then be prohibited from visiting their own child.

Visiting day, depending on the Home, was once a week, fortnight or month, for a short period only and usually within the Home grounds. In Cooinoo, in inner-suburban Sydney, visits were once a fortnight, on a Sunday afternoon, for an hour only. 'That was all that was allowed. Matron said we were spoilt because our mother came regularly,' said Marigold Kendall. Doreen Ferris, in Burnside in the early 1950s, said, 'You were allowed to see your family once a month, and once every three months were allowed out for the day.' Verneta Lohse recounted a poignant incident from her years in the 1950s in a Catholic Home, Mater Dei, in northern New South Wales. Visitors were allowed once a month and her mother came the long distance from Sydney as often as she could. One day she missed the train but caught the next one and arrived about 3.30, when visiting was officially over. A nun told her mother to get back in the taxi she had caught from the station, as it was too late. 'We were so upset. She was crying and so were we, for you would have to wait another month.'

Things were different in the Salvation Army Home at Bexley in the same years. 'You had a visit every week,' said Brian Jones, '[and] were allowed out on a long weekend if you were good.' David Walshe's account of visiting in the Gill Salvation Army Home is particularly interesting for the contradictions it reveals in that Home's practices. He says that once a month they were allowed out of the Home on weekends, with a family member. But he says, 'no boy was allowed out with anybody else'. For example, you could not go out with school friends, even if they lived less than a block from the Home. This presumably was to ensure the safety of boys by keeping them away from strangers — a particular irony in this Home, where, from the evidence of many submissions, the greatest danger to the boys came from the adults who 'cared' for them. Further, said David, 'Due to my age, it was only in the last year that I was allowed to visit my grandmother on weekends — a grandmother I saw every Sunday in church.' This is a prohibition that appears to have no grounds in necessity at all. It was, however, entirely characteristic of this Home regime: as David put it, 'on our return, our fault or not, if late even five minutes, [we] missed out on the privilege next month'.

Visiting, then, like most other events in the Home, could be used to create tension, anxiety and further loss in children's lives, rather than provide the comfort and interest which might reasonably be expected to be its purpose. For some children it just reinforced their feeling that they were alone in the world, like John Brown, who had gone into care straight from the hospital where he had been born to a single mother, and who knew no visitors were possible. 'I feel the pain started when I was at Cheltenham [Boys' and Girls' Home, Victoria] from not getting visitors.' Staff seemed to do nothing to help children with such feelings, and may have made them worse, as Dorothy Ashby's story shows. Dorothy related how at the Morialta Home in Adelaide in the early 1950s:

> Visiting days were held on the first Saturday in the month and we would be all dressed up, I would be so upset. I knew that no one would be visiting me, but the staff would always say, 'You never know, some one may come today.' I used to invent big stories about my parents to the kids that taunted me about having no

visitors. When all the visitors arrived I would go off by myself away from everyone. I had a favourite place at the top of the outside stairs where I could watch the other children with their visitors but they couldn't see me. I really got to hate visiting days.

'I was not allowed to see him because he'd been naughty': the Home as total authority

As I have said previously, one reason parents might have preferred institutions to foster homes was that they could visit their children frequently. However, as we have seen, visiting was fraught with stress for children — and, sometimes, for their parents. There are few accounts of Homes where visiting was frequent and flexible and where parents were regarded as having a right to vary visiting hours or days, or indeed to specify anything about what they required for their children. Homes provided a service, but they operated as if they were bestowing a favour. Some of the large Catholic (and other) Homes, for example, where parents made little financial contribution, had grounds for this view, at least in their own eyes. In many Homes, however, parents were paying the required fee, and they paid it punctually. Furthermore, as I have related previously (Chapter 5) state wards were subsidised by the government, and in many instances the parents were contributing to this government payment.

But regardless of the actual financial arrangements with parents, Homes were a law unto themselves. The efficient running of the institution was the paramount consideration, and it overrode any parental needs or desires. Parents accepted this, because they had no option but to accept it. Goffman makes the point that in total institutions, 'significantly, institutional plant and name come to be identified by both staff and inmates as somehow belonging to the staff'.[14] The name 'Children's Home' might imply an enterprise run for the benefit of children, but this can only ever be an ironic connotation, since the only human subjects considered were the staff, and their aim was just to make the institution run smoothly.

Another way to put this might be to say that the end was completely lost in a focus on the means. If visiting had been more frequent and flexible, less subject to regulation, efficiency would have been sacrificed. That children would have been happier and felt less abandoned was not a consideration, despite the assertions in the annual reports of the various institutions that the wellbeing of children was their goal.

The other dimension here is that parental control was conceived of as exclusive, and therefore could not be shared. As I related in the previous chapter, we can see this in state ward histories: the state showed little consideration for parents once a child had been removed. The same thing happened once a child was living in an institution. The Home, as revealed through care leaver histories, appeared to take on a parental role because it had physical custody of the child, and this was linked with having control. That is, Homes did not operate as if they were carrying out a duty of care towards children, for which they were accountable to the children's parents (including the state, where the state was the parent) — who, if that duty were breached, would be entitled to complain and demand that standards improve. This is not explicitly stated, and may not have been conceived of in this way at the time, but it is expressed in the way Homes operated.

The status of parents can be seen clearly in one story related to me. After I had interviewed Jim Mallory, who was in Burnside from 1947 to 1952, he rang back to say that his mother wanted to speak to me, to explain why she had put her children in a Home. Mrs Mallory, as a widow who had been evicted from her home, had had no option but to place her children in an institution. It was obvious that, more than 40 years later, she still felt pain about her decision and was anxious that I should understand it. She had chosen the Home carefully — a big one which she thought might have to be accountable to 'the Welfare' — but still found its rules inflexible and even callous. She was not allowed to visit her son Jim when he was ill in hospital. On another occasion she visited the Home at the correct time but was not allowed to see him 'because he had been naughty', even though it would be a month before the next visiting day. On another occasion when she visited she found her son in bed, as punishment. 'Matron will be very annoyed with you if you take him out of bed,' said the sub-matron when she lifted him up to put her arms around him. When she attempted to give her boys some slippers a staff member laughed at her and said, 'We're teaching them to be men, not cissies.' 'I was broken-hearted,' said Mrs Mallory. 'They were in Burnside five years. I'll never ever be the same. I still cry over it. I loved my children.'

Relations between staff and children

As must be clear from previous chapters, staff related to children almost solely in terms of servicing them, and that often with obvious reluctance. With a few exceptions, accounts by former inmates indicate that personal relationships with children were not considered at all, let alone thought important or necessary. This is the 'lack of love, affection and nurturing' referred to by the Senate committee as such a dominant feature of the histories they received. If we judge by the separation of siblings, the restrictions on visiting, and the strict rules about talking, it was not apparently considered important that children in institutions have personal interaction with others at all. Dealing with children in this way sends a clear message to children that they are *not worth* relating to; it is what the philosopher Gemma Corradi Fiumara has called 'the animal-husbandry approach'.[15] This term is a most apt description of the way that adults related to all children in Homes and certainly describes accurately what I experienced, and observed, and came to regard as 'normal' in my Home. To be singled out, as an infant, as somebody worth interacting with is developmentally crucial to the creation of self, says Fiumara. For older children it is significant because it is a marker of existence as a self, a self worth relating to personally. Kerry Blake, in her submission, said that 'there is a sense for me that I have no legitimacy', and that this feeling was a legacy of 'beginning life in an institution, where you are fed, watered and bathed'. 'That sort of "bedrock",' she said, 'is just not enough to develop that crucial sense of self we all need to carry ourselves through life with any success.'

This mode of care can be seen in all the Home practices, but it is also spelled out in annual reports of institutions and child welfare Departments across Australia. The 1954 Burnside annual report notes that 'our children are weighed and measured periodically while their medical fitness is constantly checked'; indeed most of the data which I studied in the Burnside archive about children's lives there concerns primarily their material environment and the monitoring of their physical conditions. This is not to deny the excellent intentions behind such care, but to highlight the almost total absence of any attention to the non-physical side of care. LO Bailey's Hopewood 'experiment' (see Chapter 2) could only have occurred within a paradigm of child development which found nothing lacking in the following statement:

> When children are nourished by an adequate supply of natural foods, eaten in correct order, and properly masticated, they will escape most of the ailments suffered by the majority. If, in addition, they had the benefits to be derived from exercise, physical culture, fresh air, sunshine, recreation, suitable companionship and guardianship, hygiene, suitable housing, clothes and

> instruction, plus the affectionate attention of the people who will be carefully selected for that purpose, will it not be strange if they do not emerge from such a home with qualifications much above average?[16]

This sounds like a formula which, if followed, will produce a highly desirable product. Even 'the affectionate attention of the people who will be carefully selected for that purpose' barely sounds as if it refers to human beings.

One of the major emotional deprivations for children in Homes was the extremely restricted possibility of personal relationship with adults, particularly with the adults in charge of them. 'They didn't have the time to treat you as individuals,' said Joy Hewitt, in a UPA Home, The Laurels, in Sydney. 'You come, you go, someone else comes, they go. But it's a sad thing for any child to be like that; it's terrible.' In another UPA Home, Rathgar at Grafton, New South Wales, said Christine Lang, 'there was absolutely no feeling of belonging, of having anybody, and some of the kids had been there for years'. Alice Nanson, however, observed:

> It wasn't intentionally cruel. It was complete and utter starvation of affection. Everyone wanted to be thought special but most had nobody. They just never got any personal affection or attention.

Or as Jennifer Richards in St Brigid's Ryde, said, 'As much as I was never mistreated, nobody ever looked out for you. I didn't even have a toothbrush.' None of the staff gave her one: it was Jennifer's problem, and the solution would have to wait for one of her mother's infrequent visits.

In all my interviews, and also in the submissions to the Senate Inquiry, there are few positive memories of staff members. The majority of staff who were remembered were remembered as either indifferent to children or brutal. Interviewees said that the 'nice' staff were always overruled by 'awful' ones, who somehow had more influence, and that 'nice' staff tended to leave. Ralph Doughty, in his account of the almost unremitting brutality of his 10 years in the Salvation Army Gill Memorial Home, recalled with 'great softness' one lady officer:

> who would give me and other boys a nice smile as she passed by or a nice smile if she saw me in the distance and if I was close enough and she knew that I could hear, she would speak my first name and say 'hello Ralph'. You were never ever called by your first name; it was either your surname, or your number or 'you' or simply nothing.

But as Ralph observed, 'it was a great risk to a lady officer to smile at a boy or speak to him' except to give him an order, and this same lady officer 'was in great fear of the manager'; and since the boy would also be punished for her action, she was very limited in expressing kindness to the boys. There are nevertheless some accounts of staff members showing kindness and interest to children. Douglas Mann, in the Parkerville Home in Western Australia in the late 1940s, recalled fondly his experiences in 'babyland', where he spent two to three years:

> Miss Holt cared for me at babyland. She really loved the children and I was one of her favourites. Even after I joined my brother at St Gabs, she was the only person who showed me any affection at Parkerville. She was like an angel.
>
> I also remember Ron the truck-driver who was good fun and mucked around with us. He never got angry and was like a father figure to the kids.

Another such account comes from John Brown, in the Tally Ho Home in Victoria from 1939, aged nine. The manager there was Edgar Derrick (see Chapter 4). John described him as 'a terrific person and he always listened', and remembered him as 'very caring to all the boys' (there were 100 in the Home). John remembered him 'lancing our boils, giving us haircuts'. Even with the 'bad eggs' who came from 'broken homes and other institutions', said John, Derrick was always patient, though he would 'pull them into line'. John concluded:

> I never saw him punish anyone or ever belittle anyone. All the staff were good. I liked all of the staff, but especially Edgar Derrick because of the way he treated everyone, including staff. He cared about and for everyone in the home. He was just such a wonderful man.

John's account also shows that even where there were 100 boys, it was possible to have a humane system of care if these were the standards set by management. 'All the staff were good,' said John — perhaps Derrick did not tolerate staff who were not, and was aware enough to know how his staff were treating the children. But a kindly superintendent did not always make a difference. Peter Brownbill, in his submission, recalled his experiences in Royleston, the NSW state receiving Home for boys, and the superintendent, a Mr James:

> I was to enter and leave this institution several times over the next decade [from 1953] and I cannot remember an unfair or unpleasant episode with Mr James. I only remember him as a warm and kind man, with the whitest of white hair.

Nevertheless, said Peter, despite Mr James, 'Royleston was a terrible place to find yourself, at any age' — this was perhaps because in a Home that was part of a highly bureaucratic state welfare system, it was not possible for the superintendent to have the personal influence that Derrick was able to have on Tally Ho. Tally Ho was conducted under the aegis of the Methodist church, which left him to do things in his own way (see Chapter 4).

Inmates often related how staff played favourites or, like Betty in my Home with my sister, singled out one particular child to persecute. Matron 'was very cruel to children she didn't like (we children used to call it 'pets and spites'),' said Shirley Banks of her Burnside matron in 1942. Sometimes interviewees recalled particular incidences of kindness as oases in their bleak lives: Joy Hewitt, for example, remembered how once, 'the cook brought me up a hot chocolate when I was sick'. The children in Else Ferguson's Roslyn Hall Children's Home in the 1960s got some cuddles from the matron, as Frank O'Leary did from the nuns who cared for him as a little boy in his rural Catholic Home. 'Cuddle' is a very rare word to find in a submission, however; these two examples come from my thesis research.

In all my thesis interviews, the couple who ran Judith Barry's Barnardos Home were the only staff (apart from Else's matron) who attempted to act as significant and positive figures in the children's lives, and Judith, as a middle-aged adult, remembered them with affection. Leonie Sheedy, in St Catherine's Geelong, also paid tribute to the benign influence of Sister Genevieve, whom she named her second daughter after. 'Good' staff had a huge effect on insecure children starved for attention and affection, and may well have made a significant long-term difference for children who were fortunate enough to experience them. I was lucky in the older woman who ran my Home, for she encouraged me to read, but my best memory of an adult in my childhood is a warm, encouraging teacher called Mrs Chapman, whom I had for two years in primary school and also for English in high school.

Other children got emotional response where they could. Anne Martin-Smith, in the Church of England Girls' Home in Sydney in the 1930s, had to get up and milk the cows at 4.30 in the morning, but said that 'it was one of the best things that ever happened to me — to sit and cuddle a warm cow and get a drink of milk which you never ever got at any other time'. Peter, separated from his sister in his Salvation Army Home, also remembered cows fondly: 'There was a cow called Daisy, my sister's name. I used to talk to her, the cow.'

Children were entirely dependent on the goodwill (or not) of strangers, people who were for the most part unaccountable for their actions since the only witnesses to them were children, whose opinion did not count. Barry Cook, in the Children's Aid Society Home in Parkville, Victoria, illustrates just how arbitrary staff behaviour could be. One of the tasks the children had to carry out here was to transport the laundry from an upstairs bathroom down to the back of the Home, quite a long journey and generally carried out at night in the dark. A favourite amusement of the staff, said Barry, was 'to make the sounds of wolves and barking dogs, thus causing the duty carriers to wet their pants'; I have already related the consequences of wetting your pants in a Home.

In fact, punishment was for many children the only physical contact they had with adults. In the UPA's Rathgar, 'There was no love, no physical contact at all unless with a strap. If you fell over, bad luck. Even the little ones,' said Christine Lang. The people in charge of this Home were, she said, 'completely devoid of any emotional feelings toward the children. I can never recall any affection whatsoever being shown by the staff toward anybody in the Home, including the babies'. State Homes were similar. Daphne Calhoun, at Weroona in the 1950s, said that she was *not allowed* to show the children any affection — this presumably reflected the same call for 'professional detachment' reported by Norma Reading, working in the Waitara Babies' Home. Chrystal Lennox's memory of the staff at Bidura in 1962 was that 'if you looked sideways, they'd hit you', or as another interviewee summarised it, 'If one of the staff didn't like you, you were history.'

What is particularly significant here is the influence that staff had on the atmosphere of a Home. It could be positive, as John Brown related of Tally Ho. Or it could be as Sylvia Baker described it — the matron of her Home 'used to terrorise our lives'. The Burnside board would not have approved of this woman's behaviour, but the board probably knew nothing of the detailed and ritualised torments she inflicted on the children. It is important to note that the adults who behaved with violence, cruelty and brutality towards children were women as well as men. One of the fallacies of this era, that all women are 'naturally' good with children or that all women like children, may have rendered particularly invisible the cruelty that women inflicted on children.

Everyday rough handling

> As a child, under care at Royleston, I felt the heavy hand of adult men, men employed to care for us ... We were their job, and when they weren't happy, we suffered, ie. at a line up you would be picked up by the collar of your shirt, your ear, or hair, it really didn't matter, and heaved to the correct position. This kind of treatment could be inflicted with malice, [by] officers who did not like you, or just an act of impatience ... they were devastating. Over time this treatment developed your sense of hopelessness, worthlessness, and aloneness. At times even the good guys had a heavy hand.
>
> Peter Brownbill, NSW state ward

The way that children were physically handled — very roughly, with so little of even ordinary care — is an aspect of Home life that was so much a part of everyday living that it is hard to define clearly. This is not the cruel corporal and other punishment described previously, although it is related to it. Interviewees did not refer to it except obliquely, but I think that is because for others, as for me, it was a standard feature of daily life, and thus unremarkable. Peter Brownbill's quote above expresses it absolutely accurately. This is not physical punishment; it is a continually reinforced reminder that 'unwanted' children do not deserve to be treated with care. It is another place where the absence of parents is felt — we all look after our own possessions with much greater care than we do those of other people. Franny Mason, in Sydney's Dalwood in the 1940s, wrote that her random memories of 'that place' were:

> chicken pox, where they used to pull our singlets off, taking all the scabs with them. It was very painful. They also sent us all off to have our tonsils removed ... sitting on mattresses on the floor in white shirts with white napkins around our heads, watching other children being wheeled past us, with blood all over them.

And as a little boy in WA's Parkerville, Douglas Mann describes this same absolute indifference to children's feelings when he says that 'an awful memory' of that time was going to the local school, a walk of two to three kilometres each way on a gravel road:

> This was really painful because we weren't allowed to wear shoes. I can remember crying all the way to school in winter as my feet really hurt — chilblains were common — and in summer we would get blisters because the road was so hot.

I remember small children shaken like rag dolls, dangling from the ankles before being thrown into cots; children crying endlessly with runny noses; Betty digging into the scalp of a child she particularly disliked as she washed her hair, the child's face contorted with pain she dared not express; tiny children sleeping on hard ridges of plastic under their sheets, not worth smoothing out; the bruises on small limbs; a toddler's hair sticking up in clumps where it had been pulled, above her flushed and tear-stained face. Witnessing this careless brutality day in and day out reinforces the feeling of emotional insecurity that starts when your parents abandon you — you are now in danger, living a precarious existence.

Some children were sexually abused, and many were physically assaulted; their bodies were at others' disposal, but even where this did not occur, *the possibility was always there*, unpredictable and unavoidable. Judith Herman, in *Trauma and Recovery*,[17] says that children in an abusive environment face a formidable task if they are to preserve hope and meaning. But they must do this, she says, for 'the alternative is utter despair, something no child can bear'. Even in Homes that were less punitive, the impersonal nature of relationships between staff and children meant the absence of any solace or comfort. Speaking specifically of the child who is sexually abused in the family, Herman notes that 'the child feels that she has been abandoned to her fate, and *this abandonment is often resented more keenly than the abuse itself*' (emphasis added). I think this can also be applied to being placed in a Home. How could my mother, my father, not only abandon me, but abandon me *here*? Children felt deeply betrayed by their parents. Jim Mallory, whose mother so reluctantly put him in a Home, reflected that he and his siblings 'had talked to her too much about it', but he added that:

> it did tear us apart in the way we were affected by it for many years. My brother turned against my mother for putting us there when he needed her. He said he didn't love her.

In my case, once I left the Home I got to know my mother (at least on the surface) and to understand something of how difficult her life had been when we were young. I was attracted to her warm, lively personality, her sense of humour; I felt the affinity of our minds. I loved her, but I kept her at an emotional distance. We never talked of the past. Never talked about what had happened or why, never talked about my father, or of how she herself felt about her life without us. I did not even try to, probably afraid of the huge abyss of pain — and all the other feelings I had never examined — that would open up. When she was dying of cancer, although I went all the way from Australia to Britain to see her, after a couple of weeks I could not stay in London. I began to feel overpowering anger towards her, and I would not believe she was dying. I told myself it was all an act. I went away to a Greek island for a holiday, abandoning her in a National Health hospital. It was only for a week, but she was dead when I returned. I feel shame — and, finally, pain and grief — as I write these words. Yet I still can't imagine doing anything different at that time, before I had help in facing my feelings about my childhood. I could not have watched her leave me again.

Relationships between children in the institutional environment

Relationships between children were surely an important part of orphanage life but there is not a great deal written in submissions about their significance. I think it is, however, a complex subject, one that would fill a book on its own; what I say here is only a few impressions. Bernard Brady, who was in the Catholic St Joseph's Orphanage in Surrey Hills, Victoria, said in his submission that 'despite the restrictions imposed by the physical containment of the orphanage environment, I entered into and enjoyed the vibrant orphanage sub-culture'. Every CLAN newsletter has a section with notices from care leavers looking for people they remember from their Homes, so it seems that often other people could make a difference, and that other inmates are remembered as significant. But the degree to which children could enjoy the company of others in a Home must surely have varied, depending, perhaps even to a large degree, on just how punitive the environment was. Where children lived in fear, personal survival became the priority. In the many accounts I have read and heard, it is not common to find former Home inmates talking about solidarity and close friendship among the children.

This is perhaps partly because, as I have discussed, staff made this difficult, or impossible — in some Homes, friendship and family relationships were used as tools for punishment, which would have discouraged overt expressions of closeness. Unhappy children, like unhappy adults, need scapegoats, and submissions show that sometimes older children would brutalise or sexually and physically molest younger ones. Undoubtedly the brutality of 'carers' was passed down the line.

Where Homes were more humane — Else Ferguson's Baptist Home in Sydney, in the 1960s, for example — and children were treated much more as individuals, they could perhaps find more comfort in each other's company

* * * * *

The impression I had initially, from my thesis interviews, was that each child, individually, hoped for rescue, and that family, whether within the Home or without, was more important than other children. Janet Maxwell, who I quoted above as feeling lonely in her large Barnardos Home. When I asked her if she had good friends in the Home, she said: 'Good friends? I don't think so. I felt terrible. I think because there were so many kids and no family.'

There were certainly some exceptions in my group of interviewees, though. Ray Lennox, a Fairbridge immigrant, spoke of the solidarity of children in his group; perhaps this was because all these children knew they had nobody in Australia. Their families, or what remained of them, had been left behind in England. (By contrast, Janet, above, had a mother who just didn't visit.) Similarly, Jane Hamilton, an orphan, made good friends, some of whom she is still in touch with. 'That was a very important thing at the time,' she said. 'You had each other. We shared a lot of things, humorous things too.' Catherine Harrison, in Hopewood, where none of the children had any family that they knew of, said that at school she was 'picked on', but that was bearable because 'there was a great feeling of brother-and-sisterhood. Eight of my "brothers" were in the class and they all stood up for me.' The Hopewood children regarded themselves as a family, all 86 of them, at least in childhood. Perhaps Cheryl Hannaford, who grew up in the typical Home of this era, voiced a common response when she said, 'There was a thing about being together, even if you didn't get on with them — like a security blanket.' Cheryl added that this was why a lot of girls who grew up in a Home went on to train as nurses, 'living in', as was customary then: 'they were used to all those people, to living in a large institution'.

Institutional colonisation

> Time spent sitting in a corner with a dunce cap on my head, and a sign on my back saying the devil is in me, this was a punishment I quite often received. I now understand why I am bad and the devil was always in me: we joined together to help each other cope.
>
> Lynette Hyde, St Joseph's Orphanage, Bathurst, NSW

In his submission to the Inquiry, David Forbes expressed what I think may be true for a great many of us who grew up in Homes that were predominantly threatening. David was a NSW state ward, taken from a chaotic and violent family but subjected while in care to institutional environments and sexually opportunistic 'carers' that made these childhood years an experience far worse than anything his family had inflicted upon him. As I noted in the previous chapter, he was eventually consigned to a home for 'subnormal' children, his emotional damage construed by the NSW child welfare system as evidence of defective intelligence. David said:

> When I was eight, I learned that if I was going to survive
> I needed to hide my true feelings; in fact I had to hide
> my true self. I had to protect the real me by shutting
> down and withdrawing into my own world ...

Some children, like me, could pass for 'normal' or even 'good' by being withdrawn and compliant. The childhood 'culture' of the postwar decades was very different from the childhood culture of today. Highly conformist, excessively 'good' children were, in the period of my childhood — predominantly the 1950s — regarded with approval, not viewed with concern, as they may be today. Many Home children survived this way, both in the Home and at school. As Terry Langham said (see Chapter 3): 'You be quiet, you do not say anything. You make yourself a small target.' You act out the role of 'the perfect inmate', becoming what Goffman describes as 'colonised' by the institution.[18] Or as Catherine Harrison, a Hopewood child, said:

> I learnt at a very early age that if you misbehaved you
> ended up getting the strap, or you got into trouble. So I
> became what was known as a 'goody-goody' and I didn't
> step out of line. It was a measure of safety, you know,
> self-preservation.

In fact, many of the children who ended up with the label 'uncontrollable' were simply children who were too visibly non-compliant to the adult norm of what a 'good' child should be. In March 2004 a report in Melbourne's *Age* newspaper about the dearth of foster carers quoted the president of the Foster Care Association of Victoria as saying that one factor in this is that 'The children that are coming [into care] now are so much more damaged and more challenging.'[19] How do we know this? Or to put it another way, what do we know about how disturbed children in care were in earlier periods? During my childhood, and for a couple of decades afterwards, 'damaged' was not a description used by welfare authorities, state or charitable, to describe Home inmates. Children exhibiting the behaviours that today get them labelled 'damaged' were called 'recalcitrant', 'insolent', maladjusted, 'uncontrollable' and other words used to describe behaviour that was 'unacceptable' — including 'mental defective'. All the children who wet their beds in Homes were 'damaged', for instance, but the treatment they got was a belting, along with any other ritual of humiliation on the agenda of their institution.

Resistance

Some children quite deliberately resisted, took what Goffman calls the 'intransigent line' and refused to co-operate. Children who did this within the institution, or who absconded from care, truanted from school or engaged in what we now call 'risk-taking behaviours', invited ever more severe punishment, including extreme physical assault and eventually incarceration in increasingly punitive environments until their spirit was finally broken — by the penal brutality of Hay and Tamworth in New South Wales, Winlaton in Victoria, Westbrook or Wilson in Queensland, or any of the Catholic Magdalen Homes, to name only a few. Many submissions to the inquiry tell this story.

Despite all this, children did take steps to change or improve their situation. The social powerlessness of children is often presented as evidence that it is natural for them to be subject to adult formulations of their 'needs' and abilities,[20] so it is important to put on the record children's attempts to have an effect on their own destiny. This could range from writing letters asking to be rescued, as Ellen Brown did at Bidura. She wrote to every person she could possibly think of that she had ever known, even the next-door neighbour and the lady who had made her best dress (which she'd worn to Bidura and never worn again). She would throw the letters over the wall of the Home in the hope that somebody would post them. Similarly, Dawn Burridge, in the rural Anglican Home Coventry in 1952, having unsuccessfully tried running away, 'used to write letters and put them in the post box and hope that they would be delivered, without stamps'.

Care leaver accounts are full of runaways: 'There were always absconders and they always got caught,' said Brian Jones of his time in the Bexley Salvation Army Boys' Home. Many children ran away to find their parents. Stephen Madison, for one, escaped from NSW state Homes on many occasions, and once, at the age of 12, got away completely, to Queensland: 'I knew I had family there somewhere.' Children who ran away knew that almost invariably they would get caught, but did it anyway, even when the punishment was a beating or being locked in a dark cupboard. They also knew that their behaviour would not be interpreted as a sign of something amiss or a cry for help; indeed they knew nobody was interested in the 'why'. As Deirdre McCourt, who was at St Joseph's Neerkol, in Queensland, observed, 'Kids ran away and no official ever asked why.' Undoubtedly, many children ran away for the same reason Lynette Hyde did. Lynette was in the Sisters of Mercy orphanage at Bathurst, NSW, where one nun beat her very brutally:

> I was absolutely terrified of her. I would tremble at the sound of her voice, or wet myself in fear. I hated her so much my life became unbearable, so I ran away about fifty times, only to be returned back to the orphanage to another belting.

Welfare authorities in fact regarded running away as an infallible indication of increasing incorrigibility. Charmaine, a NSW state ward, recalled that she 'took off a few times' but it was 'not because I was boy mad, like we were told we were, but because I wanted to be with my mother. I yearned for her affection.' For her attempts, Charmaine earned a stint in the

Training School for Girls at Parramatta, incarcerated there on her 15th birthday.[21] In Queensland the punishment could be even more severe. Patricia Pascoe, labelled by the Department a 'chronic runaway', was sent at the age of 15 to the state's mental hospital at Wacol, where she was housed with extremely disturbed psychiatric patients. Like the patients, she was given a cocktail of 'mind-boggling' drugs to keep her quiet, and was severely beaten by the 'nurses'. When Patricia attempted to escape, she was made to spend periods of from two weeks to two months in solitary confinement, some of it in the dark.[22]

But even if running away was not an option, it was still possible to make a protest. David Walshe, in his submission, recalled what happened when one of his younger brothers was required to attend the funeral of the hated manager of his Home, the Salvation Army's Gill Memorial Home:

> As the coffin passed by them in church, Frederick, my brother, put a rock on his coffin as it was the nearest thing that he could obtain that resembled a grenade.

'There was a stigma about not having a family'

'Some statuses, in our society as in others, override all other statuses and have a certain priority,' said Howard Becker in his 1963 study of deviance.[23] Becker called his work *Outsiders*, and certainly this is what Home children felt themselves to be. They were marked out as different and 'inferior' in the eyes of others and in their own eyes, because they were no longer members of viable, and visible, families. Having a stigmatised (because deviant) status, says Becker, 'will override most other status considerations in most other situations'. People are marked with this 'master status' because they have broken a rule. Breaking such a rule immediately makes you suspect, puts your moral status in question: what kind of person can you be, to break such an important rule? The answer, says Becker is '[o]ne who is different from the rest of us, who cannot or will not act as a moral human being and therefore might break other important rules'.[24] As I have suggested in previous chapters, this describes precisely how welfare authorities, institutional staff and the wider community regarded Home children. They had broken a cardinally important rule: they were not able to be cared for by their own family. The deviant identification became the controlling one. The important consequence of this, says Becker, is that:

> treating a person as though he were generally rather than specifically deviant produces a self-fulfilling prophecy. It sets in motion several mechanisms which conspire to shape the person in the image people have of him.[25]

'You're the odd ones out,' said George Murray. 'You're treated as if you're not part of society.' '"State ward" was a dirty word,' said Joy Hill. 'You wouldn't get a job if you said you had been a state ward.' Feeling stigmatised, different, a second-class citizen, not as good as other people — these self-descriptions litter care leaver accounts. The stigmatisation began when you were 'charged' with being 'neglected', or when you entered the Home. Entering the institution, as Goffman says, 'is *prima facie* evidence [to the staff] that one must be the kind of person the institution was set up to handle'.[26] Why else would you be there? This automatic labelling of inmates is not mere name-calling — it is the lynchpin of a form of social control. A speaker at the Queensland Forde Inquiry described it this way:

> People respond to the expectations that a particular environment sets for them. If the institutional environment projects a fortress-like mentality, it sets up an expectation that young people will behave in a dangerous and violent way, which in turn may influence the way in which they choose to behave.[27]

Penny Walton, living back with her mother after years in Homes, recalled:

> [Even] back in society, you were 'the Home kids'. You were never invited into people's homes. It was as if we were outcasts, even though we had enough material things. We were not wanted.

Penny's statement sums up what care leavers commonly feel about themselves and their parents. Children consigned to care suffered a double deprivation: apparently unwanted by their parents, they then, through being in a Home, also became unwanted by society. For all such children, the original feeling of being given away, abandoned, by parent or parents was reinforced by the public attitude to Home children and state wards and by the way Homes were run: a constant reinforcement of the message that they were unvalued. Ken Carter, born in 1945 and in care from babyhood, at the Victorian state Home, Turana, and the Salvation Army Boys' Home in Box Hill, Victoria, summed it up exactly in his submission:

> I feel that I'm the guilty one. I feel that I'm — it's hard to describe. You just have this sense of guilt that you, as an orphan, were trash. You are nothing, nobody wants you, and that was repeated to me on many occasions throughout my years in the penal system. It is a terrible feeling.

School became an ordeal for many if not most children: they already felt what Ken described, and then were made to feel even more different. 'We went to the local public school where we were "the Home kids", "Homeys", and were made to feel terrible,' said Jilly Marsh, who was in Dalmar from 1961 to 1968, 'and very few of us had friends outside. Others were looked down on if they befriended us.' The effect is the self-fulfilling prophecy Becker describes: 'We used to get tormented, and it makes you very aggressive, horrible,' said Jilly.

'They *expected* kids to be bad because they were not with their parents,' said Susan Fitzgerald, 'so the kids played up.' School life featured invisible social boundaries — Home children ate together, they rarely mixed with other children and 'were never allowed to go to a friend's place — and I don't remember being asked,' said Susan. 'By definition, of course,' says Goffman, 'we believe the person with a stigma is not quite human, ... [and so] ... we exercise varieties of discrimination, through which we effectively, if often unthinkingly, reduce his life chances'.[28]

One of my interviewees was Phyllis Keane, who had not been a Home child, but who contacted me to tell me her observations about the stigma attached to being one. She had spent time in the 1950s in a complex of Catholic Homes in Goulburn in rural New South Wales. One building was a hostel where country girls who lived too far from a high school stayed in order to attend school, and this was where she lived. One building, however, was a Home for girls who were orphans or from 'broken homes', children without their own families to care for them. Phyllis recalled that she felt sorry for these children, but that:

> I hated being lumped in with them in the public mind. We didn't mix socially, even when we all went to church on Sundays and chapel on Thursdays. There was a stigma about not having a family. People were very conscious of who the 'Home girls' were.

It is hardly surprising that Phyllis felt as she did. The administration had made it clear through the explicit segregation of the two groups that Home girls were 'different', and 'undesirable'. All these girls went to the same school, but 'I was in the "A" classes and none of them were,' she said. Once again, the expectation that none of these children will be 'bright' is fulfilled, particularly since some, as Susan Fitzgerald said, 'play up' and are sent out constantly, their behaviour taken as a sign of both lack of intelligence and of 'insubordination' and 'waywardness'. Thus life chances for these children, as Goffman says, are unwittingly — or perhaps not so unwittingly — reduced.

Identity

> The thing that hurt me most of all was that I didn't know who I was. No one ever told me where I came from or what. I was just an individual person that knew no one. I never ever knew how old I was. I never knew my birthday ... I just think this whole thing has had a profound effect on me. I used to wait for somebody to come and see me, just as I saw parents come in and see their kids. I was always waiting for somebody.
>
> Ken Carter, b. 1945, Victorian state ward in care from babyhood at the state Home, Turana, and the Salvation Army Boys' Home, Box Hill, Victoria

These are some of the complex questions around identity which arise out of the care experience. Who are you if your parents do not claim you? Where do you belong? Is there an identity 'Home child', a separate identity created through specific experiences, particularly stigmatisation? How does your identity as a Home child or state ward relate to your family identity when all except minimal contact has been lost with your own family, or you have seen them so little that you hardly know them? Peter Brownbill, a NSW state ward in care from age two in 1953, related how on one occasion he and another boy whom he calls simply T—— ran away — 'absconded' — from Royleston, the state boys' depot in Sydney. At Central Station, the police picked them up and took them to Balmain police station, 'where the police sergeant disclosed that he knew T——'s father, but not mine!' Peter said:

> I left that station asking … what is a father? Later that day we were returned to Royleston, [and] I was still asking that question, what is a father? T—— had one, the police knew who he was. No one seemed to know who mine was. Did I have one? I had no idea!

How does a person construct their identity when all the usual culturally determined 'normal' shaping influences of childhood — like parents! — are missing? Most of my childhood experiences occurred in the Home, not within my birth family, and this is true for many care leavers, although it may be different for older ones who already had established relationships with siblings and parents when they went into care — and who now can only grieve for what they lost.

The Home — for better or worse — played a big role in making us who we are; it was the scene of our childhood. To reject that experience totally is to reject part of our own lives and our own selves. This may be why some people go back year after year to reunions of their Homes, where they still exist. They do this even where it stirs up mixed feelings, often including pain; they cannot resolve this, but at least on these occasions they can share their feelings with others who understand. They need, perhaps, to connect again with something that was part of making them who they are.

Growing up outside your own family inevitably raises a big question: what would have happened if I had grown up 'normally', with my family? I feel a quite terrible, very painful, regret that I will never know what I would have been like as a child if I hadn't had to be a robot. And I feel as if there is a whole other parallel life 'out there' somewhere, the one which I didn't have with my parents, brother and sister. What would it have been like to be part of an 'ordinary' family? What sort of person would that have made me? Life would have been so different, so would I have been different? Or, if not different, would I have done quite different things? Been capable of other things? Things which can never be discovered now, because they have been sealed off behind the wall of defences that I set up in order to survive. Of course I can never answer these questions.

Leaving 'care'

> Home is the place where when you have to go there, they have to let you in.
>
> Groucho Marx

It must be obvious from all I have related that few children growing up in institutional care had any preparation for life outside the institution. Care leavers often found the period of their life after leaving the Home indescribably difficult, as it highlighted yet another dimension of how alone they were in the world. In one annual report of an institution — the Tasmanian Clarendon Home — I found a note that an after-care committee had been started in 1955. This committee tried to keep close contact with girls who had left the Home and also offered hospitality to children on the verge of leaving so that on departure 'they will not be without friends'.[29] This appears to have been unusual; perhaps it is partly accounted for by the size of the Home (40 to 50 children at any time) and its location in a small community, Kingston, in a small state, Tasmania. It was more usual that institutions would find work for inmates regarded as old enough to leave care, or would find them temporary accommodation and farewell them with a suitcase of clothes. Helena Dam was sent from her Catholic orphanage in 1942, aged only 11½, to work as housekeeper to the secretary of the Queensland premier. More often, young people aged around 15 or 16 were found jobs as domestics, farmhands or labourers, or occasionally a clerical position in an office.

Caroline Carroll, a NSW state ward, said that once she reached 15, in 1967, 'the Department told me I was old enough to look after myself! After never being allowed to make a decision on my own I suddenly had to make them all. I didn't even know how or what bus to catch to and from work':

> When I look back at that scared lonely kid I am amazed she survived. How did she survive? Luck. How could they put a naïve, ill-equipped, confused kid on the streets? They found me somewhere to live and a job but I had no one. They had taken my family, my confidence, stole my education, left me with huge guilt that it was all my own fault.

Nigel Shew, in Queensland in the early 1960s, though a state ward until the age of 18, supported himself by working in a factory from the age of 14½; the government showed no further interest in him. 'I found my own way,' he said, '[but] I was very unprepared for adult life':

> I lacked work, social and communication skills which in return caused anger, frustration and loneliness. I used alcohol and sometimes drugs to try and ease the pain. But that created more and bigger problems.

Many girls, as I mentioned above, went into nursing: another institution, but at least they would have a roof over their head. For boys, the armed forces could provide the same refuge. One of my interviewees, Cheryl Hannaford, said what I think is true for many, especially women:

> I think you want to get married as quickly as you can and have a family of your own and do the rose-covered cottage thing and have it all go right. But it doesn't work like that; your wrong decisions start there.

Perhaps what we want to do is go back to the beginning and

do what our parents didn't or couldn't do — but this time change the ending. People who have grown up in a Home, however, have possibly the least idea of anybody how to be a parent and how to have a family.

This last point resonates with another, compelling observation of Goffman's. In many total institutions, he says, there is a strong feeling that time spent there is 'time wasted or destroyed or taken from one's life', and as long as they are there, the inmates feel that they have been 'totally exiled from living'.[30] This feeling cannot be entirely accounted for, he says, by the harshness of life within an institution. What it must be attributed to are what he describes as 'the social disconnexions caused by entrance, and ... the failure (usually) to acquire within the institutions gains that can be transferred to outside life'. For adults who have been institutionalised — for example in a mental hospital or in a prison — the 'disconnexions' are obvious: loss of money, work opportunities, relationships. It is perhaps even worse for Home children, exiled from life on the 'outside', a term many care leavers use. The 'disconnexion', or more accurately the *waste*, in Homes is of the growing and developing and learning time of childhood; that time is spent in survival, not in gathering useful skills, knowledge, experiences and self-perceptions which can be 'transferred to outside life' — to life as a young adult.

Institutionalised children are not only burdened with their childhood losses and the legacy of their 'care'; they are also not equipped by the institution to become well-functioning adults. Life on the 'inside' does not fit you for life on the 'outside'. In fact it robs you of the possibilities offered by 'outside'. In his submission, Mark Greenhalgh, a Queensland state ward from the age of seven (in 1948), after experiencing the 'care' of both the Sisters of Mercy and a Queensland 'training' school, describes just what this could mean:

> Upon release, I was not prepared for living in 'the outside world'. All my life I had been forced to fight for survival, to take any opportunity that offered itself, with only my own well-being in mind. Consideration for others was never taught and never learned. When you grow up in an institution you know better than to trust another human being – it could cost you your life.

In a very fundamental sense, children who have never been interacted with have no idea how to interact with others — and no idea that they are not actually doing so. This can lead to what the *Bringing Them Home* report identified as a major effect of such childhood trauma: the 'failure to learn the art of living with other people'.[31] Marigold Kendall summed up this effect when she said of her six years in Cooinoo:

> I left when I was fourteen and found later how naive I was, how unaware, in dealing with people. Just the way people used to speak to each other … I was totally unprepared when I got out — it was so sheltered. It felt like I was from another planet.

Another planet that gave no clues about how life on this one might be conducted. Here is a list of things that go with being a Homie. It's not exhaustive; sometimes it seems the list could be endless:

> Nobody teaches you to think for yourself, judge for yourself, or know yourself, or how to go about making decisions.
>
> Nobody teaches you to cook, though you probably know how to clean anything at all — floors, clothes, dishes etc (if a girl) — or do hard manual work (if a boy).
>
> Nobody teaches you to ride a bike.
>
> Later on, there's no Dad or Mum to teach you to drive.

> It's very hard to choose clothes that suit you when you've never been allowed to make choices and never worn things that suit you.
>
> Birthdays are fraught — you didn't spend them with Mum and Dad when you were a child so they're not happy occasions.
>
> Christmases are even worse, sometimes indescribably terrible: the whole idea of it, it's all about families.
>
> Not to mention Mothers' Day and Fathers' Day.
>
> You're extremely unlikely to inherit money or property.
>
> There's nobody to ask about anything, from simple to important.

As a final point I would add: 'You don't trust anybody.' Which leads to another serious consequence of spending your childhood merely surviving: in order to do so you set up defences which in adult life are inappropriate, usually self-destructive, and often destructive to others. David Forbes expressed this when he said that he shut down and withdrew into his own world in order to survive. 'This worked well when I was a child,' he says. 'As an adult, though, it caused me a lot of problems':

> Since I was never able to be myself as a child, the real me was never able to fully develop as an adult. I hid myself for so long, it became very hard to stop. It was like the real me was frozen somewhere in time.

Chapter 7

The aftermath

Society continually tells victims to 'get over it', or 'it's in the past'. I can assure you that the treatment of those of us who survive will not be 'in the past' as long as one of us draws breath, for we suffer the consequences every second of our existence.

Ray Flett, NSW state ward

I could have ended up just another statistic, but I am alive, I am capable of love, friendship, a profession; I have survived. The Government needs to accept that these terrible things happened to children under their care and so-called protection. It is truly a breach of duty [of] care, to which all children have a right. People should hang their heads in shame. It was an outrage then and it remains an outrage today.

Elizabeth Behrendorf, Victorian state ward

The emotional consequences

It is clear that a childhood spent in the type of care described in this book will have far-reaching effects on the lives of the people who experienced it. However, what we know about these consequences we know mostly through anecdotal evidence, for, as the Australian Institute of Family Studies (AIFS) notes in its submission to the Inquiry, there is little longitudinal data on outcomes for Australian children who have been looked after away from home, 'and none that specifically focuses on institutional out-of-home care'. About state wards today we know somewhat more: as the AIFS submission acknowledges, they 'constitute one of the most disadvantaged groups of young people in the community'.[1] We know this because research is, finally, beginning to be done on outcomes for children growing up in care. However, this is a very recent development: in the past it was simply taken for granted that once you had removed children from their 'bad' home situation, you had done all that was required — they had to be better off. This has meant that, as the AIFS submission notes, 'children's welfare services in Australia and elsewhere have rarely gathered information to find out how the experience of being looked after affects children's subsequent health and wellbeing'. The AIFS itself, a national research institute, has also apparently not regarded such children as coming within its ambit, although these, too, are children from Australian families — even if they are families that have broken down.

We do have some indications of outcomes within a broader context. The submission from the WA Department of Community Development states that contemporary research shows that 'the links between childhood abuse and the use of health, mental health care, justice and other welfare services cannot be under-estimated': 50–60% of psychiatric inpatients, it says, and 40–60% of psychiatric outpatients, have 'childhood histories of physical or sexual abuse or both'. These figures refer to the effect of childhood abuse in all contexts. There is little statistical material that documents the measurable effects of institutional care on its survivors: and this is what is needed to convince governments that, as a matter of social justice — or even economic commonsense — they are obligated to do something to help people from this background.

We are fortunate, then, to now have the Senate Report, which draws together into a coherent pattern what care leavers themselves have always known about the effects of their childhood. It can be summed up by a statement from *Forgotten Australians*: 'the outcomes for those who have left care have, in the main, often been significantly negative and destructive'.[2]

The Report begins with a consequence which probably applies to every person who was raised in care: 'a fundamental, ongoing issue' related to 'the lack of trust and security', which impacts on every area of life. Care leaver accounts referred constantly to 'the skills required to survive in an institutional setting being quite different and inappropriate for normal social interaction in the outside world'. One person put it this way:

> How do you know how to be a parent if you have never been parented? How do you know love, if you have never been loved? How do you know how a normal family functions if you have never been in one? These handicaps have been far more pervasive and devastating to my life than the experience of being sexually abused.[3]

Care leavers typically live, permanently, with the following: low self-esteem, lack of confidence, depression, fear, distrust, anger, shame, guilt, fear of authority, obsessiveness, social anxieties, phobias, recurring nightmares, tension migraines. All of this finds concrete expression in people's lives, of course, so it is imperative, says the Report, 'to recognise and acknowledge the magnitude of contemporary social problems that are the long term effects stemming from care leavers' past experiences'. The behavioural and social effects include:

- speech difficulties (stuttering is common for care leavers);
- alcohol and drug problems;
- homelessness;
- unemployment;
- incarceration in mental health systems;
- difficulties forming and maintaining relationships;
- prostitution; and
- more serious law-breaking offences.

The last has resulted in a disproportionate percentage of the prison population being care leavers.

Anecdotal evidence shows that for far too many, emotional pain has resulted in contemplation of or actual suicide. At CLAN, our observation is that care leavers seem to die younger than the population as a whole, and have a higher than average level of debilitating illnesses at a relatively young age. I have heard more than one care leaver say of a sibling who died young, 'He died of his childhood.' Brian Hart, in his submission, summed up the legacy of this 'care':

> My life has been extremely hard, due I believe, to the treatment meted out to me whilst I was in the care of the Salvation Army. I am still trying to come to terms with it. I am now on a disability pension, my health is deteriorating, I have had bypass surgery, suffer with anxiety, depression and obsessive-compulsive disorder. I have also had ongoing counselling throughout the years and am still having counselling to this day. I have had several broken marriages and relationships, find it extremely hard to trust other people and am a loner. I believe that I am a survivor despite what happened to me as a child.

There are also indirect consequences. One woman who had endured the Training School for Girls at Parramatta described the most terrible consequence for her of her 'care' under the NSW government:

> My fear of living in Australia forced me to live apart from my mother. I have not lived in Australia since 1971. I lost my desire to live in my own country, because it let me down so badly.[4]

The partners and children of care leavers also testified to the Inquiry about the pain and difficulty, and sometimes the impossibility, of living with somebody haunted and driven by their past. How do you express emotion when you were never loved and nurtured as a child? 'I thank the system for denying me the feeling of love, for the inability to either give or accept it and for the hurt this has caused to anyone close to me,' wrote G Hampton in a submission.

'Relationships were often characterised as a desperate search for love,' says the Senate Report: 'I had never been really loved and that was the most important thing for me', for example.[5] Submissions spoke of multiple failed relationships, and of physically and emotionally abusive relationships and marriages that were tolerated 'because it was more important for me to have someone than no one'. Many do have no-one, as Ronald Pritchard related:

> I have never married I would liked to have but feel embarrassed as I still blame myself with what had happened to me. I still have to leave the light on in my house every night time. I have flashbacks seven days a week three hundred and sixty five days a year of the people performing sexual activities on me and I still blame myself for allowing this to happen. Even so, I was only a child.

One of the most disturbing results of this kind of 'care', says the report, 'is [its] impact on the ability of care leavers to successfully parent and raise families'. This has an ongoing impact, for 'Each new generation, lacking a sense of security and parental role models, is unable to provide these vitally necessary foundations for the next generation.'[6] When you grow up parentless you do not know how to be a parent, but you still love your children, and to know that you have failed and even damaged them adds to the pain, anguish, and crippling weight of your own experiences.

Caroline Carroll, in her submission, spoke for countless numbers of us when she said:

> It has taken me **50 years** to be able to say I am a former state ward. From age 15 I did everything in my power to hide my past. I carried (still do) such guilt & shame, I was told nearly every day of my life I was worthless unlovable, **I believed it.** I suffered physical/sexual & emotional abuse. Because of this harsh early treatment I feel my life has been a huge struggle. I have always felt alone. I married young, had 2 children. The marriage didn't last; was it because of my background? Without doubt it would have contributed to it. I knew so little of what family life should be like. I know I was incapable of trust, I longed for love but was unable to accept it or know how to give it. I worry what insecurities I have inflicted on my kids. Have I damaged them with my inability to reveal myself even to them? That fear of rejection never leaves. I feel they have suffered by never knowing maternal grandparents/aunts/uncles/cousins.

It's all here in Caroline's statement, and could not be better expressed:

- the stigma, so the silence and the secrecy;
- the guilt, the shame, the feeling of being unlovable and worthless;

- the feeling of unceasing struggle;
- the feeling of always being alone;
- the marriage/relationship breakdown because you have no model of family life;
- the inability to trust and to love, hand in hand with the longing for love;
- the fear of how this has affected your children;
- the fear of revealing yourself ('unlovable', 'worthless');
- the feeling that your children may also be deprived because you could not give them 'normal' family connections; and
- the 'fear of rejection that never leaves'.

We are now beginning to be able to directly link these emotional effects to medical conditions. For example, a recent US study of 17,500 adults found that a childhood involving abuse and neglect increases the risk of heart disease in adulthood, and that 'the link between these adverse childhood experiences and heart disease seems to be mediated more by psychological factors than [by] traditional risk factors'.[7] One of the most significant risk factors was emotional abuse. As the number of adverse childhood experiences increased, so did the risk of heart disease: having seven or more adverse childhood experiences (as opposed to none) nearly quadrupled the risk. How do we quantify in physical terms like this a childhood characterised by unremittingly adverse experiences — so many that they cannot be counted? 'Heart disease cannot be looked at just in terms of risk factors in middle life,' said the authors of the study. To assess the risk, 'you really need to go back to childhood. Adverse childhood experiences definitely affect future health.'[8]

All of this tells us that older care leavers must be disproportionately represented in the national statistics for relationship breakdown, drug and alcohol dependence, depression, anxiety and other mental and emotional problems, early death and suicide. It is also clear that a significant number of people, especially men, do not marry or have other long-term relationships — including friendships — and many care leavers of both sexes make a conscious decision not to have children. Others, in contrast, have many partners and children in the search to create the family they did not have themselves; often they find it difficult to sustain those relationships and parent those children. It is inevitable that a disproportionate number of children in care today will have parents or grandparents who were themselves in care. Again, we do not collect the statistics that would tell us this, although social workers are familiar with this phenomenon.

People who have lost contact with siblings and parents, who have no children themselves, or have difficult relationships with their children, do not have family bonds to sustain them through crises in their lives. For them, the standard problems that come with ageing are magnified. For most people in the general population, the capacity to remain independent is reduced as they grow old. This is exacerbated for people who have been so marginalised all their lives that they have not been able to build up enough financial, emotional or social capital to support them in their later years. So people who were emotionally neglected and abused in Homes as children come full circle by ending up even more vulnerable than most when they are old — once again they may well end up in an institution. Care leavers often express their fear of this, and their determination not to let it happen. The sad truth, though, is that through lack of resources they may well have no other option but an aged care home, and it may be run by a church or charity, perhaps even the same one that ran their childhood institution.

As *Forgotten Australians* says, the impact of this experience on society is profound, and it occurs on many levels:

The indirect costs to society of the harm done to children in care are as large, if not larger, than the direct costs but also unquantified: What has been the cost to the economy of care leavers not fulfilling their potential? What is the cost to the economy of lost productivity? What is the cost of human suffering of the child or of the family? These costs represent a loss to the economy and to society generally.[9]

Homes that were like prisons create the prison of the damaged self that people then live in for the rest of their life, unless they are fortunate enough to get the help and love required to repair that damage. Although many people show extraordinary courage and resilience in overcoming their care experience, many others are broken by it. An illustration of the terribly circumscribed life experiences of many care leavers is revealed in a newspaper report from the 2003–04 Ombudsman's inquiry into abuse in care in Tasmania.[10] It tells the story of a man who had been suing the state for its failure of duty of care, but who died in his sleep, at the age of only 41, before his case could be concluded. He was suffering heart disease, and was frail and unwell due to psychiatric illness and drug use after a childhood of psychological battering at the hands of his various 'carers'.

We know, and deplore, the fact that Aboriginal people have poorer life outcomes and lower life expectancy than the rest of the Australian population. Since a background in care is not recognised as a factor that would be valuable to record statistically, we do not have the data that would undoubtedly tell us that care leavers also constitute a group of Australians who fall below the rest of the population in quality and length of life. One of the recommendations of the Senate Inquiry seeks to remedy this knowledge gap: Recommendation 31 urges both the federal and state governments to record the care backgrounds of clients on forms already in use by agencies such as Centrelink and Medicare, and on admission forms to prisons, mental health and aged-care facilities. This recommendation, and others, urges governments to 'explicitly recognise care leavers as a sub-group with specific requirements': that is, to recognise that this is a severely disadvantaged group which needs services tailored to its unique needs.

The physical consequences: injuries

These are some of the emotional effects. Some Home inmates also have physical injuries as adults that can easily be traced back to childhood: they are a direct result of assaults. Ken Carter, in his submission, told of his experience with a doctor who, looking at X-rays of his back, asked what had happened to him when young. It was obvious to the doctor that as a child Ken had suffered an injury that had severed a disc in his back and affected subsequent growth. Ken said, 'I knew what had happened, but I didn't want to talk about it then. I just said that I didn't know.' But he did know: 'the injury obviously related to the flogging etc. with S—— [a Salvation Army officer in his Box Hill (Victoria) Home], when he laid into me behind the shower block.'

The extent of beatings in Homes suggests that damaged vertebrae and their ongoing effects must be a quite common outcome. Other survivors describe persistent migraines, deafness from being boxed on the ears — or poor hearing from untreated childhood middle-ear infections — poor teeth or loss of teeth from blows, and ongoing pain from other untreated injuries. A related issue is the long-term effects of the forced administration of drugs. The Senate Report quotes from several care leavers who experienced this: the Wilson Youth Hospital in Queensland, for example, was from the 1960s to the early 1980s, as one inmate, Beth Wilson-Szoredi, described it, 'a cross between a mental health unit and a jail'. Here, inmates were routinely dosed with heavy sedatives and antipsychotic and other experimental drugs.

Beth, who was incarcerated at Wilson in 1976, said in her submission that few of her peers from that time were still alive:

> Some did not make it out of their teens. Many died in their twenties, some before my eyes. Some decided it was all too hard and took their own lives. Many more, however, fell into the addiction trap, self-medicating, so to speak. I strongly believe there is a direct correlation between the relentless medicating of inmates at Wilson Youth Hospital and the self-medicating that people mimicked that would eventually end their lives. The drug scene is a high-risk way of life, so not surprisingly some of our peers were murdered.

In the early 1970s, in another 'training' institution, Victoria's Winlaton, girls who were considered to be at 'high risk' of pregnancy on release were given injections of the drug Depo-Provera, which at that time had been authorised for use in Australia only to treat cancer but which had a contraceptive side-effect. Other known side-effects were obesity and loss of libido.[11]

It was also not uncommon for children in institutions to be used as guinea pigs in drug trials and medical experiments; some were reported in medical journals.[12] Diphtheria immunisation, for example, was trialled on 600 children at Queensland's Nudgee orphanage — when no ill effects were reported, it was extended to the general population. And babies in two Victorian orphanages were used in experiments on the effectiveness of a herpes simplex vaccination. This raises a great many questions, beginning with, who gave consent? As the Senate Report notes, 'not all the children were orphans, yet there appears to be no record of a parent's permission ever having been obtained'; if, as was reported, the sisters who ran the orphanage gave consent, did they have this right? Do any of the people concerned know they were used as experimental subjects? Did they suffer any long-term adverse health effects?[13]

A recent newspaper article revealed that between 1959 and early 1961 the Commonwealth Serum Laboratories (CSL), a federal government agency, used babies in Victorian orphanages and Children's Homes to test a new polio vaccine — this vaccine is now thought to have been contaminated with a monkey virus since linked to cancer.[14] When this story broke, the director of public affairs at CSL is quoted as saying that community attitudes at the time of the trials in Melbourne were very different. It would have been a logical decision to trial the new vaccinations in such institutions, she said, because 'lots of kids died of communicable and vaccine preventable disease' in them.[15] Just as lots of kids did in the general population — but nobody suggested trialling the vaccine on them. Perhaps their parents would have objected.

Finally, if these are the experiments we know about, what other experiments do we not know about?

Identity

Peter Brownbill said in his submission:

> Circa 1953, I was charged a ward of the state, and remained so until 1970; these dates could be considered benchmarks. Between these benchmarks, I lived a life outside the normal experience of average Australians, male or female. The cumulative effect of this experience is so pervasive, that today, I'm 52 years old, and still a state ward!

As I said in the previous chapter, growing up in an institution means your identity is not shaped primarily by being a member of your family. So who are we, and where do we belong? This confusion about identity is aggravated by the fact that most care leavers do not have either information or documents about the families they come from. I am lucky to have the photos that I do of my family. Very few people who grew up in institutional care have any photos, either of themselves when young or of other family members. They also do not have any medical records, school reports, their own original birth certificate, their parents' birth certificates or marriage certificate. Often we know nothing at all about our parents' lives or the families we came from. We have no memories — or at best, very few memories — of family get-togethers, holidays, Christmases and birthdays. We have no family stories. I am only now beginning to piece together some of my family history. At least I still have relatives to talk to about it; many people have nobody. They did not know their parents, and they often lost their siblings in care and never found them again. Leonie Sheedy, in her submission, called it 'genealogical bewilderment':

> Being a parentless person is a most difficult thing. I feel like a second class member of the community. I feel different. I have no sense of belonging to a long line of extended relatives, no parents, brothers, sisters, aunts, uncles, cousins, second cousins. My loss is also my children's loss, as they have no extended relatives on their mother's side either. I feel that I have no past, that my life only began at 3 yrs old. The documents and family photos of a normal family life are missing.

Leonie's history is in many ways a typical state ward's, or Homie's, experience. The second youngest of seven siblings, she went into care, at St Catherine's Geelong, as a Victorian state ward, at the age of three, in 1957. She was separated from her brothers and her sisters, except for two of them, and forgot the elder ones. She now has no contact with three of her sisters, and one has died. She found her elder brother Anthony in 2002 after a separation of 40 years. When her husband Warren organised her first ever birthday party — for her 40th, in 1994 — she realised that not one member of her own family would be there:

> The lead up to this event triggered feelings of wanting to be the same as other families and have my family there. I needed to find my [younger] brother James. It took me a year to locate him and thousands of dollars spent looking for him. I even wrote to Paul Keating (the PM and my local member) to see if he could help. There was no service to assist with searching or locating family members. We even paid for a private detective to find him, to no avail.

Leonie is far from alone in this; many care leavers spend a great deal of time, money and emotional energy looking for lost relatives. Many were separated from them by state governments who have done little to date to help reunite them with their families. Many care leavers do not know the reasons they went into care, or the sequence of events, or why they were moved from one Home to another; they have no way of making sense of their childhood experiences, of piecing together the events which make up their past. And the search to find out who you are is not assisted by the records of your past which do exist — or, more accurately, which sometimes exist, since there is never any certainty that they do.

Personal records of time in care

As I have said earlier, with few exceptions, record-keeping about children in care has not been a high priority with the providers of that care, whether government or charitable. This is one of the reasons why it is impossible to accurately assess the numbers of children who grew up in care over the past century (see Appendix). Since the children cared for in the private sector were not regarded as being the responsibility of the state, the state did little or nothing, through legislation, to ensure that those institutions even kept records, let alone kept appropriate records.

On the whole, time and resources were not spent on recording, cataloguing and storing information about the children; there are significant gaps in records and records are sometimes inaccurate.

Sometimes they have simply not been kept: the Salvation Army, for example, appears to have no records for some of its Homes. Other smaller agencies, as well as many one-off Homes, have long since disappeared, along with any records of their inmates. Floods and fires, along with demolition of premises or removal to other premises, are often cited both by agencies and governments as the reason for the non-existence of records. And while obviously all these could have happened, it is evident that preserving records was not a high priority to begin with.

State wards, from any state, have a reasonable, although not guaranteed, chance of getting their personal files from the Departments involved. If there were problems in their care history, it may even be a substantial file, but it will still be impersonal and often judgmental. It will be 'personal' only in the sense that it has their name on it: it will not be a record of their development through childhood, except in terms of how the authorities regarded them — terms such as 'high grade mental defective', 'slow, but not mentally retarded', 'backward', 'difficult', 'insubordinate' and so on. There are state governments, however, that have destroyed some of their state ward files. The WA government told the Senate Inquiry that until 1980 or even later, the relevant Department had a policy of systematically culling files; the SA government, too, destroyed hundreds of state ward files in the late 1970s and early 1980s. This was only discovered when archival searches on behalf of individuals wanting to retrace their past turned up only index cards. Explaining this policy decision, the manager of the relevant section of the current Department was quoted in a newspaper article at the time as saying this:

> I suppose in some section of this department, and I am sure in others, they took action to do something about

not keeping files that were long since closed and considered to be historical information on people that the Government had no current use for.[16]

I suppose she did not mean this the way it sounds, but inadvertently she was perhaps close to the truth.

People who were not state wards have nothing at all from the relevant government Department. I, for example, did not exist for the NSW Department in a personal file, and this is the case for all children growing up in non-government Homes. I am a statistic in the table at the end of the Department's annual report, which says how many children are residing in non-government Homes at that time (the Homes are not named). Other states did not record even this. What non-wards get from their institution varies greatly; when they do manage to get their records, they generally find that there is almost nothing written in the file about them, sometimes for their entire childhoods. Often they appear on an admission and a discharge register, with nothing at all in between. Details of parents and siblings, and the reasons children have come into care, are not always recorded; and sometimes birthdays and other details are actually incorrect. It can be almost guaranteed that nothing will be written about their development or individual characteristics — there will be nothing personal at all.

Mim McKew's experience is fairly typical. After years believing there was no record at all of her childhood years in Victorian Homes, she discovered that the records of one of the Homes she and her sisters had been in for a long period had been placed in the State Library of Victoria. 'Finally,' said Mim, 'everything we imagined we needed to know — medical history, photos, school reports, holiday visits — would be there to see.' She travelled to Victoria from her home in Far North Queensland:

> I got to the State Library early and paced the foyer. The head librarian led me to the desk where a large book lay

all by itself. My heart was thumping as he opened it. So there was the three-page history of our childhood. Mine was a whole two lines:

> M.S., born Dec 1957
> Sister of H.

Mim was both astounded and devastated. 'That 60-year-old book,' she said, 'contained hundreds and hundreds of lost children's names.' What she then said sums up what many care leavers feel about the sheer indifference of the system of 'care' to which they were subjected:

> 'How can that be?' I kept repeating to myself. Our whole depraved and abused childhood. Silenced. Vanished. Gone, just like that. I cried for myself and my sisters. I cried for all of the thousands and thousands of dysfunctional adults I have never met, who have experienced the same trauma as me. If we had been disabled, adopted, or if we had been imprisoned or sent to a mental asylum, would we not have had more documentation of our lives? Was that as far as the state's duty of care went?[17]

The Senate Report contains several recommendations, directed to both state governments and non-government agencies, which are designed to address, and attempt to redress, the failures in the documentation of institutional care. They deal with locating, preserving and giving access to records, as well as with funding programs to identify and preserve records, compile directories of records, and establish services to help people search for their records — including a dedicated information and search service in each state and territory. It also recommends that support and counselling services be provided at the time of viewing records, and afterwards, if required.

The response of government and other past providers to our history

Forgotten Australians includes this statement:

> The Committee further considers that many comments in recent years by governments, churches and care providers reveal a complete lack of understanding of or acceptance of responsibility for the level of neglect, abuse and assault that occurred in their institutions.

In his 2000 UK study, *Forgotten Children: The Secret Abuse Scandal in Children's Homes*, Christian Wolmar observes that although the events he documents in his book raise many questions, 'there has been little will among policy makers to ask them, let alone answer them'.[18] So it is in Australia — or was, until the Senate Inquiry. Until this Inquiry, and despite the many signs that there were questions to be answered about the past care system (see Chapter 1), the response of all past providers of institutional care, whether governments or the non-government sector, has been characterised by both ignorance and indifference.

It is true that revelations of sexual abuse in the context of care, especially by priests and clergy, are being addressed: these are criminal acts and something has to be seen to be done. They also require damage control, because they threaten the reputation of the organisations involved. But sexual abuse is only one aspect of the story; what is most obvious about the response of all past providers is their unwillingness to acknowledge that the system they administered was so profoundly damaging *in itself*: that this is not just about individual perpetrators but about the fundamental emotional neglect, as a matter of everyday practice, of extremely vulnerable children towards whom they had a duty of care. This response is particularly inexplicable when we take it for granted, today, that early childhood experiences are crucial to adult wellbeing — hence the emphasis, both in child-care practice and in government policy, on 'early intervention' in families. In the light of this, it would seem axiomatic that people who have grown up without their parents, in institutions, whether they were sexually and physically violated or not, would have to be regarded as suffering particularly severe disadvantage. Furthermore, contemporary child welfare or 'child protection' practice begins from the premise that living in care — which today is not even institutional care — rather than with their family of origin, presents children 'with a significant number of issues which impact on their ability to grow and develop', as a recent publication puts it. The very title of this publication — *Improving Outcomes for Young People Leaving Care in Victoria*[19] — is a recognition of the risks inherent in growing up away from your birth family.

Nevertheless, no state of Australia recognises the significance, and the significant consequences, of this history. Most states have no services to speak of for care leavers, apart from supplying their state ward records. Where there are services for us, they are — like the guides to records which I talked of in Chapter 1 — usually the result of an inquiry. They are not initiatives of government set up as a considered response to a perceived need. They are specific to each state, very poorly resourced, and offered only to people who grew up in care in that state and are still living there. Care leavers who grew up in another state are not eligible. In none of the 'human services' departments in any state is there a section dedicated to addressing our issues, and only Victoria has a designated ward worker. Any services for wards — which are mainly about access to records — are located in the adoptions branch of the Department; state wards and Home children seem to have been tacked on as an afterthought. Nor is there any education for Departmental staff in any state about the past care system, so that they can help older state wards deal with the information contained in their records.

Without that training, younger staff must find the past system as incomprehensible as do the middle-aged, and older, adults who apply to them to see their records.

New South Wales presented no submission to the Senate Inquiry and sent no representative to the two days of its hearings in Sydney. Presumably this state believes there are no issues which it is required to address from its past delivery of care — despite the fact that because of its much-vaunted fostering policies, it probably separated many more children from their parents than did any other state (see Chapter 5). Neither, however, did Tasmania or South Australia send a submission to the Inquiry.

In his submission, NSW state ward Ray Flett offered the following account of what happened when he tried to obtain redress from this state for his 'care':

> The state of NSW and the ministers I have written to over the past few years refuse to acknowledge the reality of the life I have undergone. They have constantly refused to investigate my allegations of abuse and have refused to respond to any of the statements I have made. These actions have trivialised my life and the effects which I endure today. I was undergoing counselling paid for by NSW but following its constant refusal to acknowledge or apologise for what I suffered I have now rejected any more until they are willing to accept and acknowledge that the treatment I underwent was abusive and has led to a life of trauma which is getting worse as I grow older. I am frustrated and angered by this constant refusal and firmly believe that this attitude has led to this worsening of symptoms.
>
> I might add that the only reason I was eligible for this counselling was because at the age of sixteen I consented to being adopted by my foster parents of eight years. Had I remained a ward of the state I would not have been eligible for any assistance whatever.

What Ray is referring to in his last statement is that adoptees' needs are recognised by all Departments, in all states of Australia (as, of course, they ought to be). There are several workers in the NSW Department whose job is to address the needs of past adoptees, yet there is not one worker with the task of providing this for older state wards — except for one who will do so *if the ward was also adopted*. Adoptees, once they were formally signed over to their new 'parents', were no longer a state concern; the state had nothing further to do with them. State wards, however, were the state's children: the state stood for them *in loco parentis*, and had a duty of care for wards usually until they were 18 — certainly at least 16, and occasionally 21. And we who were not state wards lived in Homes licensed and inspected by the state. So in the end, the responsibility for all of us rests, directly or indirectly, with the state, for the entire period of our time in care. The difference in what states are prepared to do for these two categories of Australians could be called an anomaly. Or it could be called unfair discrimination.

'Towards Healing'

Non-government agencies vary greatly in their willingness to address care leaver issues. For reasons of space I will present here just one example, but a significant one because it is from one of the most prominent past providers of institutional care, the Catholic Church. This organisation has set up a protocol, called Towards Healing, for dealing with allegations of sexual abuse against their personnel, including, of course, those who worked in institutional care. Point 19 of the 2000 version of this protocol states:

> Whenever it is established, *either by admission or by proof*, that sexual abuse did in fact take place, the Church authority shall immediately enter into dialogue with victims concerning their needs and ensure they are given

> such assistance as is demanded by justice and
> compassion. (emphasis added)

It is safe to say that the church's reserves of justice and compassion will not be called upon very often, for few religious personnel are likely to admit their crimes, and it is extremely rare that any victim of sexual abuse can 'prove' the perpetration of acts carried out in secrecy, with every precaution taken to avoid detection. Maureen Green's submission to the Inquiry showed what is likely to happen. Maureen made a complaint through Towards Healing about her sexual abuse by a nun in the Sisters of Charity St Anne's Home in Liverpool, New South Wales, where she was placed, at the age of 15, in 1966. In this Home, she says, not only were the girls physically assaulted, and poorly fed, but 'there was no privacy: we couldn't bath, we couldn't dress', for the nuns would watch the adolescent girls in the shower and the bedroom, insisting that they leave their doors open at such times. One particular nun assaulted Maureen sexually on more than one occasion, when 'there was no one else in the room', hitting her afterwards. On one occasion, Maureen became hysterical; after this the assaults ceased, but she told nobody what had happened:

> A few weeks after the last occasion, she come up to me
> and asked me not to tell anyone or I would get a lot of
> beatings and be made a spectacle of. I wouldn't tell
> anyone, I felt ashamed. I also thought I wouldn't be
> believed. This was a nun, a respected member in the
> community; who would believe that someone like her
> would do this to me?

This nun has now left the order and is apparently teaching in a school in Sydney. Maureen included in her submission the documents relevant to the complaint she made through Towards Healing. The final one from the church authority informs her that the nun who abused her has been interviewed, and that of two others implicated in her complaint, one has dementia and one cannot be located. Having completed 'a search for the facts as far as they can be discovered', the investigation was unable to find any evidence of physical abuse or 'any other evidence indicating that children had been sexually abused as you described'. The assessor was also unable to substantiate any of Maureen's other complaints. It hardly needs saying that that was a foregone conclusion.

Sandra Pendergast, in a submission which related partly to her incarceration in 1958 as an unpaid worker in the laundry at the Good Shepherd Home in Ashfield, NSW, added a note to the end of her account in which she asked the Inquiry to 'look into this so-called program' which, from her experience of it, she felt had been 'rigged to give the outcome the church wants'. In particular, she said, the Inquiry should investigate who it was who acted as judge, since 'it seems the Order of the Good Shepherd will judge itself, and only it hears the other side's evidence'. Sandra received no answer to most of the questions she raised about her treatment in the Good Shepherd Home. When she asked why the girls had not been paid, the Order claimed that the Arbitration Commission had given them permission not to pay these workers. But, says Sandra, 'they won't tell when and where this decision was handed down so I can check it myself'. Broken Rites, an independent support and advocacy group for people who have been abused sexually, physically or emotionally in religious institutions, observed in its submission that obtaining financial compensation through Towards Healing 'has turned out to be a lottery, and a person who enters the process can encounter major problems'. The group noted that 'some victims have been coerced and intimidated by aggressive lawyers representing the church authority' and that the church authorities 'have approached it as a legal process rather than a mediation'.[20]

A final, very important point that needs to be made about this process is that once again it is a response which confines itself to abusive acts by individual perpetrators: it does not even begin to acknowledge that it was the system of care itself which failed children so badly. On this point the Catholic Church has always been silent.

What they say

The Catholic Church, however, is not alone in this, as is clear from what other past providers of institutional care, both government and non-government, have put on the public record. Here are two representative examples. The Salvation Army, in its submission to the Inquiry, and referring to one of the Inquiry's terms,[21] acknowledged that:

> sadly there have been some instances where unsafe, improper or unlawful care or treatment has occurred. The Salvation Army takes these instances very seriously. *However, such occurrences have been relatively rare and not endemic to our services.* (emphasis added)

This statement appears to be contradicted by what *Forgotten Australians* describes as the 'overwhelming majority of submissions' from ex-residents of Salvation Army Homes, which describe 'negative experiences'[22], or what I would describe as the endemic and systemic abuse of children. Ken Carter said, in his submission, about his Salvation Army Home in Victoria:

> Let me tell you one thing. When this story is told there are a lot of people out there who will remember, they know what went on in the Box Hill Home [Victoria] as it housed 150 boys ... The reason why I held back so long is that compared to the other institutions like the Catholics, nuns and brothers etc. the Salvation Army was never mentioned — they were squeaky clean. I tell you the same thing happened there too, the things I saw at

the Box Hill Home — we just had to shut up about it. I know from the bottom of my heart that if you spoke to any of the 150 boys they would say the same as I.

Many of those 'boys' did say the same thing, in August 2003 on ABC TV's current affairs program, *Four Corners*, which presented, through the survivors, the experience of living in the brutal institutional culture that characterised Salvation Army Homes in more than one state of Australia. The Senate Committee said in its report that it believed that 'there has been a notable reluctance by the Salvation Army to acknowledge past practices, in particular the nature and extent of abuse in its institutions'.[23] That opinion is unlikely to be altered by the apology posted briefly on its website by the Salvation Army immediately following the release of *Forgotten Australians*. It said, in part:

> The Salvation Army is deeply regretful of any incident of abuse perpetrated by its staff. It acknowledges that during the 1940s, 50s, 60s and 70s some children in our care were subjected to abuse ... We had more than 30,000 children in our care throughout Australia during this time and the vast majority of children regarded the time spent with us as a positive experience but some have reported abuse.

And for a government perspective on our experiences, here is what the Victorian government submitted to the Inquiry. I quote at length because this represents such a typical response to our history:

> In the past, some children were abused and neglected while in care, and a larger number of children were subjected to standards of care which would not be considered adequate by today's standards. However, it is also important to recognise that the people who cared for children in the past, either in Children's Homes or in their own homes [i.e. foster care], generally did so as well

as they could in the circumstances of the times, and that auspice organisations for Children's Homes and foster care programs generally sought to provide the type of care which they believed to be best. There are many former children in care who acknowledge the individual kindness of carers and the general care that they were given.

It would be hard to find a clearer representation of the attitudes that former inmates of Homes struggle against when they attempt to raise the issues I have discussed in this book. The overall effect of such statements is to create the impression that we are unfairly judging the past by the completely different standards of the present, and further, that a few instances of abuse and neglect are being held up as typical, when the reality is that providing care for children in this era was generally a worthwhile and decent effort if judged within the framework of the period. In fact, even judged within the framework of the period it was deficient, as governments and charities and churches knew at the time. Nobody working in child welfare could have believed that the practices which characterised institutional care were acceptable, even then. They would certainly not have believed they were acceptable for their own children.

Kate Gaffney, the Melbourne academic I quoted in Chapter 1, made this point very precisely in her submission:

> In response to the ... statement that standards were different 'back then' I have one thing to say. The acts which it has been alleged ... occurred in institutions were the very same standard of acts which, if perpetrated by a parent or relative, would have resulted in the child being taken into state care in the first place. Parents were not allowed to deny their children education or send them to work or allow them to mix with known criminals, yet the protection system did this on a regular basis. Many institutions did not have educational facilities and

therefore, a child who had been taken into care due to truancy may well be denied an education even when taken into state care. A child taken into care because their parents kept them from school in order to work may well find themselves at the age of eleven or twelve working in an industrial laundry for a religious order. Finally, a child taken into care because one of his or her parents was a convicted criminal may well be accommodated in an institution where they mixed with, indeed lived and worked with, children committed to state care as a result of criminal activity.

The title of an article on state care of children in March 2004 in the Adelaide *Advertiser* begins with words which could have been applied to any state at any time over the last century: 'System fails to protect …'[24] It includes a statement by the SA opposition's youth spokesman that 'figures showed that children under the protection of the minister were at much greater risk of being abused than all other children in the community'. This has always been the case. The only difference is that in the past, 'figures' didn't show anything at all, since none were collected; nor was it even thought that they should be.

The media response

There is a similar indifference, and unwillingness to engage with the deeper issues, in the media right across Australia. The part of this history that tends to get media exposure, as I have said previously, is specific abuse allegations. Even after the release of *Forgotten Australians*, journalists have shown little interest in this as a political and social history, instead focusing almost exclusively on the 'abuse' and 'scandal': — the sensational aspects, or the emotive ones. They are not interested in interrogating either agencies or governments about being accountable now for their clearly deficient and often criminal practices in the past. No journalist has picked up on the recommendations of the Senate Report and made it their business to pursue the parties implicated and get some answers from them.

But as well as this, the way the press actually presents our stories also indicates how reluctant people still are to take seriously (or sometimes even to believe) the reality of children's experiences. Here is just one example. In 2002, five women lodged a case seeking compensation for alleged abuse at Nazareth House in Wynnum, Brisbane, in the 1950s and 1960s. One woman, who had been in this Home from age three to 16, alleged that she had been assaulted sexually, including being raped with a broomstick or flagstick, by a Sister Bernard and another nun, who was second in charge at Nazareth House at that time. Other allegations were that children were forced to eat faeces and rotting food. The national newspaper, *The Australian*, reported the story under the title 'Nun denies abuse claims',[25] saying that Sister Bernard was 'bewildered by the accusations'. '"I find some of [the allegations] quite disgusting — that anybody could even think those thoughts", she said in a soft, almost timid, voice.' The report went on to describe how the nun, now aged 69, 'and just 157 cm tall', asserted that 'there is no truth in them, absolutely not' as she sat 'perched on a chair' in the sitting room at the Sisters of Nazareth old people's Home she runs in Christchurch, New Zealand, 'blinking and squinting from behind spectacles'. The report concluded:

> Far from being abused, the children she looked after had 'on the whole a very happy life', she said. 'Really they had a lot of fun to try and make up for the fact that they had missed out on the love and support of family.'
>
> Sister Bernard, who joined the order at the age of 22, was at Brisbane's Nazareth House from 1958 to 1962. Discipline was tougher in those days, she conceded. It

was acceptable to smack children but there was never anything more than a smack with an open hand; nothing that could be construed as abuse.

Sister Bernard's explanation for the allegations was that she was the victim of a conspiracy. Children rejected by their mothers often turned their anger on the very person who looked after them, she claimed.

The language of the media report tells us who we are to believe: the words used to describe the nun — 'soft', 'timid', 'blinking', 'perched' and 'just 157 cm tall' — invite us to believe the nun, not the 'girls'. And the good sister is still engaged in selfless enterprise, now running an old people's Home. But let us step back from the biased language and look at the situation. How likely is it that this nun, or any other person so accused, would admit that the allegations were true? This report brings irresistibly to mind what the callgirl Mandy Rice-Davies said in cross-examination during the 1960s Profumo spy trial in the United Kingdom. When she was told that a government minister denied the allegations brought against him, she said, 'Well, he would, wouldn't he?': he might be a government minister, but he is also a man, an ordinary mortal like the rest of us, trying to save his skin.

Why are people so ready to believe the denials? It is at least as likely — if not more likely, in light of the sheer weight of evidence of clergy abuse that we now have — that the accusers are telling the truth. This nun, now a frail 69-year-old, was at the time concerned a young woman in her twenties, forced by her *own choice* of the religious path to repress all sexual desire. The children in her care presented her with readymade scapegoats for the manifold frustrations of her restricted life — one she could use with impunity. That scenario is at the very least as persuasive and as likely as the one that the nun herself offers. How likely is it that people would make up the type of accusation regularly brought against 'carers' from this past system? Is this another conspiracy?

Given the similarities among the stories of both men and women who grew up in all states of Australia — and in fact in institutions all over the Western world — the balance of probability is on the side of the accusers. But to accept that proposition, we have to relinquish the completely unanalysed but oft repeated belief that 'nuns don't do things like that'. This still seems to be, for many people, an impossible task, even though there has in the past two decades been overwhelming evidence that many nuns, and priests, and other religious personnel *do* 'do things like that'.

The establishment of CLAN

It was in this climate that Leonie Sheedy and I set up CLAN — Care Leavers Australia Network — in 2000. We had two objectives: to have care leavers' experiences acknowledged by making them visible; and to get some services, nationally, to help us deal with our past. We lobbied anyone we could think of, but we battled, most of the time, against indifference and lack of interest: people did not know what we were talking about, and they weren't interested in understanding it. 'Come back when you've got the numbers,' said the NSW government minister, Faye Lo'Po, when we approached her in 2000 for funding for CLAN. For two and a half years CLAN operated out of the back room of Leonie's home. We had only membership donations — $5 per care leaver — to help the two of us provide support and advocacy to all care leavers across Australia, until we got some larger, one-off donations from a few past providers. With a couple of exceptions, these donations, it needs to be said, came not 'officially', as a matter of policy, from past provider agencies but through the personal intervention of one or two individuals working within them who offered their personal support and encouragement and put pressure on their agency to authorise a small financial contribution to keep us operating. Three years after we set up CLAN, with the passing through federal Parliament in March 2003 of Senator Andrew Murray's motion that there be an Inquiry into Children in Institutional Care, we knew that we were at least on our way to achieving the first of our objectives.

The Senate Report

> For the people who have shared all those experiences with us, [and] in the hope that we may be able to very belatedly help right some of the wrongs, it is a weight we were prepared to try and lift. I hope that we can meet some of those expectations.
>
> Senator Sue Knowles, deputy chair of the Senate Inquiry, presenting the *Forgotten Australians* report to Parliament, 31 August 2004

I hope it is now clear why the 2004 Senate Inquiry was so significant for care leavers. This history that we have experienced is now on the public record, for all to read and understand. *Forgotten Australians: A report on Australians who experienced institutional or out-of-home care as children* was released on 30 August 2004 by the Senate Community Affairs References Committee. Of the 614 submissions received to that date, 174 were confidential, a reminder that many people who found the courage to write down their experiences still found them too painful, shameful or overwhelming to be made public. In the three months following the release of the Report, the committee sent out more than 2000 copies of it — more copies than have been sent out of any previous Senate Inquiry. And even though the Report has been released, the committee is still receiving, and accepting, submissions, in recognition of the need of care leavers to have their history on the public record.

On the day the Report was released, there were historic scenes in the Parliament of Australia. Over 100 care leavers packed the public gallery, having travelled from several states to be there in Canberra. They clapped the speeches, an offence which normally gets you smartly evicted; this time, the attendants simply stood by, sharing in the powerful wave of feeling that engulfed all of us there. More than one senator, in tabling the report, broke down while detailing its contents — and some wept openly at the press conference that followed. It was an extraordinary occasion; extraordinary, too, to hear a senator say, having described the neglect and cruelty described in the majority of submissions:

> Those of us who have never experienced that do not know what these people have gone through. As someone who has experienced love from their parents and from their entire family, it is incredibly difficult to look these people in the eye. They are brave, they are tough, they fight and they do not ever stop. Those of us who have had that love and care can only say, 'We love you; we cherish you.'[26]

The report is a large and comprehensive one, testimony to the commitment and empathy of the senators and the committee staff. Over its 11 chapters, and quoting extensively from submissions, *Forgotten Australians* shows conclusively the reasons for the statement I quoted in the Preface to this book:

> The Committee considers that there has been wide scale unsafe, improper and unlawful care of children, a failure of duty of care, and serious and repeated breaches of statutory obligations.

There are 39 recommendations in the Report. If they were taken up by all governments and by non-government past providers of institutional care, care leavers would feel assured that their rights and needs were being comprehensively addressed. The broad areas these recommendations cover are:

- acknowledgment and apology;
- a national reparation fund;
- internal church redress processes;
- records: locating, preserving and access to;
- advocacy and support groups;
- support services: this includes counselling, but also covers the general areas of health care, housing, aged care, and education; and
- raising the profile of care leavers and their history through data collection, research, oral histories and memorials and exhibitions.

I will not go through every recommendation, but will instead focus on key areas which must be addressed if justice is to be done for all who have lived this history — and if we are to receive both acknowledgment and the help we need to start repairing our lives.

Apology and acknowledgment

The first two recommendations concern an apology. They urge the Commonwealth government, and all State governments, churches and agencies, to:

> issue a formal statement acknowledging, on behalf of the nation, the hurt and distress suffered by many children in institutional care, particularly the children who were victims of abuse and assault; and apologising for the harm caused to these children.

Some care leavers feel an apology is meaningless, a hollow gesture that is easy to make. Others do want an apology; for them it is an acknowledgment that what they say about their experiences is true. It often seems that agencies feel that what they are required to apologise for is sexual or physical abuse, and they are prepared to do that — it is not a difficult matter to apologise for something we are now so vigilant to prevent and which we all agree is abhorrent. To apologise for the inadequate and endemically abusive system of 'care' that I have described in this book, on the other hand, is where sincerity is tested.

Some of the churches have issued apologies, and they vary considerably. At one end of the spectrum we have the Salvation Army apology cited above, which sits comfortably beside the Catholic Church apology issued in December 2004. The Church notes that an apology was first made in its 1996 version of Towards Healing. That apology reads:

> We acknowledge with deep sadness and regret that a number of clergy and religious have abused children, adolescents and adults who have been in their pastoral care. To these victims we offer our sincere apology.

And now the 2004 statement:

> We formally renew our apology to those whose abuse was perpetrated by Catholic Church personnel. The revelations contained in the report are the very opposite of all that we would wish to stand for. We are also deeply regretful for the hurt caused whenever the Church's response has denied or minimised the pain that victims have experienced. And we regret the hurt and distress caused to the many good people who have worked in this area.

It is difficult to work out here just who is thought to have suffered most, care leavers or the Church. And the Church is silent, once again, on the broader issues, the system abuse. Alternatively, we have the apology from the NSW Benevolent Society (BenSoc), which conducted one Home, Scarba House at Bondi, NSW, over a long period. This apology is part of a long and thoughtfully worded statement:

> We wish to make a public statement of apology about past practices in our provision of residential care. The

> Board and staff feel strongly that we should acknowledge our history and the role that we played in providing any inadequate care for children placed with us. The Benevolent Society apologises unreservedly for any abuse, mistreatment or harm experienced by children in our care ...
>
> The Benevolent Society feels deep sadness and regret for the children in our care who did not receive the consistent, loving care that they needed and deserved. We welcome the Senate Inquiry into Institutional Care and its recommendations. It gives agencies such as our own the opportunity to acknowledge past wrongs and try to address them appropriately.[27]

More than five months after the release of *Forgotten Australians*, as I completed this book, no government, state or federal, had yet issued an apology. The exception, in a sense, is Tasmania, where, in the context of its own Ombudsman's inquiry, which I mentioned above, the Premier has apologised to Tasmanian care leavers.[28]

Reparation

The sixth recommendation of the report is that 'the Commonwealth government establish and manage a national reparations fund for victims of institutional abuse in institutions and out-of-home care settings', with funding supplied by both the Commonwealth and the state governments and the churches and other agencies. Although care leavers have occasionally obtained payouts through victims' compensation schemes, the two major ways of attempting to obtain redress for abuse have been through the courts, or through the organisations which ran the survivors' institution. A number of the churches have their own internal redress mechanisms. I described the Catholic Church's Towards Healing above, and outlined some of the problems encountered by care leavers who have used it. The Senate Committee found that although such processes could be valuable, they needed to be more accountable, transparent, informal and rigorous (several of the Report's recommendations address these issues).

In an article written for the CLAN website,[29] Angela Sdrinis, a personal injury specialist with a Victorian law firm, shows clearly why a compensation fund for care leavers is necessary if survivors are to find both justice and closure. All other avenues of redress, she says, present formidable barriers. Compensation systems set up by church organisations, while they claim to be about compensating the victims, are 'really about controlling the process', since 'the fact is victims go to these panels virtually cap in hand', and 'often leave ... again feeling powerless and further abused'. Survivors who take this route are handicapped by the knowledge that if they go to law instead, they will face almost insurmountable obstacles. As the Senate Report notes, these obstacles include limitation periods (statute of limitation law, which means a person has only a specific number of years after an event in which to bring charges relating to it), the difficulty of establishing liability, the adversarial nature of the system, and prohibitive costs.[30] As Sdrinis has written elsewhere, churches also often argue that 'they cannot be sued because they are not legal entities, but simply religious associations'. This argument, she says, has had some success:

> notwithstanding that they are of course quite happy to be regarded as legal entities when it comes to holding and disposing of property and the accumulation of wealth.[31]

Other difficulties, she says, are that 'where victims are state wards, state and church each try to duck and shove responsibility', arguing about who should be liable. It is also difficult to 'prove' abuse in a court case, and to counter the argument often put up by defendants that the abuse had occurred before entry to care and therefore the organisation was not liable. In sum, the odds are stacked against care leavers, who are already unlikely to have the resources, either financial or emotional, to mount an extended court case against organisations which have huge reserves and are prepared to use them. It seems naive, though reasonable, to ask: where are Christian principles and where are Christian truth, compassion and charity? Where is a sense of what is ethical and moral? Where is a sense of social justice? 'If that's Christianity, then I'd rather be a heathen,' said Teresa Pollard, who experienced her 'care' in the laundry of the Good Shepherd Home in Ashfield, Sydney. Many care leavers do want their day in court, but it can leave them feeling worse than before, as one person wrote to the Inquiry:

> My case has been through our so called judicial system only to be let down by the legal crap that was so unbelievable that I reverted back into my world of hatred and depression.[32]

For all these reasons, there is no doubt that, as Angela Sdrinis concludes, 'we need to find an alternative'. The alternative proposed by the Senate Report is a national reparation fund similar to schemes already in operation in Canada and Ireland. All governments, federal and state, would fund the scheme, in conjunction with the churches and agencies who provided care in the past. The Report notes that while such schemes vary in their design, they share a common goal: 'to respond to survivors of institutional child abuse in a way that is more comprehensive, more flexible and less formal than existing legal processes'.[33]

A national reparation fund would operate through a board established and managed by the federal government. The board would consider claims and award monetary compensation for physical, sexual or emotional abuse suffered while living in an institution or other 'care' situation away from family. In assessing claims, the board would have to be satisfied that there was a 'reasonable likelihood' that abuse had occurred, but the mode of assessment would be informal and non-adversarial, in contrast to court procedures, where care leavers have to 'prove' within the narrow parameters of allowable legal evidence what they have suffered through their 'care' experiences. In 2001 the Irish government introduced just such a scheme, known to care leavers as the Irish Redress Board,[34] to distribute compensation to however many of the approximately 150,000 people who had lived in Irish residential institutions wished to apply. Some Australians who grew up in Ireland have already received compensation payouts; they average AUD$136,000. This is a no-fault scheme in which abuse is very widely defined. Applicants need only demonstrate that they have suffered 'physical, psychiatric or other injury consistent with that abuse' — not a difficult task for most care leavers. This scheme is funded primarily by the state, but the Catholic Church agreed to contribute AUD$218 million if guaranteed indemnity against future abuse claims.[35]

There is, then, a readymade model available for Australia to follow. It needs to be emphasised, however — and the extensive recommendations of the Senate Report recognise this — that reparations should not be seen as an indication that nothing more needs to be done, that now the subject is closed. Financial payouts can never compensate people for what has happened to them. They can help them have better lives now, but they are only one strand in a package of what is required: other measures to support and assist care leavers are also essential.

Services

Support services are indeed what care leavers most desperately need. And it cannot be stated too strongly that care leavers are entitled to their own independent and dedicated support services, not services tacked on to existing ones for other groups. Australia recognises that child migrants, adoptees and the Aboriginal stolen generations both require and are entitled to services tailored to their unique needs. It is patently discriminatory for care leavers to be treated differently, as they have been to date, and it also seems inexplicable given that we constitute the largest group of children damaged by past child welfare policies and practices.

Recommendation 20 recognises this when it proposes that governments, churches and non-government agencies contribute to funding CLAN, which, as I said earlier, relies on donations and memberships to cover running costs. One of the great strengths of CLAN is that it is a national consumer group: it is run by care leavers, for care leavers. This is vital, given the high level of mistrust that a very large number of care leavers feel about dealing with authorities or officials who might be connected with their past care. CLAN provides something that no agency, church body or government department can provide: connection with other people who experienced the same desolate childhood and understand the feelings from the inside — who have 'walked the walk and talked the talk'. Whatever other services are set up, care leavers need their own forum, their own safe place. They should never *have to* return to their childhood provider agency for assistance; if they do that, it should be by choice. The federal government has moved quite promptly to recognise this: in December, three months after the release of *Forgotten Australians*, it granted CLAN $100,000 for counselling support, as an interim measure while it considers its response to the recommendations of the report.

The existence of a peer support organisation such as CLAN is not, however, a reason to let the past providers of care off the hook. Recommendation 21 states that all state governments, churches and agencies should provide a comprehensive range of services and assistance to care leavers and their families; and social justice indicates that all agencies should be prepared to take responsibility (not to be confused with blame) for their own past practices. Furthermore, services should be available wherever the care leaver now lives; that is, they should cross state boundaries. This is essential, because a great many care leavers, in an effort to put their past behind them, have deliberately left the state where their 'care' occurred.

Services provided by agencies must include, as Recommendation 23 proposes, long-term counselling as required (not merely a limited number of sessions) — including, as an option, counselling external to the provider agency (though still paid for by it). This last stipulation reflects the very significant aspect of service provision for care leavers that I have raised previously: many care leavers would never return for assistance of any type to the agency that had provided their childhood 'care'. They cannot trust their healing to the agency that caused them so much pain and suffering when they were children; many are still very angry about what happened to them, because of the impact it continues to have on their life.

Other recommendations are for services that CLAN has always said are needed: health care, housing and aged-care programs that will 'recognise and cater for the health needs and requirements of care leavers', and education options that recognise the disadvantages suffered by people growing up in institutions, such as lack of literacy.

The need for a Royal Commission

There can be little doubt that there was a high incidence, across decades of institutional care, of criminal physical and sexual assault and that, as Senator Jan McLucas said when tabling the Report in Parliament, 'the evidence is there that authorities in the church and in governments either knew or should have known that much of this horrific activity was occurring'. Recommendation 11 addresses this issue: the Commonwealth government, it says, should require all charitable and church-run institutions to open their files and premises and provide full co-operation to authorities to investigate the nature and extent of such events within their institutions — as well as the extent to which this has been concealed. The time frame proposed is within six months' of the tabling of the Report (that is, by the end of February 2005). Failing this, the Commonwealth government should consider establishing a Royal Commission into state, charitable and church-run institutions and out-of-home care during the 20th century.

Many care leavers feel that only a Royal Commission can do justice to the gravity of their experiences. The frequency with which both sexual and physical abuse is detailed in submissions indicates, I think, that the incidence of criminal acts discovered by a Royal Commission would be very high. Another issue that I believe needs to be investigated is unpaid wages — for the children who worked in laundries, on Home farms, and doing the domestic work necessary to keep the institutions going. It would be interesting, to say the least, to document the amount earned by churches and charities in the 20th century from the illegal and unpaid labour of children.

Remembering care leavers and this history

The final recommendations of *Forgotten Australians* are about making our history known: through a National Library of Australia oral history project, a National Museum of Australia permanent (but also travelling) exhibition of institutional life, through federally funded historical research into institutional care and its social and economic impact, and through incorporating the study of the effects of institutional care on Australian society into courses of study at universities. The history documented in *Forgotten Australians* and in this book is not currently taught, even in social work, social welfare or child protection courses. It is not part of the mainstream consciousness of our country's history. It has been forgotten, as we have been, but it should not continue to be forgotten. The most visible expression of it, says the report, should be in memorials commemorating care leavers: memorial gardens, plaques at the site of former institutions, or heritage centres on the site of former institutions. This we would really like to see.

Where to from here?

As I conclude this book, eight months after the release of *Forgotten Australians*, the federal government, and the state governments and other past provider agencies, are still considering their response to the 39 recommendations.

In recent years, states all over Australia have, quite rightly, been forced to address the consequences of past adoption practices by the pressure of changed attitudes, which led to changed legislation and to services to address the consequences of ill-conceived past policies. This change was driven by the fact that within the adoption community there were forceful, educated, articulate advocates for social justice who insisted on change, and on services. That is not the case for care leavers, and here is one of our greatest obstacles. Unlike adoptees, the adults who survived the 'care' experience are not likely to be able to articulate their needs and to insist on redress. The cruel irony is that this state of abjection has been created by the very experiences for which we need redress. We never thought, when we started CLAN, that we would get this far, and without the support of Senator Andrew Murray we would not have had the Inquiry. It is significant that he himself, as a child migrant, is a care leaver. Care leavers have few champions outside themselves: so few, in fact, that we know exactly who they are.

Forgotten Australians has given us our blueprint for redress and for healing, but now we must take it to the next stage. There is no obligation on government to implement the recommendations of an inquiry, even where the claims of social justice would seem to demand — and demand loudly — that they be implemented. We are nevertheless hopeful that over time we will begin to see things happening. We have heard, at CLAN, that state governments have set up 'working parties' to consider a response; as have some of the church organisations. So we try to resist the feeling that if care leavers themselves don't keep up the pressure, it's possible that nothing much will happen. It was the silence of the survivors of the past system that allowed the past providers of institutional care, including governments, to take no action.

Despite the Inquiry, those past providers still appear reluctant to take responsibility for this history. Perhaps this is because to acknowledge it means entering into an agreement to pay the huge debt that the inadequate and under-resourced care system of the past has bequeathed us, as a society. That cheap care could cost us dearly: the money we did not spend on children then we might be compelled to spend now, in order to address the damage that system caused to half a million Australians. 'Maybe it is too hard for the state government to accept responsibility,' said one NSW state ward in her submission,[36] but 'we've had to cope all these years, so why shouldn't they?' It's a fair question.

Appendix

Numbers of children in 'care' in 20th-century Australia

The postwar growth in the number of Homes which I described in Chapter 4 matched the growth in population in those years. Between 1947 and 1954, in New South Wales alone, there was a 29 per cent increase in the juvenile population — from 878,812 to 1,126,010.[1] In terms of numbers of babies born, this meant a fairly sharp rise: from a low of 16.94 per 1000 in the late 1930s to a high of almost 30 per 1000 in 1951. The birthrate did not begin to decline until 1970.[2] However, although the birthrate, along with other barometers of Australia's social development in these years, was formally recorded, the statistics on children in care were only ever recorded haphazardly. It is impossible estimate the number of children in care during the 20th century — whether they were in institutions, foster care or a mix, and whether they were in care provided by the state or by the private sector.

The Senate Report came to the conclusion that while 'any degree of accuracy' is not possible, extrapolating from the data which is available indicates that 'the numbers could be up to 500,000 and possibly more'.[3] As the Inquiry committee discovered, it is not a case of looking up a series of accessible records and making a calculation; this is amply demonstrated in submissions from state governments or past providers of institutional care that attempted to make estimates of numbers for the Inquiry.

When looking at numbers, we have to remember that we are counting two categories of children: children who were state wards, or in some way under state control, and children who were 'voluntary admissions', still 'owned' by their parents. As I have indicated previously, in the non-government institutions, record-keeping was neither detailed nor always inclusive. It was common practice, for example, simply to take a census count of children in a facility at the end of the year — which gave no indication of how many had been and gone over the period, or how many living there now had also been there the year before. This could allow the number of children in the system over a period of time to be over-reported. At the same time, it seems that considerable under-reporting also occurred, since the children who were not subsidised by the Department as state wards were often not counted at all.

There is a telling insight into how numerous, but at the same time how statistically excluded, these children were, in the submission from Mercy Community Services in Western Australia,[4] which ran St Joseph's Orphanage for Girls from 1901 to 1972, and St Vincent's Foundling Home from 1914 to 1972. They note that usually it was only the state wards in the Homes who were counted as being children 'in care', but that there was one period, 1957–68, when counting practice changed to include *all* the children living in each Home. What this showed was that in fact there were far more private — 'voluntary' — admissions than there were state wards in their Homes. Only between 15 and 17 per cent of the children in either Home over that 11-year period were state wards. If the previous counting practice had been used for this period, the only children counted as 'in care' would have been these ones, a very significant under-reporting of the *total* number of children in these Homes. And not only in these Homes, presumably, but in many other Homes in that state.

Number of state wards

Even the total number of wards for each state — that is, the government's own children — is at best an estimate, as the relevant Department itself usually acknowledges. A significant problem here when attempting a national tally is that each Department tended to arrive at its estimates differently, and so the parameters are not always the same, as can be seen in the following.

In New South Wales, between 1883 and 2001, there were apparently 135,000 state wards; perhaps we could, then, estimate 100,000 NSW state wards in the 20th century.[5] The Victorian government, in its Inquiry submission, arrives at a figure of 59,000 state wards between 1928 and 2003, but admits it is conservative, arrived at by a considerable degree of extrapolation from available, but incomplete, statistics. In 2001, the Minister for Families in Queensland replied to a request from CLAN for figures on children in care over the century by saying this:

> Regarding the figures for state wards, it is not possible to provide the data for the last ninety years. However the figures that are available are the numbers of children admitted to institutions in the period 1900 to 1980. During that period there were 72,000 admissions. If a child were admitted to more than one institution they would be counted more than once.

This statement appears to refer to all children, both state wards and 'voluntary' admissions. There is no available data before 1925 in South Australia, but from that date there are figures available for the children under the guardianship of the minister in South Australia each year.[6] The method of counting is one of the least useful possible, since figures are given for each year singly, from 1925 to the present. They vary from 1007 at the lowest (1949 and 1950) to a high of 3330 (1970). It is impossible to get an overall figure from these statistics, since there is no indication whether children who remained wards from year to year are included in each year's total, and so are counted over and over. There was also a change in the mode of counting at one stage, to include some children who had not previously been counted, which confuses things even further. The WA Department made an estimate for the Senate Inquiry that from 1920 to the present there had been 56,000 children in care who had had some contact with the state. No figures appear to be available for Tasmania.

Number of children who were not state wards

As noted above, 'voluntary' admissions were often ignored in counting; in the figures given above by different states, only the Queensland figure appears to include these children. So while Departments can at least make an estimate of state ward numbers, it is almost impossible even to *estimate* the numbers of children who were not state wards who lived in Australian Children's Homes over the 20th century: they inhabit a statistical limbo. The Victorian government was quite blunt in the conclusion it came to when it attempted in its submission to make an estimate of the number of 'voluntary admissions' in that state:

> In the period from 1949 to 1954 there were at least 1,900 children in Children's Homes who were not wards at any one time, compared to 1,100 state wards in the same Children's Homes. It is not known how many of these 1,900 children went on to become state wards, and it is not known whether periods of time in care were similar for both groups. As a result it cannot be estimated how many such children need to be added to the 59,000 children known to have become state wards.

They are speaking here of a relatively short period of time, and do not address the years before or after it, but their example is perhaps representative over time. And it is worth noting that there were actually significantly *more* 'voluntary admissions' than there were state wards. The overall Victorian estimate they arrive at, which again they admit is conservative, is that there were more than 100,000 children in care, both state wards and not state wards, between 1928 and 2003. But even in this loose estimate, they acknowledge that 'there are also probably many disabled children placed in care [who are] not captured in the numbers for wards and voluntary placements'.

For New South Wales, some idea of numbers can be gained from a 1961 article that calculated the numbers of children under 16 in non-state Homes for that year using child endowment statistics. The figure arrived at was 3890, including 'mentally defective', 'deaf, dumb and blind' and 'aborigines'. The number of children cared for by the NSW Department in this year was almost exactly the same: 3893.[7] If there were approximately 100,000 NSW state wards in the 20th century (see above), I think we could therefore estimate a similar number of 'voluntary placements' and arrive at a figure of 200,000 children altogether growing up in care in New South Wales in that period.

If New South Wales and Victoria between them account — apparently conservatively — for around 300,000 children, both state wards and others, we can see why *Forgotten Australians* estimates that at least half a million children grew up in care in Australia in the 20th century.

Picture credits

Cover: Detail from a photo of children in Dalmar Children's Home, Seaforth, Sydney. Thanks to Manly Library, NSW, for permission to use this photo from the Wellings Local Studies Collection.

Page 2 (opposite title page) and page 119: Provided by Wesley Dalmar who kindly authorised their use.

Page 175 Used with the kind permission of Child & Family Services Ballarat Inc., the organisation holding the records and memorabilia from Ballarat Orphanage.

Page 209 Victorian Children's Aid Society receipt kindly donated to CLAN by D Cook, Victoria.

FOR SUPPORT, UNDERSTANDING AND ASSISTANCE CARE LEAVERS CAN CONTACT CLAN:

Care Leavers of Australia Network
www.clan.org.au
support@clan.org.au
PO Box 164 Georges Hall NSW 2198.
02 9709 4520 or 0425 204 747

Senate Inquiry submissions cited

Anson, William 274
Ashby, Dorothy 262
Banks Shirley 310
Behrendorf, Elizabeth 239
Blake, Kerry 418
Bradshaw Paul 85
Brady, Bernard 73
Brown, John 153
Brownbill, Peter 321
Carroll, Caroline 258
Carter, Ken 296
Cook, Barry 156
Corbett, Pippa 95
Cremen, Bill 297
Cronin, Brian 297
Dam, Helena 237
Davis, Hector 133
Davis, Lorraine 182
Dekker, Muriel 86
Dethlefs, Rev. WA 48
Devereaux-Dingwall, Mavis 24
Doughty, Ralph 282
Dravine, Denise 298
Flett, Ray 20
Forbes, David 94
Formosa, Bette 136
Fraser, Georgina 8
Gaffney, Kate 207
Geldard, Kerry 311
Gesch, Mary 101
Giles, Maree 284
Golding, Frank 18
Green, Maureen 348
Greenhalgh, Mark 141
Hampton, G. 320
Hart, Brian 231
Hepton, John 336
Hyde, Lynette 114
Knight, Ivor 11
Lin, 271
Lohse, Verneta 187
Luthy, James 286
Mann, Douglas 181
McKew, Mim 6
McLeary, William 143
Name withheld 214
Name withheld 279
Name withheld 330
Pendergast, Sandra 93
Pollard, Teresa 236
Pritchard, Ron 106
Rees 'Ben Smith's' Story 329
Robb, Wilma 280
Rodgers, Lorraine 103
Sheedy, Leonie 33
Shew, Nigel 339
Smith, Rachel Ann 293
Snell, Kerry 112
Stevans, Leesa 5
Turnbull, Margaret 111
Walshe, David 248
Wilson-Szoredi, Beth 58

Submissions can be accessed through the Australian Parliament website at:
http://www.aph.gov.au/Senate/committee/clac_ctte/inst_care/index.htm

Notes

Foreword
1 de Swaan 1990: 197.
2 Not their real name.
3 Herman 1992: 105.
4 Laing, 1972a: 98.
5 ibid. 104.
6 Miller 1991: 37–38.

Preface
1 *Forgotten Australians* 2004: 4.
2 ibid. xv.
3 Bauman 1991: viii.

Chapter 1
1 Evidence to the Perth hearings of the Senate Inquiry into Institutional Care, 08.12.03.
2 Laing 1972b: 126.
3 The PhD was submitted in 1999 and the degree awarded in 2000 through Macquarie University, Sydney. My supervisor in the latter stages, who helped me so much, was Dr Anna Yeatman, who was then the Professor of Sociology at Macquarie University.
4 The hearings were as follows: Melbourne 11–12 November 2003; Adelaide 13 November 2003; Perth 8–9 December 2003; Sydney 3–4 February 2004; Brisbane 12 March 2004.
5 There are some valuable specialised studies. Kerry Carrington, in her 1993 study, *Offending Girls: Sex Youth and Justice*, analyses the NSW experience for girls, and in a recent PhD thesis through Sydney University, '"Unenlightened efficiency": the administration of the juvenile correction system in New South Wales 1905–1988', Peter Quinn analyses the administration of the juvenile correction system in New South Wales, 1905–88. Donella Jaggs, in *Neglected and Criminal* (1986), discusses the foundations of child welfare legislation in Victoria, including that relating to 'juvenile justice'. Rosemary Kerr's thesis, '"Potential inefficients at best, criminal at worst": the girl problem and juvenile delinquency in Western Australia 1907–1933' (1998), looks at government and community attitudes and responses to delinquent girls during the first third of the 20th century in Western Australia. These are just a

few examples and there are undoubtedly others, particularly unpublished academic works. However, there is no national history of the experience embedded within an analysis of the legislation and attitudes which underpinned and shaped it; that is, no companion volume to what I am attempting to do in this book with regard to dependent children in need of out-of-home care.

6   Lyman 1981: 55.
7   Lesley Hughes' interviews with retired NSW Department field officers, for her 1990 MA thesis covering the period from the 1950s to the 1970s, show the obsessive concern of this Department with the completion of paperwork in the form of reports, files, daily diaries, monthly summaries, lists of clients and so on. The NSW Department, she says (1990: 85), was 'an almost textbook example of Weber's formulation of the purest form of "legal authority system", i.e. the "rational bureaucracy"'.
8   Wolmar 2000: 1.
9   The CLAN website, http://www.clan.org.au, has details of many institutional histories and personal accounts by care leavers.
10 For example, Robert van Krieken's *Children and the State: Social Control and the Formation of Australian Child Welfare* (Allen & Unwin, Sydney, 1992); and Donella Jaggs' *Neglected and Criminal: Foundations of Child Welfare Legislation in Victoria* (Centre for Youth and Community Studies, Phillip Institute of Technology, Melbourne, 1986), to name but two.
11 Pierce 1999: xi.
12 Van Krieken 1992: 72–73.
13 ibid.
14 For the history of 'boarding-out', see van Krieken 1992: 72–79; Mellor 1990: 21–27; Picton & Boss 1981: 73–74.
15 Mellor 1990: 94.
16 Quoted in Mellor 1990: 27.
17 Hendrick 1994: 214–22.
18 Curtis 1946: 160.
19 Quoted in Brown 1947: ix.
20 Van Krieken 1992: 118.
21 *Forgotten Australians* 2004: 14.
22 *Lost Innocents* 2001: 40–41. The British inquiry was conducted partly to determine whether or not the UK government would continue its policy of child migration to Australia.
23 Forde 1999: 277–99.
24 See also Gill 1997 and Bean & Melville 1990: Chapters 9 & 10, which deal with the history and the experience of child migration.
25 Cashmore et al. 1994: 1.
26 *Lost Innocents* 2001: 69.
27 Manne 2001: 27.
28 Gittins 1998: 10.
29 I found this term in a 1971 NSW Department of Child & Social Welfare memo about the children who would be using a new government residential facility. 'Few will be orphans in the strict sense,' observed the anonymous author, 'but many could be accurately described as "orphans of the living".'
30 Bird 1998: 132.
31 Hendrick 1994: xi.
32 Platt 1969: 176.
33 Kociumbas 1997: 234.
34 For a discussion of this see, for example, Scott & Swain 2002: Chapter 1.
35 Waksler 1991b: 62.
36 Scott & Swain 2002: xiv.

37 Archard 1993: 93.
38 Waksler 1991a: viii.
39 *Sydney Morning Herald* 27.08.99: 5.
40 See, for example, *Sydney Morning Herald*, 04.06.97: 2; *Bulletin*, 10.06.97: 20–22. For an account of the resistance to acknowledging this history, see Manne 2001.
41 David Horton, reviewing Carmel Bird's *The Stolen Children: Their Stories* (1998): 205.
42 Inquiry s. 207. Kate Gaffney is a PhD candidate at the University of Melbourne. Her research examines the application of the Parens Patriae doctrine in the areas of child welfare and juvenile justice in Victoria. Her Masters degree at Monash University was a history of the state-run Winlaton Youth Training Centre (1956-1993) in Nunawading, Victoria.
43 Marcus, in Jaggs 1986.
44 Jonathon A Weiss 1972, 'The emerging rights of minors', *Toledo Law Review* 4: 25, quoted in Foreman 1975: 32.

Chapter 2

1 Her real name. Joy has written her own (self-published) book about her care experience: *Unloved, Unwanted But Undaunted*, Dunorlan Press, Tasmania, 1999.
2 Waterstreet 1998: 103–104.
3 This is explored in *A Cup of Tea, a Bex and a Good Lie Down* (1993) by Elaine Hennessey, a study of the widespread use in this period (mainly by women) of potentially lethal — through renal damage — but freely available analgesics such as those Waterstreet names. These were promoted in particular to housewives who needed 'a lift' to get through their daily routine.
4 See, for example, the experience of Lin, in 1968, described in Chapter 5.
5 Townsend 1988: 9.
6 MacKenzie 1961: 4–5. For an interesting overview of Australian society postwar see the chapter by Alomes, Dober & Hellier, 'The social context of postwar conservatism' in Curthoys & Merritt 1984.
7 McCalman 1993: 210.
8 See Brett 1993; Townsend 1988: 9; MacKenzie 1961; Ritter 1994: 1–2; Gilding 1991: 121.
9 Bowley 1947.
10 Roe 1983: 13.
11 See Watts 1983; Higgins 1982; Cunningham 1991.
12 The Queensland Premier, Peter Beattie, may have been one of the children covered by this type of state allowance. His mother died when he was four, his father left the scene, and Beattie, the youngest of seven children, was sent to live with his maternal grandmother. Beattie remembers that he got his school books free, which meant 'having to go to the principal's office to collect them, and all that sort of bullshit' (*Sydney Morning Herald*, Good Weekend, 08.05.04: 36).
13 Ludlow 1994: 32–33.
14 Davoren 1974: 1.
15 Chisholm 1979: 191.
16 Corkery 1951: 2.
17 Townsend 1988: 9.
18 Freeman 1996: 3.
19 For a full discussion of 'poisonous pedagogy' see Miller 1987: 3–102. See also Greven 1992.
20 Berg 1972: 20. See also Hardyment 1983: 176–82; Reiger 1986: Chapter 6.
21 See Ritter 1994.
22 Miller 1985: 192.

23 In his works *Attachment* (1969), *Separation Anxiety and Anger* (1973), and *Loss, Sadness and Depression* (1980).
24 Bowlby 1997: 276. See also Ritter 1994: 4–5.
25 Reiger 1993: 18–19.
26 Greven 1992: 97.
27 Forde 1999: v.
28 Greven 1992: 51, 46–54.
29 *Sun-Herald* (Sydney), 16.06.57.
30 His real name. LO Bailey's Home and his philosophy have been extensively documented, including in the press. See, for example, Trop 1971; Ambery 1998; Gill 1997: 194–204; *Sydney Morning Herald*, 05.02.94.
31 Trop 1971: 25.
32 ibid.: 22; Ambery 1998: 93–94.
33 Ambery 1998: 94. Ambery's PhD thesis on Hopewood is called 'A design for better living: the bio-politics of eugenics, diet and childhood in the Hopewood experiment of LO Bailey', University of Western Sydney, 2000.
34 Trop 1971: 18–19.
35 Gill 1997: 194–204; *Sydney Morning Herald*, 05.02.94.
36 Trop 1971; *Sydney Sun*, 15.09.50.

Chapter 3

1 Goffman 1978: 11.
2 Goffman 1978: 80.
3 Goffman 1963: 5.
4 Senate Inquiry hearings, Adelaide, 13.11.03.
5 Hendrick 1994: 2.
6 Forde 1999: 154.
7 Her real name; she is identified in many submissions to the Senate Inquiry.
8 Goffman 1978: 76.
9 ibid.: 31–32.
10 Name withheld, s. 330.
11 Herman 1992: 98–99.
12 Levi 1989: 97.
13 Quote from 'A day in the life of a girl incarcerate at The Ontario Training School For Girls, Galt, later known as Grandview', by Donna Lee, available at www.grandviewsurvivors.on.ca/.
14 This was the title of an ABC radio program in 2002, in which women told of these experiences.
15 CLAN Newsletter No. 2, November 2000.
16 Winnicott 1986: 143.
17 Hilliard 1997: 135–36. Hilliard notes that what he describes as the 'long 1950s' (late 1940s to 1963–64) 'are remembered and portrayed in the religious history of Australia as a time of confidence and expansion … The conventional view was that religious institutions, by undergirding moral values with divine authority, provided the only firm foundation for personal morality and social cohesion. The alternative, which appeared to be demonstrated by the recent experience of the Second World War and the troubled state of the world during the Cold War, was chaos.'
18 See R Freeman Butts 1970, passim, but see also the foreword (Butts 1970: vii) by the director of the Australian Council for Educational Research, Dr K.S. Cunningham. Similar disciplinary measures are described by Clive James in his *Unreliable Memoirs*, about his 1950s childhood (James 1981: 106). See also Townsend 1988: 81; Disher 1997.
19 Quoted in McLeish 1992: 50–51.

20 'Holystoning' as Robert Adamson, poet and former inmate of the NSW state 'training school', Mt Penang, reminds us (2004: 61), was 'an activity left over from the First Fleet'. At Mt Penang, he says, it consisted of 'getting down on your hands and knees on the verandah and pushing a heavy stone brick away from you and pulling it back again across one spot ... an inherently futile activity and thus all the more degrading'.
21 Name withheld, s. 279. She does not give a date, but from other statements in her submission it seems to be around 1960. The writer was aged 12, the youngest child, she says, ever to be sent to Winlaton, which usually housed girls aged 14 and more. The writer had been in institutions since the age of four, and ended up in Winlaton for running away from the Church of England Home in Brighton, Victoria, which from her account was a very brutal expression of the standard institutional regime.
22 Christine, CLAN newsletter no. 16, July 2003.
23 Church 1997: 92.
24 Brison 1997; her essay is called 'Outliving oneself: trauma, memory and personal identity'.
25 Christopher Niesche, 'Nun Denies Abuse Claims', *The Australian*, 18.09.02.
26 Senate Inquiry hearings, Sydney, 03.02.04.
27 Watson 2003: 3.
28 Laing 1972b: 156, 164.
29 CLAN newsletter no. 15, May 2003.
30 CLAN newsletter no. 17, October 2003.
31 Foucault 1991a: 235–36.

Chapter 4

1 The CLAN website lists many of the available histories: http://www.clan.org.au.
2 UPA Souvenir Pictorial, no date (but from internal evidence, c.1962).
3 *Connecting Kin* 1998: 285, 283.
4 Keen 1986.
5 Howe & Swain 1993: 141.
6 See *Lost Innocents* 2001; Gill 1997; Bean & Melville 1990.
7 Berreen & Tyrrell 1975.
8 Mellor 1990: 16.
9 Shurlee Swain, 'Breaking the hearts of our children', *The Age*, 13.05.97: 11, quoted in Coldrey 2003: 14.
10 Forde 1999: 5.
11 Speaking at the Perth hearings of the Senate Inquiry, 08.12.03.
12 Forde 1999: 99, 100.
13 Victorian Government submission, s. 173.
14 ibid.
15 Forde 1999: v.
16 ibid.
17 To test this proposition, I examined the Burnside admission files from February 1951 to December 1962, and in fact there were only four children placed there by the NSW Department in that period. Burnside accommodated, at any one time, between 260 and 320 children. According to this field officer, it was Catholic state wards in New South Wales who could end up being placed in non-government institutional 'care', because there was a severe shortage of Catholic foster parents. Under the 1939 NSW Child Welfare Act, children were required to be fostered with a family of their own religion.
18 Hicks 1960: 49.
19 Parker 1961: 51.
20 Speaking on the ABC TV *Four Corners* program, 'The Homies', 18.08.03.

21 Trop 1971: 16.
22 Windshuttle 1988: Chapter 11.
23 Noted in David Forbes' submission.
24 Quoted in Windshuttle 1988: Chapter 11.
25 Jackson 1986: 94.
26 Parker 1961: 50.
27 Victorian Government Submission, s. 173.
28 Keen 1986.
29 Howe & Swain 1993: 59–63.
30 ibid.: 124; and see 123–28 for an account of Derrick's tenure at Tally Ho.
31 *Connecting Kin* 1998: 285.
32 Wolmar 2000: 212.
33 ibid.: 213.
34 Coldrey 2003: 7.
35 ibid.: 14–18.
36 Unless specified, I use pseudonyms for all staff.
37 *Australian Christian World* 31.03.50, and *NSW Presbyterian*, 20.03.64.
38 Morri Young, who when I interviewed him in the mid-1990s was the chief executive officer of the peak child welfare body in New South Wales, the Association of Children's Welfare Agencies (ACWA).
39 Coldrey 2003: 14–15.
40 ibid.: 15.
41 See *Lost Innocents* 2001: 116–17; Gill 1997.
42 Coldrey 2003: 17.
43 Quoted in Coldrey 2003: 7.
44 The undated pamphlet appears in M Carey, *Athelstane: A History of the School and the Local Arncliffe Area*, published by this school in 1998. From internal evidence of the pamphlet, the date would appear to be sometime in the 1950s.
45 Clements & Parker 1957: 181. In fairness to Burnside, it must be said here that it was one of the first of the large Children's Homes to make significant changes to its practices along more enlightened principles, beginning in 1961. See Keen 1986: 102ff. Changes in staff attitudes to children — in all institutions — were, I think, somewhat slower to occur.
46 Quoted in Hendrick 1994: 79.
47 Goffman 1978: 73.
48 ibid.
49 Findlay 1981: 4–5; Parker 1961: 54; *Forgotten Australians* 2004: 26–29.
50 Launceston Girls' Home annual report in Tasmanian Department's annual report 1956.
51 In the isolated cases where a NSW state ward was accommodated in a non-government Home, the government would subsidise that ward, as happened in other states.
52 Victorian Government Submission, s. 173.
53 Forde Report 1999: v
54 Goffman 1978: 68.
55 Dalwood began in the 1920s as a private charity offering assistance to mothers, babies and children in poor circumstances. In 1932 it was incorporated as a public hospital under the second schedule of the NSW Hospital Act, but it operated not as a hospital but as a Children's Home, taking in 'children aged between four and ten who needed care because of family circumstances', according to an article, 'The house on Happiness Hill — for one shilling a year' by Jeanne McGlynn of the Manly Warringah and Pittwater Historical Society, *Manly Daily*, 05.11.75.
56 Parker 1961: 50.

57 Forde 1999: 100; the name of the Home is also missing in the text.
58 ibid.: 98.

Chapter 5

1 Kerry Snell gives no indication of where she was in 'care'.
2 Australia's two territories of this period, the ACT and the Northern Territory, both present a different scenario from the states. The ACT had no residential institutions for children. It was the NSW government which provided child welfare services to the ACT, from 1957 under a Child Welfare Ordinance which was in effect the 1939 NSW Act adapted to the ACT and administered by a NSW Department officer. Children who were committed to an institution as offenders would be transferred to a NSW institution, but any child who was simply committed to care as a state ward under the ACT ordinance — on neglect charges, for example — had to remain in the ACT. Since there were no Children's Homes, the resident officer had to find whatever care he could, assisted by two social workers in the Commonwealth Department of the Interior who had no legal authority. My information here is from an interview with a senior executive of the NSW Child Welfare Department who implemented this plan at the time, and who concluded about it, 'Well, I made it work, but it was very difficult.' The NT Administration had a Welfare Branch which carried out the functions normally administered by state Departments of child and social welfare; most of it, reflecting the bias of the population at the time, was concerned with the welfare of Aborigines, in particular of what are termed in the annual report of this Branch for 1957/58, 'part-coloured children'. The total number of non-Aboriginal state wards for this period (1957/58) was 96. There was one state receiving Home, and of these 96 children and young people, 16 were fostered to private families, four were working (presumably being of an age to leave school) and the remaining 76 were 'resident in institutions in the Northern Territory and southern states'. Children disposed of interstate surely had their chances of retaining family contact extremely diminished, if not eliminated entirely. In this, they were in the same boat as the 'part-coloured children' described later in this report, who were sent to southern states for education, placed in either institutions or foster care under a joint state/church and mission scheme. The report notes further that the welfare branch has accepted responsibility for 'the transfer of mental patients to institutions in southern states', which seems to indicate that it was not only with regard to children that family and kin networks were disregarded. Dependency apparently cancelled out all other claims.
3 Picton & Boss 1981: 21, 25.
4 Forde 1999: 101.
5 David Forbes, s. 94.
6 Victorian government submission, s. 173.
7 Coldrey 2003: 9.
8 Jaggs 1986: 163.
9 Quoted in Jaggs 1986: 13–14.
10 Carrington 1993: 122.
11 See the remarks by Dr Peter Quinn to the Senate Inquiry hearings in Sydney, 03.02.04. Quinn worked for the NSW Department for more than 40 years.
12 Chisholm 1979: 216.
13 Foreman 1975: 11.
14 ibid.: 32.
15 ibid.: 12.
16 NSW Department of Child and Social Welfare 1972, *Child Welfare in New South Wales*, quoted in the submission to the Senate Inquiry of the Positive Justice Centre, Sydney, s. 122.
17 Quoted in Brett 1992: 13.
18 Picton & Boss 1981: 21.
19 Quinn evidence to the Senate Inquiry hearings in Sydney, 03.02.04.

20 Clements & Parker 1957: 181.
21 In correspondence between the Minister and the Association of Child Care Agencies, Sydney: Hawkins/Stewart, 06.04.59.
22 Survey Victoria 1964: n.p.; Forde 1999: 37; Picton & Boss 1981: 32.
23 Hendrick 1994: 221.
24 Child Welfare in New South Wales 1958: 20.
25 Hicks 1960: 49.
26 NSW Department annual report 1956.
27 Hicks 1960: 58.
28 Child Welfare in New South Wales 1958.
29 Van Krieken 1992: 128.
30 ibid.: 124.
31 ibid.: 128.
32 Inquiry s. 330, name withheld.
33 The case is reported in Chisholm 1980 and also online at http://www.austlii.edu.au.
34 See endnote 2 above.
35 Chisholm 1980: 227.
36 Quoted in the presentation of the case at http://www.austlii.edu.au.
37 Chisholm 1980: 228.
38 See Marie Wilkinson's 1986 article on this topic; also her unpublished PhD thesis (1999), 'From neglected to protected?: child welfare in New South Wales 1945–1988'.
39 I am indebted to Andrew G Peake for his research on SA institutions. Since South Australia has published no directory of records, information about institutions in this state is not easily accessible.
40 See Forde 1999.
41 Forde 1999: 153.
42 ibid.
43 Inquiry s. 279, name withheld.
44 See endnote 5 in Chapter 1.
45 *Daily Telegraph* (Sydney), 05.02.04.
46 Senate Inquiry hearings in Sydney, 03.02.04.

Chapter 6

1 Bowlby 1998b: 7 (writing in 1980).
2 Victorian Government submission, s. 173.
3 ibid.
4 Senate Inquiry hearings, Perth, 08.12.03.
5 *Sydney Morning Herald*, 14.06.54.
6 Miller 1988: 74.
7 Jennifer seems to have exhibited the response described by Bowlby as characteristic when a mother visits her child after a prolonged absence. 'So far from greeting his mother,' says Bowlby (1997: 28), 'he may seem hardly to know her ... He seems to have lost all interest in her — this is a defensive reaction prompted by the initial feelings of terrible grief at abandonment.'
8 Bowlby 1998b: 10.
9 Leach 1994: 259.
10 Bowlby 1997: 24 (writing in 1969).
11 Robertson is quoted in Bowlby 1998b: 10.
12 Schneider 1968: 54.
13 CLAN newsletter no. 19, January 2004.
14 Goffman 1978: 20.

15   Fiumara 1992: 159.
16   Trop 1971: 10–11.
17   Herman 1992: 101.
18   Goffman 1978: 62.
19   *The Age*, 15.03.04, p. 5.
20   See Mason-Spruell 1993: 33.
21   CLAN newsletter no. 15, May 2003.
22   Patricia wrote an account of her experiences for CLAN newsletter, no. 14, March 2003, and these events were also reported in the *Brisbane Courier Mail* on 27.02.03 in an article by Tony Koch, 'Register confirms barbaric punishments'.
23   Becker 1963: 33.
24   ibid.
25   ibid.: 33–34.
26   Goffman 1978: 81.
27   Forde 1999: 20–21 — Wortley, public hearing on 16.12.98.
28   Goffman 1963: 5.
29   Cited in Tasmanian Department of Social Services Annual Report 1956: 8.
30   Goffman 1978: 66.
31   HREOC 1997: 188–89.

Chapter 7

1   See Cashmore & Paxman 1996.
2   *Forgotten Australians* 2004: 145.
3   Inquiry s. 214, name withheld (*Forgotten Australians* 2004: 145).
4   *Forgotten Australians* 2004: 147, quoting Maree Giles, s. 284.
5   ibid.: 148.
6   ibid.: 152.
7   Online issue of the journal *Circulation: Journal of the American Heart Association*, 21 September 2004. The study was conducted by Dr Maxia Dong and colleagues, from the Centers for Disease Control and Prevention.
8   ibid.
9   *Forgotten Australians* 2004: 169.
10   Ellen Whinnett, 'Abuse hell of Tassie state ward', *The Mercury*, 18.07.03. The Tasmanian inquiry into the abuse of children in state care, conducted 2003–04 by the Ombudsman's office, was precipitated by a report on ABC TV's *Stateline* program on 11 July 2003 about a Hobart man who claimed repeated sexual abuse after being placed into the foster care of a convicted male paedophile in the early 1960s. The final report of this inquiry was released in November 2004.
11   Personal communication from a former staff member of Winlaton who witnessed this.
12   *Forgotten Australians* 2004: 114–17.
13   ibid.
14   The Homes were Berry Street Foundling Home, Bethany Babies' Home Geelong, Children's Welfare Department Home, Turana, and the Methodist Babies Home, as well as St Joseph's Hospital (CLAN newsletter no. 24, December 2004).
15   Gary Hughes, 'Polio vaccine tested at orphanages', *The Age*, 25.10.04.
16   Article by Craig Bildstien in *The Advertiser* (Adelaide), 12.07.04.
17   *The Age*, 21.06.00: 13.
18   Wolmar 2000: 1.
19   Green & Jones 1999.
20   *Forgotten Australians* 2004: 232–33.
21   Term 1(a) in relation to any government or non-government institutions, and fostering practices, established or licensed under relevant legislation to provide care

and/or education for children: (i) whether any unsafe, improper or unlawful care or treatment of children occurred in these institutions or places.
22 *Forgotten Australians* 2004: 183
23 ibid.
24 By political reporter Leanne Craig, March 2004.
25 Christopher Niesche, 'Nun denies abuse claims', 18 September 2002.
26 Senator Sue Knowles, 30.08.04.
27 BenSoc press release, 15 October 2004.
28 AAP online report, 06.12.04.
29 See http://www.clan.org.au.
30 *Forgotten Australians* 2004: 201.
31 Letter to *The Australian*, 13.01.04.
32 *Forgotten Australians* 2004: 201
33 ibid.: 215.
34 Its title is the Residential Institutions Redress Board, administered through the Residential Institutions Redress Act 2002. *Forgotten Australians* 2004: 219.
35 *Forgotten Australians* 2004: 219.
36 Wilma Robb, a survivor of both the Training School for Girls, Parramatta, and the Hay juvenile prison.

Appendix

1 These figures are quoted in the NSW Department's 1955 Annual Report.
2 Jones 1990: 86, 87.
3 Forgotten Australians 2004: 29.
4 Inquiry s. 61.
5 NSW figures were provided to CLAN by the current Department of Community Services. The figure of 135,000 is broken down, in their estimate, into 60,000 for the period 1883–1936 and 75,000 for the period 1936–2001.
6 This information was provided to CLAN in a letter from the then Minister for Social Justice, the Hon. Stephanie Key, 06.07.03.
7 Parker 1961: 51.

Bibliography

Reports of inquiries cited in the text

Australian Senate Community Affairs References Committee 2004, *Forgotten Australians: A Report on Australians Who Experienced Institutional or Out-of-home Care as Children*, Senate Printing Unit, Parliament House, Canberra.

Australian Senate Community Affairs References Committee 2001, *Lost Innocents: Righting the Record Report on Child Migration*, Senate Printing Unit, Parliament House, Canberra.

Curtis, M (chairman) 1946, *Report of the Care of Children Committee* (the Curtis Report), HMSO, London.

Forde, L 1999, *Report of the Commission of Inquiry into Abuse of Children in Queensland Institutions* (the Forde Report).

Human Rights and Equal Opportunity Commission (HREOC) 1997, *Bringing Them Home: Report of the National Inquiry into the Separation of Aboriginal and Torres Strait Islander Children from Their Families*.

Guides to records compiled by state governments and church organisations

Anglicare Australia/James Boyce 2003, 'For the record: background information on the work of the Anglican Church with Aboriginal children and directory of Anglican agencies providing residential care to children from 1830 to 1980', Melbourne.

Australian Catholic Social Welfare Commission & Australian Conference of Leaders of Religious Institutes 1999, 'A piece of the story: national directory of records of Catholic organisations caring for children separated from families', ACT.

NSW Department of Community Services 1998, 'Connecting kin: a guide to records to help people separated from their families search for their records', Sydney.

The State of Queensland (Families, Youth & Community Care Queensland) 2001, 'Missing pieces: information to assist former residents of children's institutions to access records'.

Information Services, Department for Community Development, Western Australia, 2004, 'Signposts: A Guide for Children and Young People in Care in Western Australia from 1920'.

Other

Adamson, Robert 2004, *Inside Out: A Memoir*, Text Publishing, Melbourne.

Alomes, S, Dober, M & Hellier, D 1984, 'The social context of postwar conservatism', in Ann Curthoys & John Merritt (eds), *Australia's First Cold War 1945–1953, Vol 1: Society, Communism and Culture*.

Ambery, Deborah 1998, 'The Hopewood experiment', in *Journal of Australian Studies*, no. 59, pp. 93–100.

Ambery, Deborah 2000, 'A design for better living: the bio-politics of eugenics, diet and childhood in the Hopewood experiment of LO Bailey', PhD thesis, University of Western Sydney, Macarthur.

Archard, David 1993, *Children Rights and Childhood*, Routledge, London and New York.

Aries, Philippe 1962, *Centuries of Childhood*, Cape, London.

Australian Catholic Bishops' Conference & the Australian Conference of Leaders of Religious Institutes 1996 (revised 2000), 'Towards Healing: principles and procedures in responding to complaints of abuse against personnel of the Catholic Church of Australia'.

Bauman, Zygmunt 1991 [1989], *Modernity and the Holocaust*, Polity Press, Cambridge.

Bean, P & Melville, J 1990, *Lost Children of the Empire*, Unwin Hyman, London.

Becker, Howard S 1963, *Outsiders: Studies in the Sociology of Deviance*, The Free Press, New York.

Berg, Leila 1972, 'Moving towards self-government', in *Children's Rights: Towards the Liberation of the Child*, Paul Adams et al. (eds), Panther, London, pp. 9–53.

Berger, Nan 1972. 'The child, the law and the state', in *Children's Rights: Towards the Liberation of the Child*, Paul Adams et al. (eds), Panther, London.

Berreen, R & Tyrrell, M 1975, 'Survey of Catholic residential child care settings', report prepared for the NSW Catholic Social Welfare Commission, Sydney.

Bird, Carmel 1998, *The Stolen Children: Their Stories*, Random House, Sydney.

Blyth, Bruce 1997, *In the Shadow of the Cross: The Story of VOICES*, P & B Press, Como, WA.

Bowlby, John 1953, *Child Care and the Growth of Love*, Pelican, London.

Bowlby, John 1958, 'Psycho-analysis and child care', in *Psycho-Analysis and Contemporary Thought*, JD Sutherland (ed.), Hogarth Press, London, pp. 33–57.

Bowlby, John 1997 [1969], *Attachment*, Pimlico, London.

Bowlby, John 1998a [1973] *Separation Anxiety and Anger*, Pimlico, London.

Bowlby, John 1998b [1980] *Loss, Sadness and Depression*, Pimlico, London.

Bowley, Agatha H 1947, *The Psychology of the Unwanted Child*, E & S Livingstone, Edinburgh.

Brett, Judith 1993, *Menzies' Forgotten People*, Pan Macmillan, Sydney.

Brison, Susan J 1997 'Outliving oneself: trauma, memory, and personal identity', in *Feminists Rethink the Self*, D.T. Meyers (ed.), Westview Press, Boulder CO, pp.12–39.

Brown, S Clement 1947, 'Foreword', in *The Psychology of the Unwanted Child*, Agatha H. Bowley, E & S Livingstone, Edinburgh, pp. vii–x.

Butts, R Freeman 1970 [1955], *Assumptions Underlying Australian Education*, Australian Council for Educational Research, Melbourne.

Carrington, Kerry 1993, *Offending Girls: Sex, Youth and Justice*, Allen & Unwin, Sydney.

Cashmore, J, Dolby, R. & Brennan, D 1994, *Systems Abuse: Problems and Solutions*, NSW Child Protection Council, Sydney.

Cashmore, J & Paxman, M 1996, *Longitudinal Study of Wards Leaving Care*, Social Policy Research Centre, University of New South Wales, Report of Research Project commissioned by the NSW Department of Community Services.

Chisholm, Richard 1979, 'Children and the law', in *Children and Families in Australia: Contemporary Issues and Problems*, A Burns, J Goodnow, R Chisholm & J Murray (eds), Allen & Unwin, Sydney.

Chisholm, Richard 1980, 'Children and the law', in *Children Australia*, RG Brown (ed.), George Allen & Unwin in association with the Morialta Trust of South Australia, Sydney.

Church, Jennifer 1997, 'Ownership and the body', in *Feminists Rethink the Self*, DT Meyers (ed.), Westview Press, Boulder Colorado.

Clements, FW & Parker, N. 1957, 'Family life and child care in Australia', in *Marriage and the Family in Australia*, AP Elkin (ed.), Angus & Robertson, Sydney.

Coldrey, Barry 2003, '"The devoted, the dull, the desperate and the deviant" – the staff problem in traditional residential care', in *The Occasional Papers of the Independent Scholars Association of Australia (Victorian Chapter)*, vol. 2, no. 1, May.

Corkery, EM 1951, 'Statistical survey of one thousand children committed to institutions in New South Wales', Child Welfare Department of New South Wales, internal departmental survey.

Cunningham, Hugh 1991, *The Children of the Poor: Representations of Childhood Since the Seventeenth Century*, Blackwell, Oxford.

Daniels, Kay & Murnane, Mary 1980, *Uphill All the Way: A Documentary History of Women in Australia*, University of Queensland Press, Brisbane.

Davies, Kate 1994, *When Innocence Trembles: The Christian Brothers Orphanage Tragedy: A Survivor's Story*, Angus & Robertson, Sydney.

Davoren, Rev. John 1974, 'The role of voluntary agencies in child welfare', paper delivered at the Rights of the Child Conference, Canberra, November (published 1975 by the Australian Government Social Welfare Commission as a reference paper).

De Mause, Lloyd (ed.) 1988 [1974] *The History of Childhood: The Untold Story of Child Abuse*, Peter Bedrick Books, New York.

De Swaan, Abram 1990, *The Management of Normality: Critical Essays in Health and Welfare*, Routledge, London.

Disher, Gary 1997, 'The long road', in *The Oxford Book of Australian Schooldays*, B Niall & I Britain (eds), Oxford University Press, Melbourne, pp. 315–17.

Douglas, Mary 1966, *Purity and Danger: An Analysis of Concepts of Pollution and Taboo*, Routledge & Kegan Paul, London.

Edelman, Hope 1998, *Motherless Daughters: The Legacy of Loss*, Hodder, Sydney.

Findlay, Pauline 1981, 'The history of funding of voluntary organisations in New South Wales', in *Voluntarism and Care: Contextual Statements on the Role and Funding of the Non-Government Child Welfare Sector*, NSW Association of Child Caring Agencies.

Fiumara, Gemma Corradi 1992, *The Symbolic Function*, Blackwell, Oxford.

Foreman, Lynne 1975, *Children or Families? An Evaluation of the Legislative Basis for Child-Protective Statutory Welfare Services in the Australian States and Territories*, Australian Government Social Welfare Commission, Canberra.

Foucault, Michel 1991a, *Discipline & Punish*, Penguin, London.

Freeman, Michael 1996, 'Introduction: children as persons', in *Children's Rights: A Comparative Perspective*, M Freeman (ed.), Dartmouth, Aldershot, UK.

Gilding, Michael 1991, *The Making and the Breaking of the Australian Family*, Allen & Unwin, Sydney.

Gill, Alan 1997, *Orphans of the Empire: The Shocking Story of Child Migration to Australia*, Millennium Books, Sydney.

Gittins, Diana 1998, *The Child in Question*, Macmillan, London.

Goffman, Erving 1978 [1961], *Asylums: Essays on the Social Situation of Mental Patients and Other Inmates*, Penguin, Middlesex.

Goffman, Erving 1963, *Stigma: Notes on the Management of Spoiled Identity*, Prentice-Hall, New Jersey.

Green, S & Jones, A 1999, *Improving Outcomes for Young People Leaving Care in Victoria*, Children's Welfare Association of Victoria.

Greven, Philip 1992, *Spare the Child: The Religious Roots of Punishment and the Psychological Impact of Physical Abuse*, Vintage, New York.

Hardyment, Christina 1983, *Dream Babies: Child Care from Locke to Spock*, Cape, London.

Hendrick, H 1994, *Child Welfare England 1872–1989*, Routledge, London.

Hennessey, Eileen 1993, *A Cup of Tea, a Bex and a Good Lie Down*, Department of History & Politics, James Cook University, Queensland.

Herman, Judith L 1992, *Trauma and Recovery*, Pandora, London.

Hicks, RH 1960, 'Public and voluntary child welfare services in New South Wales', *International Child Welfare Review*, vol. XIV, pp. 44–58.

Higgins, Winton 1982, '"To him that hath …": the welfare state', in *Australian Welfare History Critical Essays*, R Kennedy (ed.), Macmillan, Sydney.

Hill, Joy 1999 *Unloved, Unwanted but Undaunted*, Dunorlan Press, Tasmania.

Hilliard, David 1997, 'Church, family and sexuality in Australia in the 1950s', in *The Forgotten Fifties: Aspects of Australian Society and Culture in the 1950s*, J Murphy & J Smart (eds), Melbourne University Press, Melbourne.

Horton, David 1998, review of C Bird, (ed.) 1998, *The Stolen Children: Their Stories*, in *Journal of Australian Studies*, no. 59, pp. 206–207.

Howe, Renate & Swain, Shurlee 1993, *The Challenge of the City: The Centenary History of Wesley Central Mission 1893–1993*, Hyland House, South Melbourne.

Hughes, Lesley 1990, 'Working for the welfare — field officers' experiences of family casework in the NSW Child Welfare Department in the 1950s, 60s and 70s', Master of Social Work thesis, University of Sydney.

Jackson, DD 1986, 'It took trains to put street kids on the right track out of the slums', *Smithsonian*, vol. 17, August.

Jaggs, Donella 1986, *Neglected and Criminal: Foundations of Child Welfare Legislation in Victoria*, Centre for Youth and Community Studies, Phillip Institute of Technology, Melbourne.

James, Clive, 1981, *Unreliable Memoirs*, Picador, London.

Jones, MA 1990, *The Australian Welfare State*, Allen & Unwin, Sydney.

Keen, Susan 1986, *Burnside: 75 Years of Caring*, Burnside Homes for Children, Parramatta.

Kerr, Rosemary 1998, 'Potential inefficients at best, criminal at worst': the girl problem and juvenile delinquency in Western Australia 1907–1933', *Proceedings of the Western Australian Institute for Educational Research Forum 1998*, http://education.curtin.edu.au/waier/forums/1998/kerr.html

Kociumbas, Jan 1997, *Australian Childhood*, Allen & Unwin, Sydney.

Kociumbas, Jan 1984, 'Childhood history as ideology', *Labour History*, 47.

Laing, RD 1972a [1960], *The Divided Self: An Existential Study in Sanity and Madness*, Penguin, England.

Laing, RD 1972b [1961], *Self and Others*, Penguin, England.

Leach, Penelope 1994, *Children First*, Knopf, New York.

Levi, Primo 1989, *The Drowned and the Saved*, Abacus, London.

Lewis, J 1987, '"So much grit in the hub of the educational machine": schools, society and the invention of measurable intelligence', in *Mother State and Her Little Ones: Children and Youth in Australia 1860s–1930s*, Bob Bessant (ed.), Centre for Youth and Community Studies, Melbourne, pp. 140–66.

Ludlow, Christa 1994, 'For their own good': a History of the Children's Court and Boys' Shelter at Albion Street, Surry Hills, Network of Community Activities, Sydney.

Lyman, P 1981, 'The politics of anger: on silence, ressentiment and political speech', *Socialist Review*, vol. 11, no. 3, May–June.

McCalman, Janet 1993, *Journeyings: The Biography of a Middle-Class Generation, 1920–1990*, Melbourne University Press, Carlton.

MacKenzie, Jeanne 1961, Australian Paradox, Cheshire, Melbourne.

McLean, Donald 1956, *Children in Need*, NSW Government Printer, Sydney.

McLeish, K & V 1992, *Long to Reign over Us ... Memories of Coronation Day and Life in the 1950s*, Bloomsbury, London.

Manne, R 2001, 'In Denial: The Stolen Generations and the Right', *The Australian Quarterly Essay*, Schwartz Publishing, Victoria.

Manning, AE 1958, *The Bodgie: A Study in Psychological Abnormality*, Angus & Robertson, Sydney.

Mason, Jan (ed.) 1993, *Child Welfare Policy: Critical Australian Perspectives*, Hale & Iremonger, Sydney.

Mason, Jan & Noble-Spruell, Carolyn 1993, 'Child protection policy in New South Wales: a critical analysis', in *Child Welfare Policy: Critical Australian Perspectives*, J Mason (ed.), pp. 25–36.

Maunders, David 1994, 'Orphanage education', paper presented to the 1994 conference of the Australian Association for Research in Education, Royal Melbourne Institute of Technology (RMIT), Melbourne.

Mellor, Elizabeth J 1990, *Stepping Stones: The Development of Early Childhood Services in Australia*, Harcourt Brace Jovanovich, Sydney.

Miller, Alice 1991, *Banished Knowledge: Facing Childhood Injuries*, Virago, London.

Miller, Alice 1988, *The Drama of Being a Child*, Virago, London.

Miller, Alice 1987, *For Your Own Good: The Roots of Violence in Child-Rearing*, Virago, London.

Miller, Alice 1985, *Thou Shalt Not Be Aware: Society's Betrayal of the Child*, Pluto Press, London.

Nicholson, Joyce 1983, *The Heartache of Motherhood*, Penguin, Victoria.

NSW Department of Child Welfare & Social Welfare 1958, 'Child Welfare in New South Wales' (in-house manual).

NSW Department of Child Welfare & Social Welfare 1966, 'Child Welfare in New South Wales, 1966' (in-house manual).

O'Connor, Ian & Sweetapple, Pamela 1988, *Children in Justice*, Longman Cheshire, Melbourne.

Parker, Norma 1961, 'Differential policies in child care', in *The Australian Journal of Social Issues*, vol. 1, no. 1, Spring.

Peake, Andrew G 2004, 'Records relating to institutional care in South Australia', unpublished paper.

Peck, Janice 1996, 'The mediated talking cure: therapeutic framing of autobiography in TV talk shows', in *Getting a Life: Everyday Uses of Autobiography*, S Smith & J Watson (eds), University of Minnesota Press, Minneapolis, pp. 134–55.

Picton, Cliff & Boss, Peter 1981, *Child Welfare in Australia*, Harcourt Brace Jovanovich, Australia.

Pierce, Peter 1999, *The Country of Lost Children: An Australian Anxiety*, Cambridge University Press, Cambridge.

Platt, Anthony 1969, *The Child Savers: The Invention of Delinquency*, The University of Chicago Press, Chicago.

Quinn, Peter 1985, 'A history of the Girls' Industrial School, Parramatta, 1941–1961', MA thesis, University of Sydney.

Quinn, Peter 2004, '"Unenlightened efficiency": the administration of the juvenile correction system in New South Wales 1905–1988', PhD thesis, University of Sydney.

Reiger, Kerreen 1986, *The Disenchantment of the Home: Modernizing the Australian Family 1880–1940*, Oxford University Press, Melbourne.

Reiger, Kerreen 1993, '"I don't think we worried about whether they were happy": changes in the meaning and practices of childrearing', paper presented at Issues in Australian Childhood Conference, Brisbane, September.

Ritter, Leonora 1994, 'From the repressive 1940s to the permissive 1960s via the "Ideal Family"', paper for White Australian Dreamtime: the cultural heritage and politics of the 1950s, conference held at School of Heritage Studies and Art, Charles Sturt University, Albury, NSW, 6–11 February.

Roe, Jill 1983, 'The end is where we start from: women and welfare since 1901', in *Women, Social Welfare and the State in Australia*, C Baldock & B Cass (eds), Allen & Unwin, Sydney, pp. 1–19.

Rose, DE 1942, *A Study of Juvenile Delinquency in New South Wales*, NSW Government Printer, Sydney.

Schneider, David M 1968, *American Kinship: A Cultural Account*, Prentice-Hall, New Jersey.

Scott, Dorothy & Swain, Shurlee 2002, *Confronting Cruelty: Historical Perspectives on Child Protection in Australia*, Melbourne University Press, Melbourne

Speier, Matthew 1976, 'The adult ideological view in studies of childhood', in *Rethinking Childhood Perspectives on Development and Society*, A Skolnick (ed.), Little, Brown & Co., Toronto, pp. 168–86.

'Survey of Child Care in Victoria 1962–1964, A Report by the Committee Appointed by the Chief Secretary of Victoria, Hon. AG Rylah, MLA 1964', Victorian Government Printer, Melbourne ('Survey Victoria').

Tizard, J & Tizard B 1974, 'The institution as an environment for development', in *The Integration of a Child into a Social World*, M Richards (ed.), Cambridge University Press, Cambridge.

Townsend, Helen 1988, *Baby Boomers: Growing up in Australia in the 1940s, 50s and 60s*, Simon & Schuster, Sydney.

Trop, Jack D 1971, *A Gift of Love: The Hopewood Story*, West Publishing Corp., Sydney.

Tuck, Elizabeth 1977, 'Charitable Homes: what is the role of the District Officer?', unpublished report (presumably an internal Departmental document) for the NSW Department of Family and Community Services (the name of the Department at this time).

Van Krieken, R 1992, *Children and the State: Social Control and the Formation of Australian Child Welfare*, Allen & Unwin, Sydney.

Waksler, Frances Chaput (ed.) 1991a, 'Preface', *Studying the Social Worlds of Children*, Falmer Press, London.

Waksler, Frances Chaput 1991b, 'Studying children: phenomenological insights', in *Studying the Social Worlds of Children*, FC Waksler (ed.), Falmer Press, London, pp. 60–69.

Waterstreet Charles, 1998, *Precious Bodily Fluids: A larrikin's memoir*, Sceptre, Sydney.

Watson, Don 2003, *Death Sentence: The Decay of Public Language*, Knopf/Random House, Sydney.

Watts, R 1983, 'Revising the revisionists: the ALP and liberalism 1941–1945', *Thesis Eleven*, no. 7, pp. 67–86.

Wilkinson, M 1986, 'Good mothers — bad mothers: state substitute care of children in the 1960s', in *Gender Reclaimed*, H Marchant & B Wearing (eds), Iremonger, Sydney.

Wilkinson, Marie 1999, 'From neglected to protected?: child welfare in New South Wales 1945–1988', PhD thesis, University of Sydney.

Windshuttle, K 1988, A history of welfare services in New South Wales 1788–1988, manuscript supplied by the author (no pagination).

Winnicott, DW 1960b, 'Ego distortion in terms of true and false self', in DW Winnicott, 1990, The Maturational Processes and the Facilitating Environment: Studies in the Theory of Emotional Development, Part One: Papers on Development, Karnac, London, pp. 140–52.

Winnicott, DW 1986 [1968], *Home is Where We Start From: Essays by a Psychoanalyst*, Penguin, London.

Wolmar, Christian 2000, *Forgotten Children: The Secret Abuse Scandal in Children's Homes*, Vision Paperbacks, London.

Index

Adamson, Robert, 362
adoption, 98, 99
    records and services, 327, 328–9, 347, 350
Allambie, 259
Anderson, Maggie, 246
Anglican Church Homes, 96, 136, 156, 160–1, 264, 297
    records, 43
    see also Church of England; Cooinoo
Anson, William, 257, 260
Archard, David, 58
Arrowsmith, Norma, 192, 193–4
Ashby, Dorothy, 80, 279–80
Ashley Home for Boys, Deloraine, 248
Australasian Conference on Child Abuse and Neglect (1999), 44
Australian Capital Territory, 218, 239–40, 364
    see also 'care' providers
Australian Institute of Family Studies, 310

Babies' Homes, 85, 176, 270–1, 272
Bailey, LO, 99–101
    see also Hopewood
Baker, Harry, 126, 260
Baker, Sylvia, 52, 86, 115, 136, 189, 212, 264, 270, 288–9
Ballarat Orphanage, 130–1, 172–3, 178, 189, 227
Banks, Shirley, 287
Baptist Homes *see* Roslyn Hall Children's Home, Rockdale

Barnacle, Jeannette, 127
Barnados Homes, 156, 176, 178, 179–80, 198, 261, 270, 275, 287, 293
Barry, Judith, 287
Bartlett, Rosemary, 111, 208
Bauman, Zygmunt, 33
Beattie, Peter, 360
Becker, Howard, 298–9
Behrendorf, Elizabeth, 142, 146–7, 258, 309
Berg, Leila, 93–4
Benmore, 174
Bexley Boys' Home, Sydney, 86, 208, 278, 297
Bidura, 111, 121–2, 149, 171, 235, 237–8, 265, 296–7
    medical checks, 107–8, 241
    staff behaviour, 288
    see also receiving Homes
Blake, Kerry, 283
Blayse, Lewis, 171, 173
boarding out *see* foster care
boarding schools, 83–4
Bowlby, John, 94, 257
    grief behaviour in children, 271
Bradshaw, Paul, 256
Brady, Bernard, 68, 205–6, 292
Bringing Them Home, 60, 307
Brison, Susan, 144
Brown, Catherine, 152
Brown, Ellen, 111, 266, 268–9, 296–7
Brown, Hannah, 265–6
Brown, John, 178, 180, 279, 285–6

Brownbill, Peter, 108, 137, 274–5, 286, 289–90, 302–3, 320
Brush Farm, 236
Burnbrae, 174
Burnside, 69, 116–17, 121, 126, 136,189, 203, 260, 281–2
  Admissions file, 80, 87–8, 362
  attitude to parents, 197–8, 281–2
  care, quality of, 90, 283, 286–7, 288–9
  cottage Homes, 177
  founding, 159
  intentions of, 90, 96, 195–7, 289
  payments to, 208–10
  segregation of sexes, 262, 264, 265
  staffing, 187
  visiting days, 278
  see also Presbyterian Homes
Burridge, Dawn, 297

CLAN *see* Care Leavers of Australia Network
Calhoun, Daphne, 187, 288
Canberra *see* Australian Capital Territory
care leavers, 212, 304–8, 320–1
  birth families lost, 80, 232, 239, 246–7, 322
  compensation claims, 343–6
  continuing trauma, 64, 73, 106–7, 132, 142, 152, 184, 239, 309
  criminal records, 312
  disadvantaged group, 318, 350–1
  deaths, early, 312, 316, 319
  experiences discounted, 54–5, 328, 333–4, 336–7
  guilt feelings, 313, 314
  longitudinal studies needed, 310
  mental health, 310–11, 312, 315–16, 317, 346
  parenting skills, 306, 311, 314
  physical illnesses, 312, 318
  post traumatic stress disorders, 259–60, 313
  prejudices against, 299, 300
  relationships, failures of, 312, 313, 315–16
  services for, 327, 346–7
  social skills lacking, 307–8, 311–12
  substance abuse by, 315, 319
  see also children in care
Care Leavers of Australia Network, 4, 31, 292, 347
  aims of, 338–9
  funding, 338, 347
  website, 344
'care' providers, 156–7
  attitudes to children, 196–7
  services and reparation for care leavers, 343, 347–8, 351
  systemic problems with, 326, 332–5
  see also names of states; religious organisations; past providers
carers, 17, 63–4, 105
  attitudes to children, 191–3
  cruelty of, 136–7, 138–40, 288
  detachment from children, 270–1, 288
  insufficient numbers, 176, 177–8
  low status work, 185–6, 190
  as martyrs, 189, 190
  mother as norm, 79, 88
  own experience of childhood, 93, 183, 190–1
  qualifications of, 186–8, 190
  sexual abuse by *see* abused, sexually *under* children in care
  surveillance by, 123–4, 126
  turnover, 189
  well intentioned, 187–8
Carpenter, Mary, 222–3
Carrington, Kerry, 222
Carroll, Caroline, 110, 148, 191, 247, 221, 241, 243, 305, 314–15
Carter, Ken, 102, 141, 147, 200, 300, 302, 318, 332–3
Catholic Church *Towards Healing* protocols, 329–32, 342, 343–4
Catholic Church Homes, 78, 87, 176
  funding for, 205
  records, 43, 161
  standards lacking, 161, 166
  training schools, 248–9
  see also names of Homes
Catholic Family Welfare Bureau, 161
Chandler, Margery, 82, 109, 141, 142, 149, 208
charity, 159–60, 205–7
  dangers of, 212, 213–14
Charmaine, 297–8
Cheltenham Boys' and Girls' Home, 279
child labour in Homes, 124–7, 171
  for commercial purposes in, 127–8, 331, 349
child migrants, 51, 87, 173, 293
  care of *see* Ross Report; Senate Inquiry into Child Migration

child raising, 94–5
  emotional deprivation in, 93, 94, 95
  experimentation in, 99–101
  material benefits, 90–1
  repressive practices, 90, 92–3, 94, 96
child rescue movement, 222–3
child welfare Acts, 88, 235
  breached by Departments, 220, 334–5
  breached by Homes, 166
  child labour provisions, 124, 129
  powers of, 53, 224–5
  provisions for Homes, 170
  punishment provisions, 137–8, 253
child welfare Departments, 39
  care leavers not recognised, 326–9
  care system damaging, 326–7
  case files, 227, 229
  costs of care, 217–18, 229
  as guardians of wards, 164–5, 166, 167, 328–9
  history of, 45, 216–17, 234
  powers of, 226, 240–1
  rhetoric, 219–20, 252, 254
  role of institutions, 41, 164
  standards for Homes, 163, 164, 167
  threat of removal by, 82, 228
  wards *see* state wards
  see also names of States
childhood, 51–2
  in Australia, 45, 91, 122–3
  as experienced by carer generation, 93
  impact on adult life, 326–7
children
  adult knowledge prohibited, 91–2
  attitudes to, 92, 95, 196–7, 221
  in care *see* children in care
  as commodities, 98–9, 116, 144, 274–6
  emotional care, 93
  grief experience, 266, 271–2, 365
  informal care arrangements, 68–69, 73
  play, unsupervised, 122–3
  sexuality of, 262
  social policies about, 55–6, 326–7
  and social values, 58–9
  as threatening, 105, 221–2
  treatment by adults, 55, 58, 91–3
  unwanted, 73–4, 98–9, 103
  vulnerability of, 68–69, 145, 146
children, abused, 58–9, 291, 335
  adult health outcomes, 310–11, 315
  and attitudes of adults, 55

compliance as survival mechanism, 20–2, 23–4
  in institutional care *see* abused *under* children in care
  and sexual knowledge, 92
  and social class, 23
  see also under children in care
children, neglected *see* neglect; state wards
children, uncontrollable, 225–6, 295–6
children in 'care', 39–40, 57, 79–83, 85–7
  abandoned, 269, 270, 271, 273, 277, 291
  abused, sexually, 30, 142–7, 238, 241–5, 275–6
  abused, verbally, 130, 140, 151–2, 189–90, 191
  abusive treatment of, 30, 49, 50, 250–1, 289–91
  age at entry, 85
  animosity between, 293
  bed wetting, 131–2, 140–2, 296
  clothing shared, 108, 111
  conformity for survival, 106, 151, 295
  distanced from families, 174, 182, 277–8, 279, 293
  employment of, 173
  see also child labour in Homes
  experimentation with, 99–101, 249, 283–4, 318–20
  escapes sought, 296–8
  fear, 105–6, 147
  gratitude expected of, 62, 163, 211–12
  maintenance payments for, 198, 203, 207–11, 280
  see also maintenance payments
  numbers, 44, 51, 70, 79, 169, 176, 352–5, 364, 367
  objects of charity, 205, 212, 213–14
  oppression of, 233–5
  personal records, 227, 229, 322–5
  privacy denied, 114–15, 123–4
  punishment of *see* punishments in care
  regimented, 121–3, 124
  relationships between, 178, 275, 292–4
  relationships with carers, 284–8
  removed, 52–3, 54, 258–9
  renaming of, 110
  as rescue, 56–7, 60
  runaway *see* escapes sought *above*
  segregation of sexes, 261

self worth, 108–10, 116, 283, 300
separation recollections, 257–61
siblings separated, 70, 74, 108, 148–9, 237–8, 257, 261–6, 321
and social class, 56, 84, 193, 198, 221, 229
stigmatised, 73, 298–300, 314
uninformed, 260, 264, 266–9, 271
vaginal tests, 242–5
venereal disease tests, 241–2
voluntary placements, 43, 67–8, 245, 257, 353, 354–5
work *see* child labour in Homes
see also care leavers; Children's Homes; state wards
Children's Aid Society Home, Parkville, 117, 288
Children's Homes, 38–40, 64–5, 103
accountability lacking, 152, 281, 288
admission procedures, 107–8, 109
attitudes to parents, 197–8, 200, 210–11
autonomy of, 159–61, 162–4, 169–70
as benevolent, 63–4, 163
buildings, imposing, 171–3
food, 116–20
funding for, 168, 170, 201–3, 208
histories, 155–6
hygiene, 104, 109
as identity, 302–3, 307–8
as inappropriate, 47–8, 230, 327
isolation of, 120–1, 150, 171, 173, 257
management practices, 49, 188–9, 280–1
numbers of, 70, 157–8, 170, 232–3
official records of, 41–4
physical care as sufficient, 49, 60–1, 90–1, 164–5, 170–1, 201, 212, 283
as preparation for adult life, 151, 172, 294, 304–7
as prisons, 102, 104, 183, 221–3
public face, 194–6, 198–200, 281
quality of care, 62–4, 177–8, 179–81
and religion, 96–8, 132–3, 182, 196
remedial role, 87–8, 99, 172
sizes of, 176–7
staff *see* carers
traumatic for children, 59–60, 65
understaffed, 176, 177–8
visiting days, 252, 264, 265, 269–70, 276–80, 281

see also children in care; institutional care; names of individual Homes
Chisholm, Richard, 226, 240
Christian Brothers Homes, WA, 136, 144, 161, 164–5, 183, 256
staff, 190
Christian organisations *see* religious organisations
Church, Jennifer, 143
Church of England Boys' Home, Burwood, 160, 204
Church of England Girls' Home, Burwood and Carlingford, 84, 108, 112, 115, 177–8, 265, 270, 287
Churches of Christ Home, NSW, 188, 204–5
Clarendon Children's Home, Tasmania, 202–3, 206, 304
Coldrey, Barry, 185, 189, 190, 205, 221
Commonwealth Serum Laboratories vaccine testing, 320
Commonwealth wards, 69, 206
concentration camp parallels, 126, 153–4
Connecting Kin, 42–3
Cooinoo, 126, 133, 159–60, 204, 207
visiting days, 278
Cook, Barry, 117, 141, 265, 288
Corbett, Pippa, 82–3, 264
cottage Homes, 176–7, 220
country life, 173–4
cows, 287–8
Cremen, Bill, 78, 259
Cronin, Brian, 97, 105, 153–4
Crowley, Senator Rosemary, 54
cruelty, unreported, 139
Curtis Report, 47–8, 115, 185–6, 189

Dalmar Homes, 125–6, 135–6, 165, 186–7, 189
funding for, 205, 210
staff, 187–8, 192
Dalwood Home, Sydney, 208, 290, 363–4
Dam, Helena, 114–15, 137, 147, 191, 304
Davies, Daphne, 110, 148, 172, 191, 192–3, 236
Davis, Hector, 61–2, 83
Davis, Lorraine, 127, 128, 129, 260–1, 277
Davoren, John, 84
Dekker, Muriel, 130

delinquency, 56, 221–3, 234
  as psychiatric problem, 249
  see also training schools
depots *see* receiving Homes
Derrick, Edgar, 181, 285–6
Dethlefs, Reverend, 249
Devereaux-Dingwall, Mavis, 107, 110, 227, 258
divorce
  and placement of children in Homes, 78, 86–7
  as stigma, 73
Dr Dill Mackey Home, Sydney, 82, 141, 208
Doughty, Ralph, 106, 110, 113, 122, 125, 148, 184, 263–4, 285
  photos of mothers, 274
Dravine, Denise, 243–4

education, 130
  and early childhood experiences, 131
  minimal, 128–9, 130–1
  see also schools
Emmett, Kath, 186–7, 192, 277–8

Fairmont, Jim, 165, 187–8, 201, 205
families, 272–3
  crisis support lacking, 84
  importance of, 231, 232
  large, 87
  reported to Welfare Departments, 86, 88–9
  social norms for, 72–3
  social security for, 74
families, extended, 270
  and care of children, 71–2, 80
  unsupportive, 78, 86, 87
family group Homes *see* cottage Homes
Fanshawe, Gabrielle, 87
fathers
  care of children, 82, 86
  desertion by, 76, 79
  violent, 82–3
  see also mothers
Feinstein, Rebecca, 85, 179, 260
Fenton, Sally, 80, 125, 133, 269
Ferguson, Else, 82, 86, 181–2, 186, 287
Ferris, Doreen, 278
film censorship, 91
Fitzgerald, Susan, 205, 301
Fiumara, Gemma Corradi, 262–3
Fletcher, Jack, 123, 265, 266–7

Flett, Ray, 52–3, 309, 328–9
Forbes, David, 110–11, 122, 132, 236, 247, 294–5, 308
Forde Inquiry, 43, 50–1, 144
  critical of Child Welfare Department, 166, 167–8, 217–18
  numbers of Homes, 158
  risk factors identified, 212–13
  submissions to, 299
Foreman, Lynne, 226, 227
Forgotten Australians, 4, 30–1, 34, 339–40
  comment on previous inquiries, 49
  long term costs of care, 316–17
  recommendations, 340–1
    on apologies, 341–3
    on further investigations, 348–9
    on health care data, 317–18
    on personal records, 325
    on recording of history, 340–1
    on reparations, 343–6
    on services, 346–8
  see also Senate Inquiry into Children in Institutional Care
Formosa, Bette, 102, 120, 125–6, 135–6, 210
foster care, 46, 99, 220, 231–2, 295
  abuse in, 146, 236, 250
  and contact with birth family, 232, 245
  selection for, 274–5
  see also children in care; *and under* New South Wales
Fraser, Georgina, 64

Gaffney, Kate, 62, 221, 334–5
Geldard, Kerry, 111, 118, 143, 149–50, 208, 260, 267, 277
Gill Memorial Home, Goulburn, 87, 106, 110, 122, 125, 148, 182
  intentions of, 194
  punishments in, 113, 136–7, 184–5, 191
  visits and outings, 278–9
  see also Salvation Army Children's Homes
Goffman, Erving, 103, 107, 110, 112, 124, 142, 150, 198, 207
  on social stigma, 299, 301
Golding, Frank, 172–3, 178, 189, 263
Good Shepherd Sisters training schools, 127–8, 248, 254
  unpaid work claims, 331

Goodwood Orphanage, Adelaide, 146
Green, Maureen, 330–1
Greenhalgh, Mark, 120, 143, 306–7
Greven, Phillip, 96-7
grief *see under* children

HREOC *see* Human Rights and Equal Opportunity Commission
Hamilton, Jane, 262, 293-4
Hampton, G, 313
Hannaford, Cheryl, 109, 115, 186, 204, 267, 294, 305–6
Harrison, Catherine, 295
Hart, Brian, 35, 155, 312
Havilah, 109
Hawkins, FC, 230–1
heart disease and childhood experiences, 315
Heffron, RJ, 219
Hendrick, Harry, 55–6, 107, 231
Hepton, John, 185
Herman, Judith, 20, 114, 291
Hewitt, Joy, 260, 284, 287
Hicks, RH, 169, 213
Hill, Joy, 69–70, 110, 192, 215, 241, 243, 246–7, 295, 299
Homes *see* Children's Homes
Hopewood, 99–101, 171, 174, 178, 203, 283–4, 295
  relationships between children, 294
Horton, David, 60
Human Rights and Equal Opportunity Commission, Inquiry into the Separation of Aboriginal and Torres Strait Islander Children from Their Families, 32, 49
  report *see Bringing Them Home*
Hyde, Lynette, 139, 145, 256, 294, 297

identity, 302–3
  and body, 143–4
  denied, 36, 48–9, 107, 108–12, 144, 252
  growth of, 152
  as Home child, 300, 302, 320–1
Inquiry into Children in Institutional Care
  see Senate Inquiry into Children in Institutional Care
Institution for Boys, Tamworth, 236, 252–3
Institution for Girls, Hay, 236, 250–1
institutional care, 45–6, 103–4, 154, 198, 207
  dehumanising, 46, 48, 50, 59–60, 62, 107, 110, 263
  isolation from society, 121
  as labelling, 299
  possessions removed, 112
  privacy denied, 114
  for staff benefit, 280–1
  staff surveillance, 123–4
  see also Children's Homes
institutionalisation, 123, 306
Irish Redress Board, 346
Isabella Lazarus Home, Sydney, 85, 179

Jaggs, Donella, 63, 222
Jewish Homes *see* Isabella Lazarus Home, Sydney
Jones, Brian, 278, 297

Keane, Phyllis, 301
Kendall, Marigold, 126, 133, 159–60, 204, 207, 278, 307
King, Truby, 93–4
King Edward Home, Newcastle, 235–6
Knight, Ivor, 136, 146, 164–5
Knowles, Senator Sue, 339
Kociumbas, Jan, 45, 56

Laing, RD, 21, 36, 152
Lang, Christine, 108, 111, 284, 288
Langham, Terry, 106, 295
Launceston Girls' Home, 127, 202, 206, 260–1, 277
The Laurels, Sydney, 284
Lennox, Chrystal, 121–2, 260, 288
Lennox, Ray, 87, 293
Lin, 237–9, 245
Lohse, Verneta, 128–9, 278
Luthy, James, 68–69, 184
Lyman, Peter, 41
Lynwood Hall, NSW, 110, 140, 148, 172, 191, 193, 236

Madison, Stephen, 297
Magdalen Homes' laundries, 127–8
  see also Good Shepherd Sisters training schools
maintenance payments, 75–6, 218
  entitlement to, 77
  gaol for non-payment, 76
  to Homes, 198, 201–3, 207–11
  lack of, 78

surveillance of families, 76–7
see also under children in care
Mallory, Jim, 281–2
Mann, Douglas, 78, 120, 131–2, 142, 164, 285, 290
Manne, Robert, 51
Marcus, Steve, 63
Marsh, Jilly, 29, 37, 152, 207, 300
Martin-Smith, Anne, 84, 260, 287
Mason, Franny, 149, 265, 290
Mater Dei, Narellan, 128, 278
materialism, 90–1
Maunders, David, 130
Maxwell, Janet, 189, 270, 275, 293
McCalman, Janet, 72–3
McCourt, Deidre, 162, 297
McCulloch Report, NSW, 49
McKew, Mim, 116, 117–18, 210–11
  personal records, 324–5
McLeary, William, 116–17, 118
McLucas, Senator, Jan, 348–9
media investigations, 333, 335–7
Medway, Bob, 86–7
Menzies, Sir Robert, 229
Miles, Richard, 260
Miller, Alice, 22, 92–3, 94, 97, 151, 228
Miller, Elizabeth, 133, 199, 276–7
Missing Pieces, 43
Mittagong Homes, 137, 239
moral danger charges, 244–5
Morialta Home, Adelaide, 279–80
Morton, Liz, 178
mothers,
  desertion by, 82
  separation from, 257–61, 271–2
  unmarried stigma, 75
  see also fathers; parents
Mount Gibraltar Boys' Home, Bowral, 135, 177
Mount Penang, 253, 362
Murphy, Bunny, 273
Murray, Senator Andrew, 4, 31–2, 339, 350
Murray, George, 246, 299

Nanson, Alice, 122, 207, 262, 274, 284
Nazareth House, Brisbane, 114–15, 137, 145–6, 147, 336–7
Nazareth House, Melbourne, 114, 118, 153–4
neglect, 222, 223–5, 228
  children charged with, 64, 227

New South Wales, 217, 230–7
  birth family information, 246–7, 253
  directory of Homes, 42–3
  fostering policy, 39, 46–7, 67, 216, 230–2
  historic homes conserved by, 171–2
  inquiries into, 49
  inspections by, 165
  licensing Homes, 14, 37, 39, 41–2, 99, 138, 158, 168–71, 176
  Lin's story, 237–9
  records, 41–2
  relief payments, 75–6
  responsibilities in ACT, 218, 239–40, 364
  Senate Inquiry, 328
  statistics, 354, 355, 367
  vaginal tests, 241–4
  see also 'care' providers
New South Wales Benevolent Society, 83, 264
  apology, 342–3
New South Wales state Establishments, 168–9, 170, 232–3
  as preparation for foster care, 172, 233, 235–6
  specialised roles, 235–7
  training schools *see* Institution for Boys, Tamworth; Institution for Girls, Hay; Training School for Girls, Parramatta
Neyens, William, versus NSW Department 239–40
Nicholson, Godfrey, 48–9, 115
Norgard report, 167
Northern Tasmanian Home for Boys, 206
Northern Territory, 218, 224, 225, 364
Nudgee Orphanage, 319

O'Halloran, Mary, 266
O'Leary, Frank, 287
orphanages *see* Children's Homes
Owen, Iona, 109
Owen, Mary, 114

parent-child relationship, 15
parents
  children removed by state, 67, 227
  feelings denied, 54, 232
  incapacity of, 61, 222, 224, 226–7
  legal rights of, 227, 239–41
  loss of, 37, 54

maintenance *see* maintenance payments
selection of Home, 69
sought by runaways, 297–8
visits *see* visiting days *under* Children's Homes
voluntary placement of children in care, 43, 67–8, 245, 266
see also fathers; mothers
parents, single, 13, 70, 77
social security payments for, 72, 74–5
state relief payments, 75, 360
Parker, Norma, 197, 230
Parkerville, WA, 120, 131–2, 142, 156, 285
cottage Homes, 177
shoes not provided, 290
Pascoe, Patricia, 298, 366
past providers of institutional 'care', 54, 156, 326, 329, 332, 338, 347, 350, 351, 353,
see also 'care' providers; religious organisations; names of states
Pendergast, Sandra, 128
Penglase, Joanna, 303–4
books as escape, 22, 24
brother, 13
compliance, 20–1, 22, 24–5, 273, 295
depression, 25–6
father, 11–12, 26
her story, 9–11, 36, 111–12, 118–20, 123, 149, 165–6, 211, 261–2
see also Taylor, Betty
mother, 12–13, 15, 19–20, 75, 291–2
psychiatric help, 26
research and thesis, 31, 36, 37–8
sense of shame, 17
sister, 4, 17–18, 25
therapeutic help, 27–8
Peter, 270, 287–8
Pierce, Peter, 45
Picton, Cliff and Boss, Peter, 216–17, 229
Platt, Anthony, 56
police, role in child removal, 173, 225, 227, 258
Pollard, Teresa, 345
poverty, 83
Presbyterian Homes, 80
see also Burnside
Price, Geoff, 136
prisons, 154
Pritchard, Ronald, 313

Protestant Federation Girls' Home, Sydney, 118, 133, 143, 149–50, 260, 267, 277
punishments in care, 112–13, 118–19, 122, 126, 133, 134–42, 148
for absconders, 297–8
for non-compliance, 296
as only physical contact, 288
and religion, 96–7, 276, 294
shifting ground rules, 150
visitors denied, 276–7, 278, 280, 282

Queensland
children admitted to care, **81**, 79
cost of care, 217–18
criticised by Forde Report, 166
deserting fathers, 76
directory, 43
maintenance payments, 218
neglected children, 224
placement policies, 219
relief payment, 360
statistics, 354, 355
see also 'care' providers; Forde Inquiry
Quinn, Peter, 229–30, 253, 364

Randall, Bunty, 188, 204–5
Randle, Bruce, 66, 74, 135, 177, 267–8
rape *see* state-sactioned rape
Rathgar, Grafton, 108, 111, 284, 288
Reading, Norma, 270–1, 288
receiving Homes, 216, 259
see also Bidura; Royal Park receiving depot; Royleston
Red Cross Home, Cronulla, 260
reformatories *see* training schools
Reiger, Kerreen, 94–5
religious organisations, 96, 132–3, 156–7, 361
benevolence assumed, 98
charitable tradition, 159–60
compensation claims, control over, 329–31, 344–5
management of Homes, 159, 182
punishment of children, 96–7
see also 'care' providers
Richards, Jennifer, 284
Robb, Wilma, 250–1, 253
Robertson, James and Joyce, 271–2
Rodgers, Jim, 187
Rodgers, Lorraine, 106, 130, 140, 227, 269–70

Roe, Jill, 75
Roslyn Hall Children's Home, Rockdale, 82, 181–2, 186, 287, 293
Ross Report, 49
Royal Park receiving depot, 259, 265
Royleston, 108, 123, 265, 286, 289, 302–3
rural life *see* country life

St Anne's, Liverpool, 330
St Brigid's, Ryde, 284
St Catherine's, Brooklyn, 133
St Catherine's, Geelong, 147–8, 287, 321
St John's Boys' Home, Goulburn, 259
St Joseph's, Ballarat, 97, 105, 153–4, 256, 294
St Joseph's, Bathurst, 139, 256, 294
St Joseph's, Broadmeadows, 85
St Joseph's, Lane Cove, 205
St Joseph's, Largs Bay, 275–6
St Joseph's, Neerkol, 162, 176, 184, 297
St Joseph's, Surrey Hills, 205–6, 292
St Martha's Girls Home, Leichhardt, 87
Salvation Army
　apology, 333
　Senate Inquiry submission, 332
Salvation Army Boys' Home, Bexley, 208, 278, 297
Salvation Army Boys' Home, Box Hill, 104, 141, 147, 318, 332–3
Salvation Army Boys' Home, Hobart, 201
Salvation Army Children's Homes, 69, 124, 155, 176, 183, 332–3
　church attendance, 133
　training schools, 248–9
　see also Gill Memorial Home, Goulburn
Salvation Army Home, Indooroopilly, 171
Sandra, 264
Sawyer, Beryl, 188, 194, 208
Scarba House, Bondi, 264, 343
schools, 122
　boarding, 83–4
　education minimal, 128–9
　Home children in, 121, 131–2, 180, 290, 294, 300–1
　within Homes, 121
　see also education
Scott, Dorothy and Swain, Shurlee, 57
Sdrinis, Angela, 344–5

self, sense of *see* identity
self worth, 282–3, 300
　see also under children in care
Senate Inquiry into Child Migration, 31, 49–50
Senate Inquiry into Children in Institutional Care, 31–2
　hearings, 30, 358
　recommendations *see under Forgotten Australians*
　report *see Forgotten Australians*
　scope, 38
　submissions, 30, 38, 39, 144, 310–11, 328, 332, 333–4, 339
separation *see under* mothers
sexual abuse, 17, 30, 142–7, 238, 241–5, 275–6
　assessment of claims of, 330–1, 336–8
　recognition of, 326, 329–30
　see also under children in care
Sheedy, Leonie, 4, 31, 44, 287, 321–2
　establishment of CLAN, 31, 338–9
Shew, Nigel, 124, 305
Signposts, 44
Simmonds, Lesley, 108, 112, 115
single parenting *see* parents, single
Sisters of Mercy, 161, 162, 183–4, 297, 306
Sisters of the Good Shepherd *see* Good Shepherd Sisters
Smith, Ben, 252–3
Smith, Rachel Anne, 215, 250
Snell, Kerry, 215
social norms, 72–3
　deviance from, 298–9
　in welfare assessments, 88–90
social values
　and institutional care, 65
　and treatment of children, 57–9, 63
South Australia
　case files, 323–4
　Community Welfare Act, 1972, 226
　maintenance orders, 76
　Senate Inquiry, 328
　statistics, 354–5
　training schools, 248
　see also 'care' providers
Spence, Catherine Helen, 47
Spielman, Judy, 4, 10, 19, 27–8
state-sanctioned rape, 241–5
state wards, 39, 67, 215
　case files, 227, 229, 323

funding for care, 201–2
numbers, 353–4
placement of, 46–7, 164
prejudice against, 221, 233, 314
psychological assessments, 235
removed from families, 52–3, 245–7
services for, 327–8
see also children in care
Stevans, Leesa, 114, 118
stolen generation, 51, 53, 54, 56, 347
Sydney City Mission, 157
Sydney Rescue Work Society, 182
systems abuse, 50, 176, 203, *passim*

Tally Ho, Burwood, 180–1, 285–6
Tasmania
  apology, 343
  donations to Homes, 206
  Government payments to Homes, 202–3
  maintenance payments by parents, 218
  Ombudsman's inquiry, 317, 343, 366
  Senate Inquiry, 328
  see also 'care' providers
Taylor, Mrs, 13–14, 22
  Children's Home, 14–15
Taylor, Betty, 13, 14, 15–18, 20–23, 24–25, 149, 199–200, 287, 290
  abusive behaviour, 24–5, 290
  devotion to Joanna, 15–17, 20–2
  obsessive cleanliness, 23, 111–12
  persecution of sister, 17–18, 149, 287
Towards Healing see Catholic Church
  Towards Healing protocols
Townsend, Helen, 72, 91
Training School for Girls, Parramatta, 219–20, 225–6, 236, 298
  medication in, 251
  vaginal tests for, 242–4
training schools, 40, 183, 216, 233, 247–53, 296, 358
Tucker, Marion, 75
Turnbull, Margaret, 118, 147–8

United Nations Convention on the Rights of the Child, 92
United Protestant Association Homes, 156–7, 176, 262
  see also Rathgar

van Krieken, Robert, 233–4, 235
venereal diseases
  children tested for, 241–2
  as indicator of neglect, 224–5
Victoria, 62, 63
  Children's Welfare Act, 1954, 167
  Children's Homes, 158, 166–7, 176
  cottage Homes, 220
  relief payments, 75–6
  Senate Inquiry submission, 333–4
  statistics, 354, 355
  see also 'care' providers
Victorian Children's Aid Society Home, 117, 141

WR Black Home, Brisbane, 130, 199
Waitara Babies' Home, 270–1, 272
Waksler, Frances Chaput, 57
Walshe, David, 182, 184, 278–9
Walton, Penny, 300
wards of States *see* state wards
Waterstreet, Charles, 71–2
Watson, Don, 151, 254
Webster, Pearl, 112–13, 121, 123
Weroona, 187, 274–5, 288
Werrington Park, 132, 171–2
Westbrook Farm Home for Boys, Queensland, 120, 143, 249
Western Australia, 44, 217
  Children's Homes, 70, 164–5, 201
  files, 323
  statistics, 353
  see also 'care' providers
White, Mavis, 264–5
Whitlam Labor Government, 74–5
Williams, Joy, 60
Wilson Youth Hospital, 109, 244, 249
  medications, 249, 318–19
Wilson-Szoredi, Beth, 244–5, 318–19
Winlaton Youth Training Centre, 115, 139, 225–6, 244, 248, 254, 362
  isolation cells, 250
  medications, 250, 319
Winnicott, Donald, 131
Wolmar, Christian, 44, 183–4, 326
women
  as carers for children, 289
  employment for, 13, 14, 72, 74, 160, 186–7

Youth Welfare Association of Australia, 99–100

www.ingramcontent.com/pod-product-compliance
Lightning Source LLC
Chambersburg PA
CBHW021140160426
43194CB00007B/638